African Theatre
in Development

Editors
Martin Banham
James Gibbs
& Femi Osofisan

Reviews Editor
Jane Plastow
School of English, University of Leeds LS2 9J

Associate Editors
Eckhard Breitinger
Forststr. 3, 95488 Eckersdorf, Germany

John Conteh-Morgan
Dept of French & Italian, Ohio State University, 248 Cunz Hall, 1841 Millikin Rd,
Columbus, Ohio 43210-1229, USA

Hansel Ndumbe Eyoh
PO Box 8222, University of Buea, Buea, Cameroon

Frances Harding
SOAS, Thornhaugh St, Russell Square, London WC1H OX9, UK

Masitha Hoeane
Thaba Nchu College of Education, PB X717, Selosesha 9785, South Africa

David Kerr
Private Bag 0022, University of Botswana, Gaborone, Botswana

Amandina Lihamba
Dept of Fine & Performing Arts, PO Box 35051, University of Dar es Salaam, Tanzania

Rose Mbowa
Dept of Music & Drama, Makerere University, PO Box 7062, Kampala, Uganda

Olu Obafemi
Student Affairs Unit, PMB 1515, University of Ilorin, Ilorin, Nigeria

Ian Steadman
Faculty of Arts, University of Witwatersrand, PO Wits 2050, Johannesburg, South Africa

Contributors are invited to submit material for
forthcoming titles in the *African Theatre* series

Playwrights & Politics in African Theatre
Women in African Theatre
South African Theatre & Performance

Articles not exceeding 5,000 words should be submitted preferably on disk
and always accompanied by a double-spaced hard copy.

Format: either IBM or Apple, 3.5 inch floppy disks, preferably in Word for Windows,
Word (DOS) 6, Word Perfect 5.1 for DOS or WordStar 5.5. If using Apple format
please save all files as Word for Macintosh version 6.0. 1 or lower if possible. Please
label all files and disks clearly. Typewritten submissions may be considered in exceptional circumstances if they follow the standard double-spaced format.

Style: Preferably use UK rather than US spellings. Underline titles of books or plays.
Use single inverted commas except for quotes within quotes. Type notes at the end of
the text on a separate sheet. Do not justify the right hand-margins.

References should follow the style of this volume (Surname date: page number) in
text. All references should then be listed at the end of article in full:
Surname, name, date, *title of work* (place of publication: name of publisher)
Surname, name, date, 'title of article' in surname, initial (eds) *title of work*
(place of publication: publisher).
or Surname, name, date, 'title of article', *Journal*, vol., no: page number.

Reviewers should provide full bibliographic details, including the extent, ISBN and
price.

Copyright: Please ensure, where appropriate, that clearance has been obtained from
copyright holders of material used. Illustrations may also be submitted if appropriate
and if accompanied by full captions and with reproduction rights clearly indicated. It is
the responsibility of the contributors to clear all permissions.

All submissions should be accompanied by a brief biographical profile. The editors
cannot undertake to return material submitted and contributors are advised to keep a
copy of all material sent in case of loss in transit.

Editorial address
8 Victoria Square, Bristol BS8 4ET, UK

Books for Review & Review articles
Jane Plastow, Reviews Editor, *African Theatre*
School of English, University of Leeds, Leeds LS2 9JT, UK

African Theatre in Development

Editors
Martin Banham
James Gibbs
& Femi Osofisan

Reviews Editor
Jane Plastow

James Currey
OXFORD

Indiana University Press
BLOOMINGTON & INDIANAPOLIS

First published in 1999 in the United Kingdom by
James Currey Ltd
73 Botley Road
Oxford OX2 0BS

and in North America by
Indiana University Press
601 North Morton Street,
Bloomington, Indiana 47404-3797

Manufactured in Great Britain

British Library Cataloguing in Publication Data
African theatre in development
1. Theatre - Africa
I. Banham, Martin   II. Gibbs, James   III. Osofisan, Femi
792'.096

ISBN 0-85255-599-7 (James Currey Paper)
ISBN 0-85255-594-6 (James Currey Cloth)

Library of Congress Cataloging-in-Publication Data
A catalog record for this book is available from the Library of Congress.

ISBN 0-253-21341-X (Indiana Paper)
ISBN 0-253-33599-X (Indiana Cloth)

Typeset in 10/11 pt Monotype Bembo by Long House, Cumbria, UK
Printed by Villiers Publications, London N3

Contents

Notes on Contributors

Martin Banham is Emeritus Professor of Drama and Theatre studies in the University of Leeds, editor of *The Cambridge Guide to Theatre* (1988) and co-editor of *The Cambridge Guide to African and Caribbean Theatre* (1994).

Eckhard Breitinger, in addition to research interests that include Theatre for Development and drama in Uganda, is a Professor at the University of Bayreuth. He is editor of a series that has made an important contribution to the critical assessment of African writing, the Bayreuth African Studies Series.

Ali Campbell is a Lecturer in Theatre at Queen Mary and Westfield College, University of London. He has for many years been a Community Theatre and Theatre in Education practitioner, working extensively throughout the United Kingdom as well as in Eastern Europe, Uganda and Eritrea.

Jan Cohen-Cruz is Associate Professor of Drama at Tisch School of the Arts, New York University. She is co-editor of *Playing Boal: Theatre, Therapy, Activism*, and editor of *Radical Street Performance: An International Anthology* (Routledge, 1998).

Carolyn Duggan studied at the Universities of Natal and University College, Cork, where she is currently Head Tutor in the Department of English. She combines academic work and family life with visits to South Africa and with directing productions in Cork.

Jumai Ewu is Lecturer in Drama at University College, Northhampton UK. She is a specialist in Community and Children's Theatre.

James Gibbs teaches at the University of the West of England (Bristol) and has a particular interest in Ghanaian, Nigerian and Malawian drama.

Frances Harding is Lecturer in African Drama in the Department of African Languages and Cultures, School of Oriental and African Studies, London. She figures in this volume not only through her article and her review, but also as a participant in the June 1998 Workshop described by Jan Cohen-Cruz.

David Kerr has taught at the Universities of Malawi and Zambia, and is currently at the University of Botswana. His numerous publications include *African Popular Theatre* (James Currey, 1995).

Christine Matzke is a PhD student at the Workshop Theatre, University of Leeds. She is a qualified nurse, holds an MA in Commonwealth Literature, has travelled widely in Africa, and has published on African women's writing and Eritrean dance forms.

Chuck Mike is a theatre director with a long record of work in Nigeria. He is currently Director of the Performance Studio Workshop, Lagos.

Bantu Mwaura, a Kenyan performance artist and storyteller, is a postgraduate student in Theatre Studies at the University of Leeds.

Roshni Mooneeram is a doctoral student and graduate assistant in the Department of French at the University of Leeds.

Osita Okabue lectures at the University of Plymouth. He specializes in West African and Caribbean theatre.

Jane Plastow studied drama and English at the University of Manchester, has lectured at the universities in Ulster, Dar es Salaam, and Addis Ababa and currently teaches at the University of Leeds. Her work in the field of arts co-ordination has taken her to many places including Banjul and Harare. She has published widely on stage-craft, theatre arts and community theatre.

Agbo Sikuade was educated at Igbobi College, Yaba, and the University of Lagos. Between 1975 and 1985 he was a Producer, latterly Principal Producer, with the Federal Radio Corporation of Nigeria, and he is currently a media and public affairs consultant. He has written short stories and for the stage, as well as radio plays.

Foreword

MARTIN BANHAM, JAMES GIBBS & FEMI OSOFISAN

We are delighted to offer this new series dedicated to the theatre and drama of Africa. Practitioners, teachers and students of African theatre have long sought to establish a forum for discussion, debate and the exchange of ideas and information. Valiant publishing initiatives have been undertaken by colleagues in Nigeria, Cameroon, South Africa and in many other parts of the continent, to establish journals that would be scrupulously edited and reliably distributed. Indeed in the *South African Theatre Journal*, *African Theatre Review*, etc., important publishing footholds in the field have been established. Our hope is to complement existing work, to create a truly pan-African context of material and interest, and, through the support of our committed publishers, to offer a regular publication that will be professionally distributed.

The editors thank our distinguished board of editorial advisors for their support and encouragement; they have greatly assisted us in shaping and launching our first issue and in our onward planning. This issue, on *Theatre in Development* (broadly interpreted and *not* restricted to TfD) will be followed by a volume on the theme of *Playwrights and Politics* and by a volume on *Women in African Theatre*. Each title in the series will also include one new play from Africa, selected by Femi Osofisan. We warmly invite contributions addressing the themes of future issues, and information for our Noticeboard where we wish to record news of important activities in theatre throughout the continent. We shall devote significant space to reviewing new (and some old!) books in the field.

In a perfect world, this series ought to be coming out of Lagos or Dar es Salaam or Cape Town. Our ambition and belief, however, is that, though the series is published outside the continent, its heart, head and function are based firmly in Africa.

Dedication

As this first issue of *African Theatre* was in production, we learnt with great sadness of the death, in February 1999, of one of our Associate Editors, Professor Rose Mbowa. Rose, Head of the Department of Dance and Drama at Makerere University, made an enormous contribution to the strength and vitality of theatre in Uganda and throughout Africa.

Her play *Mother Uganda* (1987), which tells the story of an attempt to bring warring children into harmony, in its many manifestations contributed to healing her homeland and to a greater understanding of Africa outside the continent.

Rose, who received her undergraduate and post-graduate education at Makerere and Leeds, was a woman of great determination and energy. Brilliantly creative, she was loved by all who knew her, and will be very greatly missed. May she rest in peace.

The Editors

Strategies in Staging
Theatre technique in the plays of Zakes Mda

CAROLYN DUGGAN

In 1936 H.I.E. Dhlomo (quoted in Barnett) claimed that, while he accepted that all modern drama has developed from similar disparate roots, he nevertheless decried a clinging to the past simply for the sake of the past, especially a xenophobic, inward-looking cultural expression. Dramatic expression, he maintained, benefits from outside influence and, paradoxically, we become better able to express our selfhood when there is an outside reference. More specifically, African drama should not be exclusively African. Dhlomo avers that African drama:

> must be grafted in Western drama … It must borrow from, be inspired by, shoot from European dramatic art forms, and be tainted by exotic influences… The African dramatist cannot delve into the past unless he has grasped the present …To do this the African dramatist must be an artist before being a propagandist, a philosopher before a reformer, a psychologist before a patriot. (Barnett 1983: 228)

Joe de Graft, forty years later, concurred, but identified dilemmas confronting contemporary Afirican writers. While embodying a fierce pride in their individualism – a natural development from the emerging national confidence of successively independent nations – these writers feel obliged, nevertheless, to respond to the general call to a return to roots. Some writers are able to do this while some are not as the call entails a move to 'attitudes and modes of creative thinking more in consonance with a folkist milieu' which is becoming less and less relevant to more and more writers. The old Africa is perforce changing and with it its artistic expression. De Graft lists the forces for change as including:

> disbelief in magic and religious ritual; active rejection of the claims of the clan and folk wisdom; a new psychology fostered by the competitiveness attendant on urbanization, and a ruthless cash economy; and, last but not least, a growing belief in the almost limitless possibilities of technology. (de Graft 1976: 17)

The scenario, twenty years on, does not seem very different.
This change, of course, has been gradual (sometimes over hundreds of years)

under the ravages of colonization but it is now, in the latter half of the twentieth century, that the successively independent African nations must suddenly, as it were, confront an almost unrecognizable world of the arts which is, nevertheless, essentially African. And African drama depicts this change perhaps more pungently than other art forms because not only does drama draw on life for its source, but its raw materials are 'actual human bodies, attributes, and behaviour' (3). Drama always holds the mirror up to life. A distinctive feature of African society as a whole is the anomalous mix of the traditional on the one side with the most up-to-date thinking and practice on the other. Far from being an incongruity there emerges between the two a concomitance, which not only enriches the ensuing culture but is, in fact, a necessary nexus – not least so in the realm of drama.

In the case of South African writer, Zakes Mda, this dichotomy is self-evident. Mda is essentially a serious and intellectual writer. It would be very easy for him to be self-indulgent and write elitist works for the educated bourgeoisie but to do so would be to negate his intentions entirely. In his own words theatre, for him, is 'an instrument of liberation' (Mda 1990b: 358) and therefore he would ignore the call of his roots at his peril. Consequently, we find his characters, themes, and settings all firmly rooted in the proletarian. All these features are instantly accessible to his audience whoever and wherever they are. It is in his theatrical technique (language aside, as he writes in English) that Mda turns to Europe. And this is fitting. Ari Sitas acknowledges that in South Africa the theatre, as such, is not an indigenous institution but is seen rather as 'part of *okunjengokwabelungu* (the light that "shines" from the white man)' (Sitas 1986: 90) – an inheritance from Europe, as it were, tempered and adapted for the black man's purposes. From the seventies, black drama in South Africa became more and more useful to the purposes of the black man, that is, as a tool of liberation and it needed, therefore, to move away from being, as it was previously, merely an entertainment – the issues of living were too vital. It was not enough that white liberals, whether politicians or dramatists (such as Athol Fugard) should lead blacks towards freedom. In fact, Mda sees Fugard's plays, no matter how radical, as depicting blacks as 'helpless, dispirited, dumb and bereft African workers, suffering in silence and stoically enduring their tragic situation' (Mda 1983: 14), consequently unconsciously discouraging a struggle for autonomy. Fugard 'does not rally men to any cause' (14), a role Mda sees as belonging naturally to that of the playwright. Quoting from a conference in Gaborone, Botswana, he declares 'any person who stands behind a pen (a brush, camera, or saxophone for that matter) must be just as effective as any person who stands behind a gun in the service of progress' (15). In 1995 Mda had not changed his opinion of Fugard. In an article of that year he was still bemoaning the lack of agency in Fugard's black characters:

> The oppressed suffer in silence, and are not involved in any struggle against oppression. Instead they are involved in a struggle to accommodate oppression and survive it, not to confront it. They are endowed with endless reservoirs of stoic endurance. The spirit of defiance that exists in the South Africa we all know is non-existent in

these works. The oppressed let oppression happen to them, and all they do is moan and complain about it, and devise ways to live with it. (Mda 1995: 40)

Because he wishes to spur people on to action, Mda requires a reasoned response from his audience. Whatever attitude, policy or ideology he is promulgating, he demands a concomitant reaction. His audience must differentiate between reality and illusion; they must observe, think and then take agency in their lives. With this purpose then, Mda's technique is an adumbration of that of Bertolt Brecht. Both practitioners have similar aims and, therefore, it is no coincidence that they should espouse similar techniques. That both Brecht and Mda would seem to espouse Marxism as their respective basic political ideology is less relevant than that they use similar dramatic techniques to promulgate their philosophies and Mda, at least, would seem to see the value of marxist criticism as ineluctable (Mda 1993a: 33). His close involvement in Theatre for Development (described fully in his *When People Play People*) as well as the changing South Africa has focused Mda's concerns, not only with racially based but also class based inequalities. The 1970s saw the rise of Trade Unionism in South Africa, epitomized in the mass stoppages of 1973 and 1982, and the rapid growth of industrialization and the consequent changing life styles of the workers, all reflected in the so-called 'working class theatre' of the time (Sitas 1986: 85–7).

Brecht's involvement with Marxism is well documented and for him there were three essential points of contact between it and his Epic theatre: 'a materialistic conception of man, the primacy of reason, and an unshakeable belief in the possibility of changing the world' (Dickson 1978: 230). Influenced and inspired by the sociologist Fritz Sternberg, Brecht rejected the concept of individualism as outdated, collective man being the dominant idea of the age in his view. He argued, therefore, that Epic theatre was the only dramatic form adequate to such a conception and claimed that wherever historical materialism predominates, Epic forms emerge in dramatic writing (231). Mda, also, in *When People Play People*, found that in order to raise consciousness in an audience, the form of the play should suit the ideology. Not only should situations be close to the audience's experience but the audience should be challenged by the finished product. They should be encouraged to judge for themselves, draw their own conclusions and then be motivated to act on what they have experienced. Consequently, if the existing forms are found to be inadequate, the dramatist is forced to substitute a new one.

Brecht's Epic theatre has proved an excellent basis for Mda. Like Shaw, both dramatists have sought to place their plays in historical contexts. These events and these people are interesting for many reasons, but most of all for the political insight gained through the social circumstances in which they find themselves. However, unlike Shaw, both Brecht and Mda seek to stimulate a desire for change. The emphasis is on the spectator and the final effect of the play is to 'leave him productively disposed, even after the spectacle is over' (Subiotto 1982: 41). Because the spectator has, perforce, a wider view of events than the protagonists, he is able to 'assess the evidence presented and adopt an attitude as to its significance' (41). If thus roused, it is hoped that the spectator will not only be stimulated to change his own thinking but be encouraged to intervene. The spectator can therefore not sit passively and absorb an entertainment. On stage are social issues that impinge directly on his own existence and have a relevance that must be acted upon. The audience cannot sit as if drugged. It must remain detached although engaged. Brecht blamed the general passivity of audiences on the effects of Aristotelian philosophies of empathy and catharsis and Stanislavsky's developments in the realm of naturalistic acting methods and resolved to disabuse the audience of any sense of illusion. The members of the audience were constantly to be reminded that this was a theatre and that they were not to 'suspend disbelief'. Every effort was made and every method was developed to distance the audience from the play and eventually the details of the alienation-effect were developed. Later in his career, Brecht found it necessary to modify some of his more rigid views. For example, he found that it was neither desirable nor possible to eliminate all emotional involvement by the actors in their roles and that it was actually 'artistically important to leaven dry didacticism with the life blood of human emotion' (Eddershaw 1982: 141). Another danger of his earlier views (also modified later) was the emphasis on form. The focus had become deflected from what he was saying to how he was saying it. He attempted then to emphasize the importance of the dialectics so that the political, sociological and economic issues regained their original significance.

Epic theatre, then, is an excellent medium for Mda. His philosophy is appropriate and the formal techniques are admirably adapted to his intentions. The most effective alienation techniques are evident in all of the plays in question but individual plays have individual strengths. *Dead End* (Mda 1990a), the earliest play, is the most tentative, while *Joys of War* (Mda 1993b), the most recent of the period, is the most innovative and daring but all the plays succeed in drawing on the various techniques which are the most beneficial for emphasizing Mda's message of empowerment.

An overall distancing effect is most potently perceived in *The Road* (Mda 1990a). Because the play is a direct confrontation with the theme of apartheid and because this theme is explored most searchingly, ranging from its absurdities to its cruelties, it could and should be a highly emotive play. Any play dealing with the anomalies of apartheid, especially with a South African audience, is going to stir up high emotions which, according to Brecht, will cloud or numb judgement. By translating the entire concept into symbols, Mda forces the audience to interpret, assess and judge. The enormity of apartheid, sometimes too vast to assimilate and appreciate are, through symbolism, reduced to manageable terms. An entire race is encapsulated in one man. Farmer represents the Arikaner Nationalist; Labourer represents the indigenous South African. The interaction between the two enable entire political policies to be encompassed and applied within ordinary lives so that the direct effects may be judged. If Farmer steals Labourer's bundle, he steals his means of living. If the choice is between autonomy in his own life or a living of sorts at the whim of Farmer, it becomes obvious to the audience the extent of the effect of a loss of agency in a whole race. The black race loses dignity, initiative, responsibility. Its quality of life is undermined. Having made the judgement on the basis of this minimalization, the audience is then easily able to maximize (like a photographic enlargement) and see the issues for what they are.

In *We Shall Sing for the Fatherland* (Mda 1990a) another overall distancing technique is used. The symbolic nature of the protagonists and the situation, while effective, is not foregrounded. Again, the likely empathy of the audience is diffused by the ambiguity of place and time. This could be South Africa – everything points to it – but the time is wrong. This is ten years after the Wars of Freedom so is it another African country? Either way the audience is made to observe objectively that if this is South Africa, this is what could happen in the future if care is not taken. If it is not South Africa then this is what has happened in other countries and we should learn from their mistakes.

Paradoxically, *The Hill* (Mda 1990a) which is the most realistic in presentation and the play that permits its audience to empathize the most, is the play most likely to stimulate the audience in a reasoned response. Man and Young Man are extremely engaging and the playwright allows, indeed consciously manipulates, emotions in the spectator. The audience cannot help empathizing with the two men but yet is taken, step by step, through a process which demands decisions and judgements. The frustration of the two men prior to the discovery of the efficacy of the magical 'green page' is the main focus of the kaleidoscope of emotional changes that they undergo. It is the most emotional of the seven plays. However, the scenes involving the Nun serve to disrupt any development of a sense of illusion. The attack on the church is really one of the side issues, but the near surrealism of the Nun scenes shifts the perspective. The Nun, herself, is unworldly, dreamlike. She seems not to see or hear the men but mumbles on and on. Yet she is important to them as they make desperate attempts to reach her. The contrast in the method of treatment of the two themes serves to highlight each by juxtaposition.

Similarly, although Mda seems still to be exploring technique in *Dead End*, the scenes between Charley and God break from the straightforward telling of the story. When Charley tries to justify himself to God, the audience enters the 'confessional' and, through its privileged position, may and must make value judgements. Again, Charley is a likeable, witty rogue and the audience is allowed to teeter dangerously near empathy with him. Without the God scenes, all the blame might be laid on Frikkie, however in the God scenes, Charley's culpability emerges.

As far as staging is concerned, six of the plays are presented in a realistic fashion although none is illusionist in effect. *Dead End*, *We Shall Sing for the Fatherland* and *The Hill* all have surrealistic scenes involving God, the protagonists at their own funerals and the Nun respectively, while *The Road* is entirely symbolic. Symbolism disguised as realism asks the audience to stretch their powers of acceptance. *Dark Voices Ring* (Mda 1990a) and *And the Girls in Their Sunday Dresses* (Mda 1993b) are staged realistically but the lack of a conventional set in each play (as in all the plays) counteracts any visual temptation of illusion.

Joys of War, set on three distinct levels or acting areas which allow for the separation of time and place, is the most innovative of all the plays as far as staging is concerned. The two soldiers are placed on the uppermost level, and when not active assume poses in silhouette, as if statues in a war memorial. This potent image and the partly ironic title serve to remind the audience that the issue of armed insurrection is a possible answer to an impossible situation that cannot be condemned out of hand. The fact that this is the top level also places the soldiers on a pedestal, as it were: they are to be admired, aspired to, supported. At the bottom level are Mama and Nana. Apart from being the least significant or powerful in society (old people and children), they have the furthest to go. They have a long and arduous journey ahead of them and it is only at the end that they can climb up to the ironic safety of the soldiers. The middle level is the realm of dream, imagination, memory. The demonstrations of the past may be observed independently at this level or the protagonists may take an active part, willingly or unwillingly. Funerals, weddings, interrogation chambers or police cells – the shadowy figures of the mind move at this, not always tangible, level which is always *between* states of consciousness. Although the scenes on the upper and lower levels usually work independently of each other and although the characters are mostly unaware of each other, there are moments of interaction between the two. For example, very early in the play the soldiers' conversation is interrupted by Mama's laughter. They react in amazement at her short interchange with Nana, then resume their conversation as if nothing has happened (*JW* 91/2). They register the presence of the others but it is not until the end that the four actually meet up. There is no acknowledgement of the previous encounter. Although there are several clues dropped during the course of the rest of the dialogue, this is perhaps the clearest indication for the audience that there is a link between these two groups.

Usually, if the intention is merely to relate either an incident or a complex story, a logical and progressive sequence of events is followed. But when the ultimate intention is didactic, moralistic or revolutionary a logical sequence is immaterial. It is enough that the points are made and that the necessary outcome, either the persuasion to action or agreement of one's audience, is achieved. The order of the points is less important than the impact of each. Consequently, according to Brecht, the scenes in a play need not be in any specific order. It would seem that Mda also sees scenes as not necessarily sequential, plot development being of less importance than thesis. As far as scene arrangement is concerned, *Dead End, Dark Voices Ring, The Hill* and *And the Girls in Their Sunday Dresses* are sequential and linear. The other three experiment with three different types of scene arrangement. *We Shall Sing for the Fatherland* is ostensibly the story of the predicament of two veterans who are spurned by society and who eventually die of exposure. However, if the incidents during the course of the play are examined, it soon becomes evident that they are not vehicles for the development of the plot but rather commentaries on society in general and society's relationship with the soldiers. The order of the scenes is of no significance. They are entirely independent of each other and, although not extraneous to the plot, do not propel it forward.

Businessman and Banker's conversation may occur at any stage in relation to the Young Man, the Young Woman and the Old Woman. Even Ofisiri's scenes, while he does become more and more ruthless, do not really demand specific positions – whether in relation to each other or the scenes involving the other characters. Even the final stamping out of the fire and the Old Woman's offering of shelter may be interchangeable, though, because they result in the deaths of the two heroes, they must occur near the end of the play. Of course, the funeral scene must come last.

The Road presents an interesting pattern as far as scene arrangement is concerned. As in the previous play, the various scenes, such as the re-enactment of history, Labourer's 'singing' for his supper and so on, need not be in any particular order. The various confessions and activities within the play are presented to the audience for assessment without sequential direction. The initial setting of the scene and the final gunshot serve as a framing device to illustrate the inevitable outcome of the system described within the play.

In *Joys of War* the juxtaposition of scenes has a more specific purpose. It serves as both a tension breaker and a means of retaining links. For example, in the first conversation between the soldiers, Soldier One discusses, firstly, the unnecessary death of his baby due to a lack of health facilities in the squatter camp and the bureaucracy responsible for the situation. They then go on to the subject of the so-called 'suicides' of political and other prisoners. These two subjects are critical in the lives of the protagonists and the audience. They are also potentially inflammatory. Mda insists on his characters and his audience remaining focused on the issue. He has Mama suddenly stand up in the middle of a discussion and 'laugh aloud for a long time' (*JW* 91). The soldiers look at her in amazement, and then, after her short dialogue with Nana, resume their conversation. They have not forgotten their topic but the tension has been defused. Later on, when the two soldiers' conversation becomes heated, Soldier Two threatens to shoot Soldier One. The latter tries to make light of it but obviously feels seriously threatened:

> **Soldier One**   You must be crazy. Of course you are joking, eh? You are serious then? I am sure you are joking. Ha! What a joke. It's a joke, isn't it? Just a joke? (94)

After Nana's interruption, Soldier One's next words are: 'Tell me, man, have you ever been in love?' (94). This reduction of tension by means of a scene change occurs several times throughout the play.

Sometimes the break is abrupt but at others Mda allows the scenes to be linked, usually by means of a common word. While Soldier One is telling his story of being held by the police and interrogated, Mama and Nana are still puzzling over what has happened to Nana's father (Soldier One). Soldier One says: 'You know, when they ultimately *released* me I kept on thinking about the big map on the wall' (115). The scene changes abruptly to the two women and Mama remarks: 'I don't think prison agrees with your papa. He was never the same after they *released* him from the local prison' (116). The linking word (in this case 'released') is a device used several times. Early in the play the link is more elusive. The audience is beginning to suspect a connection between

Soldier One and the women when Soldier One describes the effects and aftermath of a police raid on a squatter camp. Immediately Nana, who feels that her father has betrayed her by deserting her, says: 'But others say they saw him run away. Then again they saw him at a bus stop with a luggage … running away on us' (102). 'We', however, know he is a soldier and can arrive at the right conclusion by filling in the blanks in the story.

Mda's control of form is perhaps most evident when he allows his separate scenes to merge at the end of each of the two acts in *Joys of War*. The end of Act One sees a linked but separate discussion of why Soldier One/Papa has deserted his family and joined the guerrilla army. At the end of the play the two women climb up the stage levels to the 'safety' of the soldiers. Ironically, to them, safety means freedom from the dangers of criminal types and police and what safer place for this would there be than with the underground army? Physically and metaphorically, they reach the same level as the soldiers.

If Mda does not use the independence of scenes solely to break the tension, conversely he does not break tension only by scene change. Although traditionally, humour has been treated with great suspicion in political theatre, it seems to work well for Mda as a diffusing device. Evident in *Joys of War* on two occasions, it is used more extensively in *The Road* and in *We Shall Sing for the Fatherland*. The use of humour in *The Road* is the most delicate where he is dealing with a serious and humourless subject, highly emotive whichever side of the divide the audience sits. The use of symbolism throughout the play could serve to render it pedantic and overly didactic. However, the treatment of the notion of discrimination according to skin colour as a matter fit only for derisive laughter is an effective weapon as well as a means of keeping the audience in check. If members of the public are going to allow themselves to judge the situation clearly, they simply cannot have their faculties clouded by high passion.

The play abounds with reference to colour and, in the beginning, Farmer and Labourer talk at cross-purposes about their respective relationships with blacks. Farmer, beginning with the caution against hitch hiking, says: 'You never know man, you might be stopping a black car for a lift' (*TR* 125). All South Africans would know that this means a car driven by a black person but Labourer (a foreigner from Lesotho) says: 'A hearse!' The tone has been set. The humour is wry but it is humour nevertheless, so that the audience reacts, not with a sense of outrage but – more potently – with a sense of the ridiculous. That Farmer, later on, realizes that Labourer is black only because he has been told so is ludicrous. 'Why didn't you tell me you were black, you bastard?' he yells (131). Labourer attempts to mollify him by saying: 'Now look, don't get emotional about this' – but it is too late, and it is too late for the audience as well. However, it is laughter that will be evinced from them here and this is important if they are to assess and judge. The message they get is: colour discrimination is totally ludicrous – how can we allow ourselves to be made a laughing stock? The duplicity of the pre-1994 National Government is then driven home in the later discussion on government policy towards foreign non-whites. Because of trade, i.e. money, the National Government declared the Japanese 'honorary white'. The Taiwanese, being non-communist, were also 'honorary white' while communist mainland Chinese were not. Non-South African blacks, also for reasons of trade, were given privileges not accorded to South African blacks. As it stands: irrational; but when Farmer is able to look closely at Labourer and tell that he is from Lesotho and not any other neighbouring black state this makes the whole issue laughable, especially when he had been unable to detect Labourer's blackness previously. Making fun of something is a powerful method of reform as all famous satirists have found.

The emotional control in *We Shall Sing for the Fatherland* is of a different kind. Throughout the play it is the humorous banter between Janabari and Sergeant that engages the audience in their dilemma. Derelicts though they are, and physically repulsive as the other characters find them, we, the audience, care about them and we are concerned for their future. However, lest we concentrate too strongly on their individuality and lose sight of the issue at hand, Mda will not allow any inappropriate emotion in their death scene. Here are two war veterans who are not only forgotten by a society that owes them everything, but are actively rejected. Because of the inhumanity of this ungrateful society, the two men are about to die of exposure, yet they will not sleep before singing a patriotic song to 'the fatherland' (the irony of the supposed caring and protecting 'father' is not lost on the audience) (*WSF* 44). Before the audience can lose itself in empathy with these two, Mda jolts them into laughter. The veterans, in all seriousness, stand mouthing the song because their voices will not emerge. The scene is funny. The situation would be funny were it not so serious.

The more easily detectable Brechtian devices such as narration, role-playing, music and special effects are all part of Mda's dramatic repertoire as well, although (with the exception of *We Shall Sing for the Fatherland*) narration and role-playing are the key elements.

Direct narration is a major feature of *Dead End*. Charley narrates anecdotes and explanations to God while Charley and Tseli swap experiences, either shared or individual. The action of the fabula is told rather than acted out. *Dark Voices Ring*, to a slightly lesser extent, also has Man and Woman narrate the story of Nontobeko – her birth, her expectations and her demise. The other four plays, *The Hill*, *The Road*, and *And the Girls in Their Sunday Dresses* and *Joys of War* use narration mainly to fill the audience in on the history of the various characters, but it is the area of role-playing that is most developed both as a narrative technique and alienating device in these six works.

In *Dead End*, two of the instances are mere dramatic anecdotal excerpts when Charley plays both parts in a scene. He is both Mr Koornhof and Tseli/Anna (*DE* 7) and he acts out Tseli's future problems in having to cope with a baby. Very briefly (5 lines) he and God slip into the roles of priest and altar boy (11). Again, in *Dark Voices Ring*, initially, Man merely impersonates Woman on the telephone to van Wyk (*DVR* 55/6) but later Mda skillfully interweaves narration and role-playing when the treatment of prison labour is depicted. Woman, taking the part of her *induna* husband wields an imaginary whip while she shouts at Man (as the prisoner): '*Voetsek* Janfek! Move on!' (62). She and Man mime the whipping scene whereupon he goes on to mime digging the potatoes while she narrates the next part. Man intervenes, as Janfek, and they resume their roles, reverting again to narration. And so it goes on, moving smoothly from narration to role-playing over the course of two pages.

The Hill shows a degree of sophistication not achieved in the previous two plays in the dramatic use of role-playing. Young Man acts out his supposed return to his family with the fatuous symbols of his success (the steering wheel and the car battery), simultaneously contrasting the hollowness of this success with the abjectness of the reality of their lives (*TH* 79). The scene showing the rich doctor negotiating to employ Young Man to do gardening work (15/6), emphasizes the contrast in their social situations. It highlights the lack of concern of the doctor, who compares, with cool disregard, the five rand per month he offers Young Man for labour and the 1500 rand per month he expects himself.

The other scenes with Man and Veteran in the roles of NRC recruiting officer and prospective recruit, and later with Veteran as a mine evangelist and the rest of the cast as congregation – deal graphically and yet subtly with corruption and hypocrisy respectively. A mere narration in these instances may seem like biased misrepresentation but the re-enactment is much more convincing and far more conducive to judgement-forming on the part of the audience.

In *The Road* Mda makes use of role-playing twice in very different ways. The first example is the scene when Labourer reads from 'Chapman's Travels in the Interior of South Africa' (*TR* 143) and the two men act out the roles of explorer and slave bearer/guide. The impact in this instance lies, not so much in role-playing nor in the actual roles played, but in the irony of Labourer, representing the colonized, reading out the story of his subjugation. The other role-playing scene is, typically for the characters in this play, at cross-purposes. Labourer acts out his conversation with his wife Lucy about her request for 'a big male dog' (151), while Farmer acts out his wife's recognition of him in a magazine photo taken at a Swaziland 'house of sin' (151). It is well that neither man is concerned in the other's story but tells his own independently, because both stories concern their sexual relations with their wives – did they but know it. And their sex lives are interlinked – did they but know it. The roleplaying makes the events immediate but their presentation highlights the subtlety of the relationship between the two.

In *And the Girls in Their Sunday Dresses* we also find two instances of role-playing, both with similar purpose. The first scene sees Woman as an evangelical preacher – a prostitute made good. She has 'seen the light' and now sings at evangelical rallies all round the world, having married a 'john' who fell in love with her. She urges her congregation to see the error of their ways but the message is clear to them in the words of the Lady:

> I will repent. I feel the spirit. I will repent. But first let me find myself a john who
> will marry me and take me to Europe with him, or who will build me a house in

Maseru West, and furnish it. Then I'll repent! And be saved! And work for the Lord... (*GSD* 22)

The second instance of role-playing in this play shows the Lady as one of the civil servants and the Woman as a purchaser of a bag of 'free rice'. The necessarily obsequious attitude of the Woman with her repetitive '*me*' (35) contrasts with the callousness of the person with power. The desperation of someone prepared to queue for four days for a bag of black market rice is emphasized when it is contrasted starkly in an interchange such as:

Lady You can write, can you?
Woman Yes.
Lady Then you can fill in the information yourself while I finish eating my fat cake (35).

In *Joys of War* there is a development in the technique of role-playing. Not only do the characters act out, between them, incidents in their lives, but other characters join them to re-enact their experiences in order to elaborate a point or explain an action or attitude to the other – a device not seen in the other plays. Soldier One, for example, acts out his own interrogation experience (*JW* 112), while Soldier Two acts out his rejection by his erstwhile lover (128) and then his own scene relating his betrayal, with false information to the police, of his betrayers (134).

Narration and role-playing can be seen, then, to be valuable devices in Mda's technical repertoire – not only for the frequency in which they appear in all the plays but also for the variety and efficacy with which he uses them.

Music is used in a very minor way in Mda's plays, but the fact that six of the seven feature at least one song even if it is only a silent one as in *We Shall Sing for the Fatherland* must prompt some comment. The songs are largely atmospheric, taking the form of lullabies, wedding or funeral songs and the like. Two of them are ironic: the praise song Veteran sings on his entrance in *The Hill* is ironic because it is a joyful song of optimism sung to young men on their initiation into manhood; while Labourer's song in *The Road* as he sweeps the road for Farmer, though typical because 'we always sing and dance to make our labour more enjoyable' (*TR* 140), is ironic because of the outrageous liberties Farmer has taken.

Usually in theatre, props are an adjunct to the realism of the action or as a reinforcement of the text. In Brechtian theatre props draw attention to themselves because they are an intrinsic part of the dialectic. Although Mda makes little use of props, when he does, the impact is powerful. In *The Hill*, the symbolism of the flower and rosary (grace and blessings from the church) and of the steering wheel and car battery (spurious riches from the land of gold) are self-evident, but the possession of a pair of trousers has a sizeable impact. Initially, Young Man appears on stage without trousers, emphasizing his vulnerability and the dire circumstances in which the size of his excrement indicates the extent of his success in life. Then it is the turn of Veteran to enter without trousers: he has been robbed not only of his possessions but also his dignity. He remains trouserless for the duration of the play, a visible reminder of the indignities he has and still must suffer in the mines as a migrant worker. Finally, he steals the trousers from Man, who must finish the play in total humiliation. The other two have separately improved their positions. Man is as low as he can go and we are left with the reminder, continuous throughout the play, of the right of a man to his dignity and of its fragility.

In *The Road, And the Girls in Their Sunday Dresses* and *Joys of War* props are used symbolically. The book in *The Road,* the 'chair of patience' in *And the Girls in Their Sunday Dresses* and the doll in *Joys of War* are all self-evident. That they are used so sparingly does not diminish their importance – on the contrary, they are fore-grounded by their minimal use.

Brechtian technique is better known for its devices simply because they are a little more obvious, but the essential Brechtian technique lies more in the alienation effect of the construction of its text. In inexpert hands an imbalance can sometimes degenerate into mere gimmickry. That Mda's emphasis is on the alienation effect achieved within the writing of the text shows that he understands fully what van Dijk means when he criticizes 'the overwhelming tendency to see Brecht's theory and practice as a style rather than a method' (van Dijk 1990: 121).

BIBLIOGRAPHY

Barnett, Ursula A., 1983, *A Vision of Order: A Study of Black South African Literature in English (1914–1980)* (London: Sinclair Browne).
de Graft, J.C., 1976, 'Roots in African dama and theatre', in Eldred Durosimi Jones (ed.) *African Literature Today, Vol. 8: Drama in Africa* (London: Heinemann).
Dickson, Keith A., 1978, *Towards Utopia: A Study of Brecht* (Oxford: Clarendon Press).
Eddershaw, Margaret, 1982, 'Acting methods: Brecht and Stanislavsky', in Graham Bartram and Anthony Waine (eds), *Brecht in Perspective* (London: Longman).
Mda, Zakes, 1983, 'Commitment and writing in theatre: the South African experience', *The Classic* (South Africa), 2, 1: 13–15.
— 1990a, *The Plays of Zakes Mda*, introd. Andrew Horn (Johannesburg: Ravan Press).
— 1990b, 'Marotholi traveling theatre: towards an alternative perspective of development', *Journal of African Studies*, 16, 2 (June): 352–8.
— 1993a, *When People Play People: Development Communication Through Theatre* (London: Zed Books).
— 1993b, *And the Girls in Their Sunday Dresses: Four Works* (Johannesburg: Witwatersrand University Press).
— 1995, 'Theatre and reconciliation in South Africa', *Theatre*, 25, 3: 38–44.
Sitas, Ari, 1986, 'Culture and production: the contradictions of working class theatre in South Africa', *Africa Perspective*: 84–110.
Subiotto, Arrigo, 1982, 'Epic theatre: a theatre for the scientific age', in Graham Bartram and Anthony Waine (eds), *Brecht in Perspective* (London: Longman).
Van Dijk, Maartin, 1990, 'Blocking Brecht', in Pia Kleber and Colin Visser (eds), *Re-interpreting Brecht: His Influence on Contemporary Drama and Film* (Cambridge: Cambridge University Press).

Propaganda & Mass Education
Alec Dickson & drama for development in the Gold Coast

JAMES GIBBS

Introduction

Alec Dickson, best known in the United Kingdom for his work with Voluntary Service Overseas and Community Service Volunteers, and in the United States for his contribution to the foundation of the Peace Corps, worked in the Gold Coast briefly during the late forties. He was concerned with mass education, social welfare and community development programmes. Although he was not interested in drama *per se*, his determination to use all available methods in order to challenge those he was working with, to clarify issues, communicate information and recommended solutions, encouraged him to experiment in the area that is now known as theatre for development.

For the Gold Coast, Dickson's gospel, and I use the word advisedly in view of the prophetic fervour with which he argued his case and the recklessness with which he aroused opposition, was that of mass education in a very broad sense. He had the temerity to aspire 'to change the social atmosphere'. The account that follows, using publications and documents from among Dickson's own papers as well as published sources, gives an indication of his approach, the controversy it embroiled him in and the legacy it left. Although fascinated by the light cast on the operation of colonial administration, my particular interest is in the use of drama (impersonation, before an audience, of a structured sequence). I suggest that Dickson should be regarded as a pioneer in the use of drama within the context of a national community development programme on the West African coast.

From the analysis, it becomes clear that, while he appreciated that drama, coupled with discussion and demonstration, had an important role to play in focusing community effort, Dickson did not approach the issue with clearly articulated ideas as to how precisely plays should be put together or how groups should be gathered to perform them. He was open to suggestions from those around him, but, by default, his cultural background influenced him: he was most comfortable with familiar European conventions, with carefully plotted, moral and didactic pieces. His work in drama for community development was continued by further projects undertaken by, for example, the Social Welfare and Community Development Department, by the Extra-Mural Studies Department and by the Workers' Brigade Drama Group. This work throws light on *Foriwa*, a play by Efua Sutherland that addressed development issues.

Background

In *A Chance to Serve*, the principal introduction to Dickson's life and a source I shall draw on repeatedly, Mora Dickson, his widow, edited his writings so that she created a picture that is partly a self-portrait. The effect is curiously like a brass rubbing: the original is underneath, the labour of the intermediary makes it appear on paper.

Born in 1911, Alexander Graeme (Alec) Dickson's important early experiences included public school life – he went to Rugby – and visits to Germany during the period when fascism was beginning to make an impact on old and young. Scouting, patriotism, awareness of the links established between Oxbridge and deprived communities in London – Dickson was an undergraduate at Oxford – all contributed to the matrix within which his early ideas developed.

Always articulate and anxious to communicate, he became a journalist on graduation, working on *The Yorkshire Post* and *Daily Telegraph*. Even while starting his career, he managed to combine writing with organizing activities for disadvantaged young men. The war gave his life a new direction and brought military service with the Cameron Highlanders and the 1st King's African Rifles. By 1940 he was in command of a platoon in the Abyssinian Campaign.

As for some others, the army provided opportunities to experiment and to move into new areas of activity. In the final months of the conflict, Dickson led the East African Command Mobile Propaganda Unit. This project grew out of his recognition of the advantages of using servicemen as agents for influencing the communities in which they had grown up. He argued that military training and experiences under arms had equipped the soldiers with a perspective that was of benefit to their 'home towns'.

In an article on 'The Returned Askari' that was published in *The Times* (1945), Dickson pointed out that the East African Command Mobile Propaganda Unit could be used to

> convey by display, demonstration and discussion – to illiterate farmers, herdsmen, plantation workers, copper miners and schools, what the war was about, why it had been won, and how they could contribute to victory.

There is no specific mention of drama in this telescoped account, nor is there in 'Tell Africa: an experiment in mass education' which appeared in *Geographical Magazine* during March 1946. It is apparent, however, that in addition to the methods mentioned above, 'display, demonstration and discussion', he made use of games, music and 'Janes' techniques'. Many of the ingredients of drama were, thus, present.

A Chance to Serve includes an account of the Unit putting on a 'potted, mobile edition of the Aldershot tattoo but containing as high an educational content as possible' (Dickson 1976: 28). The 'show' was performed widely in East and Central Africa by a contingent of men from different language groups and with varied backgrounds. Dickson was able to write: 'Our unit has left every village in Nyasaland and N. Rhodesia singing our songs and emulating our PT' (Dickson 1976: 31).

Dickson's awareness of the purposes of education – or propaganda – was broad. For while his views had partly been formed in England, and while East Africa had made a distinctive contribution, American and continental influences were also important. His thinking reflected the ideas about mass education associated with literacy teaching techniques developed in the Philippines by Dr Frank Laubach, and he was well aware of the achievements of the US Civilian Conservation Corps. As an example of what large-scale planning could achieve for the transformation of life in a vast area, the Tennessee Valley Authority provided inspiration.

His ideas about character formation, already fairly clear from his experience at Rugby, were influenced by the writings of Kurt Hahn and by the examples provided by the Outward Bound Movement. As far as drama was concerned, there were the pioneering ventures of the Village Theatre Movement in the United Kingdom, and of the way Moral Rearmament used touring productions of plays, such as *The Forgotten Factor*, to stress the importance of individual commitment to an ideal.

These influences were all apparent in the ideas about mass education programmes that he developed. He worked on the principle that the goal was to 'change the social atmosphere' and in order to do this, he was convinced, people should be equipped with skills. Throughout his work and writing the concern to mobilize groups for specific purposes was combined with a recognition that this implied creating opportunities for individuals to become involved and transformed. He quoted with approval Lord Elton's comment in *St George and the Dragon* that 'It was not so much the Crusaders who made the Crusade, as the Crusade which made the Crusaders.'

In attempting to 'change the social atmosphere', Dickson adopted a step by step approach. There were, as he saw it, various stages by which a community could be led to a point at which development could take place. Literacy was of primary importance, and this was linked with physical training, courses on civics, discussion groups and debates. In the broad context provided by this approach, projects involving music and drama had roles to play.

Gold Coast Experience

Dickson's work in East Africa impressed Henry Gurney, who was the Acting Governor General in the Gold Coast for substantial periods during 1945 and 1946, and led to an invitation to take up a post in Mass Communication in Accra. However, on assuming duties, Dickson found a colonial administration that was unhappy with any reference to 'Mass Communication'. Gurney had been moved on and the colonial service – partly accommodated in Christiansbourg Castle – was (in 1948) initially complacent and then, when faced by a boycott of European goods and rioting in the major towns, jittery. In this political climate there were doubts about the whole idea of 'Mass Movements' and Dickson, the apostle of mass communication, soon found himself stripped of his designation 'Mass Education Officer' and dubbed 'Social Welfare Development Officer'. Given this inauspicious start, it was not surprising his influence was more or less limited to the production of a handbook and to a few projects in Trans-Volta.

The *Mass Education Handbook* described activities for clubs and women's groups. From the sections on common ailments and domestic hygiene in that volume, it is clear that health and health education were of prime importance. The teaching techniques recommended included the use of visual aids – it was the age of the flannel-graph, and 'transparencies' – and a section on the use of Keroscope projectors. There was nothing in the book on drama as such. Only in the paragraphs on the importance of demonstration when teaching first-aid was pretence and acting mentioned. For an insight into Dickson's views of drama it is necessary to examine the Trans-Volta projects in some detail.

Dickson's account of his work in Trans-Volta, 'an experiment in mass education', appeared in *African Affairs* (Dickson 1950a) and *Overseas Education* (Dickson 1950b). In the latter, 'Condensed by W.E.F. Ward, from a longer report', and presented under the title 'Training community leaders in the Gold Coast', Dickson was, clumsily, described as 'formerly Social Development Officer'. The longer document can be found in the Dickson Papers and a substantial part is reproduced in *A Chance to Serve*. The account is of fundamental importance for the investigation of Dickson's approach – it gives an idea of the context in which he operated, contains clues to the influences on his thinking and provides information about his working methods – including his use of drama.

The title of Dickson's paper as it appeared in *Overseas Education* does not indicate the extent to which it reflects what happened on four courses in the Trans-Volta area of the Gold Coast. And it does not tell the story behind that 'formerly' – the reason why Dickson moved on shortly after the courses closed. In fact, he had lasted only about eighteen months in the country. The Castle, as indicated above, was unhappy with Dickson; and he had limited sympathy for the Castle. For example, while tactfully recognizing the value of the year-long training courses offered in Accra for welfare assistants, he was anxious to proceed in an altogether more populist direction. The courses he organized were held well away from Accra, and during them a large number of people were exposed to experiences which, he hoped, would result in radically changed attitudes. The following extract illustrates his 'gospel' – and it takes little imagination to picture the expressions on the faces of the conservative elements in the colonial administration when it was read out:

> [The] need to create a social climate of venturesome initiative, in the words of the Cambridge Report, is – in the writer's view – the vital, fundamental role of mass

education. Providing the emotional outlet needed in a society fast losing its traditional forms of self-expression: creating a people's movement for social betterment; evoking the new mental and moral qualities called for by the new order that the educated African wants; developing a social tolerance and cohesion; emphasising the obligation of service to the community by the educated elite; recognising the strong element of enjoyment, without which community development cannot succeed: these were the objects of the campaign, and not the formation of a model P.W.D. gang or a glorified sanitary squad.

The reference to 'the Cambridge Report' was to a Colonial Office document produced after a Conference held in the university town during 1948. As can be appreciated, it provided a number of statements that Dickson could use to justify the programmes he wanted to implement. But, aware that nationalist politicians were attracting large crowds, the Castle was terrified of 'venturesome initiative'. Reports from Cambridge could be waved around, but they did not impress those who sat in Christiansbourg Castle, the men on the spot.

Under Dickson's leadership, courses lasting roughly a fortnight were held at Peki, Anfoega Akukome, Kpedze Awlime and Abor. The reasons Dickson gave for concentrating on the area included the following:

> The Ewe people form a homogeneous tribal block, of a size and vigour that make them suitable for a mass education campaign. They are interested in their own language, and attempts have recently been made to produce a mass literacy primer. They are increasingly conscious of their own nationhood. They have a tradition of craftsmanship and a really outstanding aptitude for choral music. And they themselves expressed a desire for mass education to be started among them. (Dickson 1950b: 3).

It was also, in all probability, convenient for both parties that Dickson should be a long way from Accra. For Dickson, it was invaluable that involvement in the courses was encouraged by the Evangelical Presbyterian Church which had a devoted following in the area. The seeds of his secular gospel fell on soil that others had prepared.

Predictably, the programme centred on a literacy drive, but attention was also given to first-aid, hygiene, physical recreation, discussions, civics, music, cinema, drama, hobbies, and women's crafts. The report, which Ward condensed for publication in *Overseas Education*, indicates how uncertain Dickson was about the precise means by which progress could best be made. He was, with a modesty rarely encountered among, say, foreign aid workers, World Bank Officials and lecturers in Theatre Arts, feeling his way, prepared to recognize that he did not know all the answers. For example, with regard to health education, he was uncertain whether priority should be given to treating emergencies or to basic hygiene. And he wondered aloud what should be treated under 'civics'. It is apparent that under this heading he spoke about Kurt Hahn's life and career, and that George Padmore, whose very name must have given some of those in the Castle apoplexy, was afforded the opportunity

to speak. Apparently he delivered what Dickson described as 'some highly ten-
dentious effusion ... on Imperialism'.

There was, it seems, a brief discussion about what drama should be used for
and how it should be organized. This did not, however, constitute anything
like the full debate on 'Aesthetic considerations to maximise communication in
theatre for development' that was necessary. Reporting on what seems to have
been a fairly dilatory discussion, Dickson wrote:

> We toyed with the idea at first of presenting little plays featuring Ananse the Spider
> of West African folklore. We were not, however, a touring concert-party out to
> entertain native audiences – but a training team endeavouring to instruct voluntary
> leaders in how they themselves might organise village drama. We had, therefore, to
> show first how to take a social problem and dramatise it; then, how to present it.

In view of the importance of Ananse stories to Ghanaian dramatists and the use
that has been made of Concert Parties to teach and preach, this is a paragraph
full of missed opportunities. Neither playwrights nor concert partymen,
Dickson and his group were happier in the role of missionaries with a secular
gospel. They built on familiarity with a heritage they shared with many of the
local participants – and made use of New Testament parables, such as The
Good Samaritan and The Prodigal Son. Since members of the Evangelical
Presbyterian Church were supporting the courses in force, this was very
familiar territory indeed to many of those involved. Relevant secular lessons
were tagged onto or tugged out of Biblical narratives. Various modern-dress
versions of The Good Samaritan were performed and the prodigal son or
daughter lived riotously in Kumasi and Accra before returning to his or her
village.

There was, however, room for a larger measure of local inspiration. Dickson
continued:

> Other more secular themes treated were the sick-father turning from the rapacious
> futilities of the witch-doctor to the gratuitous benevolence of a Government
> dispenser (this was not meant in the satirical sense that it might appear); the responsi-
> bilities of parents in juvenile delinquency; and the scorned wife who enrolled on a
> literacy course so as to find out what was in the notes being passed between her
> husband and the Other Woman, and who eventually regained his respect and
> affection. (Dickson 1950b: 9)

Course members, it appears, actually put on their own plays. Wisely, in view
of their lack of knowledge about local conventions, leaders did not suggest
'how drama could be organised'. Dickson wrote, quite frankly, 'we had not
ourselves thought out the matter (nor is it easy to)'.

Dickson recognized that it was too much to hope that 'those attending our
courses of only a fortnight would go away and start a village theatre
movement'. There is, it should be noted, a certain ambiguity in all this, since,
despite a reluctance to 'suggest' there had been 'leadership by example' and,
thanks to the status that inevitably accompanied him, Dickson established a

particular pattern: the simple moral narrative emerged as the dominant pattern for the drama.

The situation was further complicated because, while providing leadership from the outside, Dickson expressed his conviction that local leadership was an essential part of the success of community development. He noted the contributions to the courses of the Revd C.G. Baeta, A. Kotei (an illustrator), 'Kumasi' Kassena (an ex-serviceman who led the physical training sessions), Lucy Alar (a senior nurse), William Tsitsiwu (a singing teacher), and Police Bandsman Adzaku. Dickson was not the first, nor was he the last, to find himself providing an influence while recognizing his own inadequacies, and lauding the talents of those with whom he was collaborating. Given the fact that he had been in the country only a short time, he was probably only vaguely aware of the significance of what he was doing in working with Baeta and the others. The impact of Christian missions on the Guinea Coast had been accompanied by the introduction of traditions of art, music, military training, health education and singing. He was, in fact, working with men and women who had grown up in and contributed to syncretized traditions.

Working in Trans-Volta had certain advantages – not least that it was beyond the immediate supervision of the Castle. However, being so close to French-ruled Togo meant that there were opportunities for international embarrassment. Dickson was, in any case, dangerously impressed by French patterns. It was his opinion, for example, that the French were more aware of the potential for drama in community development than the British: he referred to 'Le petit théâtre au village', which, apparently, was covered in a course given at L'Institut Français d'Afrique Noir, in Dakar. And he worked with Gabriel Johnson from Togo, who, he considered, possessed a fine sense of humour, and who brought imaginative insights to theatrical situations. As if praising a 'rival' imperial power were not enough, Dickson entertained His Excellency M. Cedille who travelled from Lome and spent a day and two nights at the course. Cedille clearly took a great interest in what was being done but the encounter was not without repercussions. Indeed it seems to have occasioned something of an international incident (Dickson 1950a: 150; see also du Sautoy 1958).

As can be appreciated from this brief description of the course and Dickson's 'general attitude', the format for mass education he encouraged could be seen as presenting a challenge to the entrenched position of colonial administrators in Accra. The involvement of 'international Communists' such as George Padmore was particularly provocative, and the collaboration with the French was clearly unpopular with those at Christiansbourg. An account of the forces perceived to be at work is provided in *A Chance to Serve* where Mora Dickson writes:

> The Colonial Service were paranoically obsessed that [Alec Dickson] was seeking to introduce some totalitarian form of organisation, equating with the Hitler Jugend his every proposal for utilising the potential energies and idealism of young people for constructive tasks.

In vain Alec Dickson cited his favourite passage from *Faith for Living*, written by Lewis Mumford…: 'But the young will care for their regional home if they have a part in creating it … They should help clear the slums as well as studying housing, they should help plant the forests as well as study conservation.' It should not need another war to effect this purposeful mobilisation of youth. (Dickson 1976: 45).

However, if mass education was viewed with suspicion from the Castle, it was, predictably, championed elsewhere. The emphasis on literacy found favour with some of 'the educated natives' to whom Dickson referred in a passage quoted earlier. In reporting one 'of the only two wise-cracks that were ever made at our expense by the African press' (a remark that after ten days on the literacy course, participants would be able to '… spell "Convention"'), Dickson was hinting at the support he received from the nationalists – particularly from members of the *Convention* Peoples' Party.

During the months that followed the Trans-Volta initiatives, the local nationalist press took up Dickson's cause and case. The flow of events can be glimpsed through the reports in the newspapers. Part of the issue was exposed in 'Mr Dickson and Mass Education' which appeared in the *Accra Evening News* on Christmas Eve 1948. There an anonymous contributor drew attention to the 'confusion' surrounding Dickson's appointment: it was stated that Dickson '[had] been denied his true professional chances [in order] to figure merely as a Social Development Officer'.

After Christmas battle was resumed with 'This team teaches people community life.' (*Ashanti Times*, 29 December 1948), where it was reported that Dickson was leaving for Trans-Volta, and it was noted that he had been, with David Kimble of Extra-Mural Studies, to 'French Sudan'. This was followed by 'The Man Dickson' in the *Gold Coast Express* (19 February 1949: 2) and, the following month, by Kofi Baako's contribution. Baako (1949) summed up much that had gone before and found someone to blame in an article in *The West African Monitor* with a title to frighten many colonial servants: 'Mass Education and Self-Government'. He said Dickson 'came and was pushed to one side', and he placed the blame for this marginalization on Tom Barton of the Education Department.

From his arrival, Dickson's work had been viewed with suspicion by many colonial officers in the Gold Coast. When he was championed in the columns of the nationalist newspapers, his exit was assured. He left having spent only eighteen months in the country. However the kind of work, including the work with drama, that he had been doing could not be 'pushed to one side'. Publications indicate that it continued.

In a *Report on Community Development* sent from the Governor General of the Gold Coast to the Secretary of State for Colonies, London, on 27 August 1949, it was noted that 'Drama instruction is given in the techniques of dramatizing local themes of social importance.' This was put in context by the following statement:

> The intention has been to instruct educated young people in the technique of such things as the organisation of mass literacy, the improvement of choirs and village

bands, the encouragement of physical training and games, the fostering of hygiene and first aid lessons, and the presentation of short open-air plays.

Owen Barton, one of Dickson's colleagues in the Social Welfare Department and not to be confused with Tom Barton of the Education Department, gave a broadcast talk on 'Mass Education' that was printed in the *Gold Coast Bulletin* during November 1949. Under the heading 'Village Drama', he referred to 'amusing sketches which have a theme of social significance'. The examples of topics treated included juvenile delinquency, agricultural techniques, and modern medical practice. Owen Barton sounded a rare note when he commented on the 'aesthetic elements' in the performances: he observed that it was 'difficult to correct the tendency to produce long dramas', and pointed out that dialogue drama was used with music, singing and discussion groups.

Drama continued to occupy a significant place in the work of what became the Gold Coast Social Welfare and Community Development Department. When the Colonial Secretary visited the country early in 1950, the *Bulletin* reported that

> [He] watched a short comedy in four acts by members of the [Mass Education] team. The play, which carried a moral aimed at discouraging the drift from the country into the large towns, showed the misfortunes which befell a farmer's son who was persuaded by a visitor, a hooligan from Kumasi, to leave his village 'to find work' in the larger town. (Anon. 1950).

By this time, Dickson was about to go to the British Cameroons. There he embarked on a very fruitful period at Man O'War Bay, developing his concern with leadership training by using challenging situations, or 'happenings', to involve the participants deeply in problem-solving exercises.

Drama for community development in the Gold Coast flourished in a Social Welfare and Community Development Department led by the influential Peter du Sautoy, where drama work was undertaken by Ken Pickering, J. Riby Williams, J. G. Wartemburg and others. And it formed part of the brief of the Workers' Brigade Concert Party that Nkrumah later set up involving Bob Johnson, Bob Thompson, Bob Cole and the Haitian dramatist and director, Felix Morriseau-Leroy. That is a story that has been touched on by K. N. Bame (1985) and John Collins (1994), and that must be told in full at some time.

Return to Ghana

In 1958, after the Gold Coast had been Ghana for some eighteen months, Dickson, who had spent 1956–8 in Iraq, returned to West Africa. He was 'wearing a different hat' having been invited to contribute to a training project in work camp methods. With Hans Peter Muller and Andrew Rutter, he spoke to work camp leaders from West Africa, and on 30 August he was one of the MCs at a dance.

Naturally, he was interested to see what was going on in terms of development work in Nkrumah's Ghana, and was particularly anxious to learn about the Workers' Brigade that had been formed. On 3 September, Ken Pickering took him to see the Brigade in action, and to meet Brigadier Turner. Much had changed since Dickson's time in the Gold Coast, and much was to continue to change – not least the Workers' Brigade.

Conclusion

Few among the younger generation of activists involved in Ghana's vigorous theatre for extension communication programmes are aware of the pioneering part played by Dickson in encouraging the use of drama in community development. But a legacy remains in the impact of mass education projects in Eweland, and in the drama work carried forward by the Social Welfare Department. And, there is a well-known text that is of significance for the history of extension work in Ghana and an account of it provides a fitting coda to this essay.

Efua Sutherland, who significantly worked in education in Trans-Volta in the early fifties, told me she had been aware that activists had made an impression on communities there: she mentioned those involved with reforestation particularly (Efua Sutherland personal communication, 27 March 1995). One of her plays, *Foriwa*, is specifically concerned with community development and grew from a short story revealingly entitled 'New Life in Kyerefaso'. It shows the way youth can work with age, and the importance of women in community life, but the catalyst for much of the action is a freelance, community development worker, a 'stranger', Labaran, who shows that he is prepared to get his hands dirty cleaning up the village. His plans for the community involve greater access to written material and improved methods of agriculture.

Sutherland uses characterization and dialogue, incorporates festival theatre and a plot which involves a marriage, in a fairly conventionally presented scripted drama. The vision of the piece is articulated by Labaran who can be linked with many, his dreams have been shared by a generation or more, but some of his lines are worth quoting in the present context to show that although Dickson was sometimes isolated, he was also part of a chorus. After the Queen Mother has issued a call to the community to end divisive bickering and bring new life to the village, and after her daughter, Foriwa, has committed herself to 'stay and place [her] efforts here', Labaran is exhilarated and decides that he too will remain in a village. He says :

> I will strike camp and build some permanence here, where the dawn for which I was waiting is now beginning ... I was seeking meaningful employment for my reserves of mind, drive, and sensitivity. (*Earnestly*) Postmaster, a university degree is a devil of a thing if all it gives a man, is the passport to a life of vague respectability. I couldn't permit myself to get caught in that ... So, I've been wandering in search of a way of

applying myself. And now I see my feet on hopeful, solid ground, am I not the one to give all the thanks? (Sutherland 1967: 53)

Clearly more remains to be achieved, but, within the world of the play, a decisive battle has been won, there has been a change in the social atmosphere. Labaran, the advocate of community development, the man who puts words into deeds, has found a focus for his ambitions.

Foriwa was first produced in the spring of 1962 when Alec Dickson, having founded Voluntary Service Overseas, 'faced', in the words of *A Chance to Serve*, 'the hard prospect of once again creating a new vehicle for his ideas'. Had he been at the Drama Studio in Accra during the run of *Foriwa*, he would, I am sure, have felt that some of the ideas that were closest to his heart had found expression in a most impressive vehicle.

ALEC DICKSON, SELECTED BIBLIOGRAPHY

— 1945, 'The returned Askari', *The Times* (21 August).
— 1946, 'Tell Africa: an experiment in mass education', *Geographical Magazine* (March): 456–62.
— 1949, 'Mass education – beginning or end?', *West Africa* (26 February).
— 1950a, 'Mass education in Togoland', *African Affairs*, 49, 195 (April): 136–50.
— 1950b, 'Training community leaders in the Gold Coast', *Overseas Education* (London), 22, 1 (October 1950): 8–21. (Draft entitled 'Mass education in the Gold Coast and Togoland'. The draft is longer and includes references to the example of *The Forgotten Factor* and to French colonial training in drama. The *African Affairs* article has details of the experience of working in French Togoland.
Also
1976, Dickson, Alec, edited by Mora Dickson, *A Chance to Serve* (London: Dobson).

GENERAL BIBLIOGRAPHY

Anon., 1948, 'Mr Dickson and mass education', *The Accra Evening News* (24 December): 2; (see also 22 December 1948: 1).
Anon., 1948, 'This team teaches people community life', *Ashanti Times* (29 December).
Anon. ('Appreciative'), 1949, 'The Man Dickson', letter in *Gold Coast Express* (19 February): 2.
Anon., 1950, 'The Colonial Secretary sees display', *Gold Coast Bulletin* (22 February).
Baako, Kofi, 1949, 'Mass education and self-government', *The West African Monitor* (11 May): 1.
Bame, K. N., 1985, *Come to Laugh: African Traditional Theatre in Ghana* (New York: Lillian Barber).
Barton, Owen, 1949, 'Mass education', *Gold Coast Bulletin*, 45 (9 November): 3.
Collins, John, 1994, *Ghanaian Concert Party: African Popular Entertainment at the Cross Roads*, PhD thesis, State University of New York, Buffalo.
du Sautoy, Peter, 1958, *Community Development in Ghana* (London: Oxford University Press).
Gibbs, James, 1997, '"Who is Kofi Basaki?" Finding out about village drama in Ghana', *West Africa* (24 February–2 March): 318–19.
Sutherland, Efua, 1967, *Foriwa* (Accra-Tema: Ghana Publishing Corporation).

Theatre in Development in Mauritius
From a theatre of protest
to a theatre of cultural miscegenation

ROSHNI MOONEERAM

Pedan Gopia Why not ask me what's my problem?
Gouvernèr *Geté! Dan sa lasal la koz lang ofisiel nou lavll. Mo pa pou axepté okenn patwa ousa djalek. konpran!*

Pedan Gopia Why not ask me what's my problem?
Governor Look! In this room we will only speak in the official language of our town. I will not accept any patois or dialect. Understood! (Virahsawmy, *Galileo Gonaz*, 1996: 72)

In this article, I consider the development of Mauritian post-colonial theatre in Creole through the plays of Dev Virahsawmy, Azize Asgarally and Henri Favory. My main focus will be on Virahsawmy, author of the first play in Creole in modern times (1972), and the playwright who has exploited the potential of this radical theatre in order to respond to changing priorities. The first part of this article analyses some of the most important repercussions that the very choice of Creole as dramatic language has entailed, before considering the preoccupations and impact of the early theatre of protest. The second section examines the transition of Virahsawmy's later plays and translations/ adaptations away from a militant commitment to a preoccupation with the emerging ideal of a hybrid cultural identity for the Mauritian nation, and with the initiation of a dialogue between local and international cultural trends. Finally, I point out the potential contribution of theatre towards the development of a literary norm.

Mauritius – a socio-linguistic introduction

Having received immigrants from Europe, Africa and Asia during French (1715–1810) and British (1810–1968) colonization, Mauritius is a multi-ethnic and multi-lingual country, with a complex socio-linguistic composition. Independent since 1968, the country has retained English as the official language although its use is mainly confined to the written medium, education, parliament and the judiciary; and French as a semi-official, prestigious language, acceptable in parliamentary debates. French is also the privileged medium of the press, radio and television. The most widely spoken language, however, the mother tongue of more than three-quarters of the population, cutting across various ethnic groups, is Creole which remains officially unacknowleged and unstandardized. Originating from early French colonization, it was seen as the slaves' deformed imitation of their masters' language, a corrupt form of French. Before independence, Mauritian Creole was considered to be inadequate to fulfil the functions of a written language and quite unsuited to be the medium of literary expression. Since independence, however, Creole has moved on considerably, both in terms of people's perception of it and in terms of the extension of the fields where it functions – not through any efforts from the State, but rather through the efforts of individual artists.

The emergence of a theatre in Creole

French theatrical activities started with the construction of the first theatre building in 1754 (Chelin 1954) and plays were performed by French artists for a francophone elite. Under British rule, theatrical activities picked up only in 1932 with the creation of the Mauritius Dramatic Club, performing Sheridan, Wilde, Shaw, and supported by various Shakespearean performances under the sponsorship of the British Council. Fifty years later, however, with the developments in the theatre in Creole, Decotter (1983: 79) suggests that a turning point had been reached in Mauritian dramaturgy. After nearly two and a half centuries of performance of canonical French and English plays, the growing popularity of theatre in Creole is impressive. By the mid–1980s, with the pioneering work of Dev Virahsawmy, Azize Asgarally and Henri Favory, the theatre in Creole had already established itself as a new but powerful dramatic expression. Virahsawmy, the first playwright to publish in Creole in modern times with *Li* (1977), and two of the most successful plays in Creole, *Zeneral Makbef* (1984) and *Zozef ekso palto larkansiel* (1984), remains the figurehead of the dramatic art.[1] Out of Favory's numerous plays produced, *Tras* (1983) his best known play, is the one to have had the sharpest impact.[2] Asgarally's *Ratsitatane* (1983) is the first historical play in Creole.[3]

To understand the replacing of Creole as the most effective language for dramatic experiment (Virahsawmy, 1995: 693), we have to go back to the militant political climate that inspired the playwrights after independence. The main priorities behind their theatre were that it should be an important vehicle for the establishment of a national culture – which goes hand in hand with the recognition and promotion of a national language – and that it should reach as wide an audience as possible. Underlying Virahsawmy's, Asgarally's and Favory's dramatic careers is the conviction that Creole is the only language that can translate the experiences and cultures of Mauritius for the stage. To write in Creole is also a fundamental step in the political struggle against the class system since Creole is identified with the exploited proletariat. The move away from a theatre relevant exclusively to an English and/or French-speaking elite to a theatre in Creole, and the valorizing of previously ignored local material entails a significant 'democratisation of culture' (Kershaw 1992: 10). The choice of Creole at once represents the interests of the majority and defies those who refuse to acknowledge Creole as a language in its own right (Ramharai 1990: 19). In an attempt at promoting Creole to the status of a national language, in a socio-linguistic situation where English and French have unparalleled prestige, the playwrights seek to put it on equal footing with the two colonial languages, by proving that it can be the medium of dramatic and literary creativity. The choice of Creole as dramatic language takes on an increasingly subversive dimension. I hope to have established, by now, that because of the implications of choosing Creole, the development of a theatre in Creole will necessarily have to be accompanied by linguistic considerations.

The theatre of protest: early Virahsawmy, Asgarally and Favory

Virahsawmy's Li, the first play in Creole
Li (1977) marks the passage from the comic sketch, farce and burlesque, associated with Creole, to a more mature theatre in terms of form and content. It describes, for the first time, a topsy-turvy world in Creole in a serious and dramatic tone. The protagonist, a political activist considered dangerous by the government, is imprisoned in a police cell while people outside demonstrate for his release. The fact that he is never once seen or heard, is referred to anonymously as 'Li' (the third person pronoun in Creole) and, yet, is at the centre of the play and most of the dialogues, makes of him an even more powerful symbol. Assassinated by the sergeant — who is himself the victim of higher powers — for his belief in and fight for justice, Li emerges as a national martyr with parallels to Gandhi, Jesus and Mandela. *Li* paints a bleak picture of post-colonial chaos, a world of corruption, prostitution, crime, injustice and political manipulation.

The history of the text is in itself, perhaps, more significant to the acknowledgement and development of the theatre in Creole. Virahsawmy wrote *Li* while he was in prison for nearly a year, in 1971–2. Believing in revolutionary action, other militants and Virahsawmy had paralysed the country through strikes. Under the decree of the subsequent State of Emergency, the militants were detained without any charges. In 1977, on the eve of the first performance, the play was banned by the national censorship board. In 1979, however, the Réunionese press dedicated a few articles to Virahsawmy and his play while Carpanin Marimoutou, Réunionese poet, critic and académic, published a trilingual version of the play in Mauritian Creole, Réunionese Creole and French (Réunion: Les chemins de la liberté[4]). Virahsawmy submitted the play to the *11th Concours de Radio-France International* in 1981 and won the first prize. It became, undoubtedly, a crucial landmark in the literary history of Mauritius. It proved that Creole could not only be the medium of dramatic expression but that it could do so with success enough to gain international recognition. The success of *Li* not only helped to debunk prejudices against a theatre in Creole but also showed that writing in Creole need not be equated to a linguistic and cultural ghettoization. The banning of the first play to be written in Creole and to be awarded a prize, however, revealed both irony and tragedy. The reason why the play was banned remains unclear. The journalist Pierre Benoit (*Week-end,* 4 October 1981: 8) believes that *Li* was not banned for political reasons since it hardly includes any highly subversive political comments. He suggests, instead, that what frightened the authorities was the idea that '*Seki ti feb vin for* ...', 'those who were weak become strong' represented through the martyred protagonist. As Kershaw questions, 'If performance is powerless to affect the socio-political future, why then has it been taken so seriously by the successive powers that be?' (Kershaw 1992: 21) The banning of the play speaks for itself about the potential impact of drama in Creole.

Asgarally's Ratsitatane*: 'recuperating' a voice*

Ratsitatane (1983), written and played in the context of the 150th anniversary of the abolition of slavery, with 22 actors dressed in the costumes of the times, is the first play in Creole based on historical facts. It dramatizes a page in the history of Mauritius and Madagascar, going back to 1821. Ratsitatane, the nephew of Radama, king of Madagascar, is exiled to Mauritius on suspicion of a conspiracy against the British authorities and a revolutionary attempt to free his country. In Mauritius, while trying to run away, Ratsitatane is betrayed, tracked down and executed in public. Although *Ratsitatane* is no more than a dramatized version of historical events, Asgarally gives a voice to the silenced, allowing the prince slave to present a different perspective to the dominant colonial one. Through his right to speak, Ratsitatane holds the power to impose his opinion not only on the audience but also on the colonial authorities within the play; to bring the self and the other face-to-face. *Ratsitatane*, in its attempt at reliving a page of history, is, however, more than a simple counter-attack on historical as well as non-historical colonial texts justifying slavery.

In denouncing the ills of colonization and slavery, Asgarally's insight into the process of the 'colonization of the mind' is particularly striking. When the man-hunt for Ratsitatane is about to start, two freed slaves offer their help to the slave owners.

1er esklav Affransi *Nou seron rekonnaissan et fiers dêtre à vo kôté dan cett lutt que vou menez kontre le zesklav marron, se bandi, se kriminel ki veull tou détruirr ici pour ensuitt implante leur kultur barbar. Donné nou de fuzis et nou montré digne de la konfiance que vou avé placé en nou.*

First freed slave We will be grateful and proud to be on your side in your struggle against the run-away slaves, those bandits, those criminals who want to destroy

> everything and then to implant their barbarous culture. Give us some guns and we will show ourselves worthy of the trust you have put in us. (59)

The fact that the slaves speak French – Asgarally's orthography is misleadingly inconsistent in a play in which all the characters, including the French colonial authorities, are made to speak in Creole – is not a coincidence. Through this disconcerting use of languages – especially in a historical context where Creole would have been the lingua franca of the slave population in Mauritius – Asgarally creates an awareness of the psychic violence of an enslavement that convinced the victims of their own linguistic and cultural inferiority and inculcated in them the will to fight for the defence of French language and culture.

Favory's Tras: *developing a performance and linguistic aesthetics*

Presented at the *Festival de Nancy* (1983), *Tras* portrays the struggle, in court, of a few labourers against the injustices of a sugar estate. The play addresses painfully real socio-economic situations. Although independence in Mauritius saw the end of a white hegemony at the head of political power, white hegemony in the sugar industry has never been contested. A series of situations in which the 'tablisman' ('sugar estate' but the Creole word is loaded with colonial politics and connotes the ongoing power relations) buys itself the lies and support of the field supervisors, police and even that of the court, illustrates how it maintains its power because the majority accepts its predominance as the norm.

In *Tras*, however, Favory gives a different dimension to the theatre of protest by experimenting with the aesthetics of his theatre rather than focusing on the militant side. The breath of fresh air is the character of the usher. From being a low-profile character, he turns into the most subversive element in the play, by constantly intervening, singing and commenting on the unfolding of events in court:

> **Zoké-wisyé** *votroner, votroner mo pa kone ki ariv mwa me depi sa dernye tan-la mo santi nu komsidire dan enn gran teat teat teat.*

> **Usher** Your honour, your honour I don't know what is happening to me these days I feel like we are in a big theatre theatre theatre (39)

The attempt at making the voice of the oppressed heard is carried out through an overt exploration of theatricality itself. The judge and the usher come to an agreement by which they respect each other's role – the judge will represent the court; the usher, the theatre. At points where we feel that the truth is being manipulated, the usher overrules the judge's words and intervenes aggressively to make the underdog's side of the story heard: '*teat ras laparol*' (101), 'the theatre "snatches" its right to speak'. The 'word' has also been 'snatched' with the installing of Creole as the dramatic language of the play, and with the more specific use of Creole as the language of the court within the play.[5] Theatre provides a safe space where the previously marginalized can reappropriate their right to self-expression. This is powerfully illustrated in the transformation of the court into a dramatic space before which the usher can raise a subversive voice to question certain assumptions and scrutinize contemporary reality with a sense of history. The usher also establishes different rules: '*byin sagrin u me dan teat penan privilez*' (135), 'Sorry but in theatre there are no privileges'. Through the usher's use of the theatrical space as an arena for the uncovering of the hegemony, Favory proposes a transparent illustration of the alternative but therapeutic potential of the theatre, where justice can follow a different and fairer course.

Favory's play, however, is far from providing a safe and happy solution or resolution. Inspired by Brecht, Favory seeks to blur the obstacles between the stage and the members of the audience by transforming the latter into active participants in the performance. In Round 6, subtitled '*ler manze*', 'lunch time', the actors share 'prawn crackers' with the audience. This not only gets the audience more directly involved with what is going on on stage but also puts them in an uncomfortable position, since '*manze*' in this context connotes the acceptance of bribes. During this round, the actors on stage will be '*manze*' both literally as well as metaphorically. The spectator is denied the complacent, passive role of a mere 'consumer'. Favory establishes blatantly transparent and often disturbing relationships between the fiction of the performance and the real world of the audience's experience outside theatre.

With *Tras*, the theatre in Creole is shaping up, not only in terms of performance but also in terms of language. It was described as 'a play which could leave its mark on the history of world theatre. (...) The language of the play is so precise, so creative, so authentic as to put the kreol[6] language amongst those in which the finest theatre has been produced' (*Week-End*, 30 January 1983). The media gave evidence of the role of theatre in putting Creole on a par with the colonial languages in use in Mauritius. There is a growing awareness that literature can serve the cause of language and give it new dimensions.

Virahsawmy, the later plays

Abs Lemanifik *and metalinguistic discourse*

In Virahsawmy's later plays, Creole is no longer merely a means of communication but assumes a poetic and artistic function. With language itself at its centre, *Abs Lemanifik* (1985) is both a reflection of this redefinition of Virahsawmy's dramatic preoccupations, as well as the sign of confidence in a dramatic culture in Creole. The play starts off with chaos, a crowd of people who, bored and desperate to find some sense of direction in life, believe they are in need of a saviour. Among them is an artist, a poet-singer-musician, but he is ridiculed and his guitar is symbolically stolen. Abs, an extra-terrestrial being with supernatural powers, descends from the skies and offers to be that saviour, and establishes a new order with hierarchies of 'Mini-Abs' and 'Siper-Mini-Abs'. The rest of the play is an unresolved struggle between Abs and Zed. The play highlights the opposition between Abs, who represents dictatorship, uniformity and political slogan and Zed, who represents emancipation, individualism and poetic language. The theatrical space allows Creole to take a step aside from itself and engage in reflexions on discourse, marking the difference between language as slogan and language as poetic. Abs, in his attempt at creating a new world, coins a new language for better control. In order to purify people's thoughts of the 'negative element', encapsulated in his enemy Zed, Abs orders that the language should be amputated of its phoneme 'z' which should be replaced by 'f', 's' or 'v'. The choice of this particular phoneme is, in itself, not a coincidence – the 'z' phoneme in Creole is also often interpreted as an aspect of corrupt French (for example 'zes' for 'geste'). This amputation leads to a serious communication breakdown and to a series of bawdy innuendoes:

> **Fam** *E!... Eta aret fer to zes.*
> **Mari** *Zes, zes, zes! To pa gagn drwa dir 'zes'. to bizê...to bizê dir...*
>
> **Wife** Hey!...Stop making a fuss.
> **Husband** Fuss, fuss, fuss! You don't have the right to say 'fuss', you have ... you have to say ... (36–7).

The audience would immediately pick up on what the substitution of 'z' by 'f' would lead to: 'fes' or 'arse'. The manipulation of linguistic features has tremendous relevance in terms of socio-linguistic relations. This attempt at linguistic 'purification' also entails the superimposition of the colonial languages on Creole. When asked whether all his words should be recorded, the representative of Abs replies in a linguistic mish-mash of Creole, English and French:

> **Mini-Abs 14** *Otomanikma! What do you think! Take down everything comme ça la posterite pu rapel mo aksio purificateur. Wi, take down tu.* (38)

The pedantic use of English and French (often clichéd) phrases, the use of slogans and the coining of new words – '*manifiksiô*', '*yerarsi Abstokrasi*' – mask the truth and only lead to a more chaotic world. In fact the repression of the language has such disastrous consequences in terms of communication breakdown that the scheme of linguistic and general repression and 'purification' has to be abandoned. Even Abs has to give in to the banned phoneme:

> **Mini-Abs 14** *Ki u desiviô?*
> **Abs** Desiviô. desoviô ... A to'lé dir desiziô! To pa kapav koz kuma tu dimun No. 14?
>
> **Mini-Abs 14** What is your decivion?
> **Abs** Decivion, decivion... Oh you mean decision! Can't you talk like everybody else No. 14? (44)

Abs Lemanifik portrays neo-colonial and other types of repressions as well as liberations as being channelled mainly through language. Towards the end, the Creole language triumphantly asserts its integrity as the 'z' phoneme comes back with a vengeance, as the following illustrates:

> **Mini-Abs 33** *Mo nepli kopran naye. Ti dir nu aret dernié let alfabet. Sâ oken eksplikasiô, tu dimun fin rekumâs servi li. Ena mem ki met dé z kot ena ên sel.*

Mini-Abs 33 I don't understand anything anymore. We were told to stop using the last letter of the alphabet. Without any explanation everyone has started using it again. There are even some who use two zs where there should be one. (59)

If in real life Creole is merely the medium of communication, the theatrical space allows the playwright to present Creole as a vibrant force, one that can fight its own battles and come out triumphant. Creole, which is seen as a substandard language in relation to the European languages in Mauritius, here, overflows with weapons for its own defence, with ironical expressions providing sharp political analysis. The real hero of the play is Creole, transformed from a medium of communication into an autonomous force, imposing a new image of itself on the audience.

In *Abs* socio-political aspects remain in the background. What comes across as more significant is the self-assertion of Creole and the playwright's ability to 'zôglé ar mo' (29), 'to juggle with words', to explore the poetics of the dramatic language and to indulge in the pleasure of subverting language. Virahsawmy exploits the resources of the language in order to appeal to an indigenous sense of humour. A sign of confidence in this relatively new dramatic culture in Creole is the cross-reference to an earlier play in Creole. There is an incident where the Mini-Abs are planning strategies to eliminate the subversive phoneme 'z'.

Siper Mini-Abs 2 *ki sa elemâ êdisipline la?*
Siper Mini-Abs 1 *Pa gagn druva pronôs so nô.*
Siper Mini-Abs 2, 3,4 Li

Siper Mini-Abs 2 Who is that subversive element?
Siper Mini-Abs 1 Pronouncing his name is forbidden.
Siper Mini-Abs 2, 3,4 Li (32)

This intertextual echo of Virahsawmy's first play points out that a dramatic culture in Creole is being consolidated.

Zeneral Makbef: *opening up to a multi-cultural dialogue*

Although *Zeneral Makbef* (1981) is an inspired rewriting of *Macbeth,* the success of *Zeneral Makbef* relies on the discovery and satirical exploitation of relevant issues for a local public. Makbef, who makes himself Emperor of a Republic, with a lust for power matched only by an unnaturally intense sexual appetite for both men and women, is a satirical comment on leaders such as Bokassa and Idi Amin Dada. Instead of the invasion of Scotland by Norway, the third world country runs the risk of being invaded by a foreign superpower. Makbef is reduced to being the comic victim of the rivalry between two superpowers, the *Yankidola*, on one hand, and the *Rouspoutchik*, on the other. *Zeneral Makbef* warns against two types of oppression which newly independent countries face, the risk of becoming puppets in the hands of superpowers and the victims of their own leaders.

Unlike in *Li,* however, we have a successful mixture of politics, satire,

Mauritian folklore and humour. *Zeneral Makbef* is a satire of those who manipulate the less politically aware through words, revealing political language as a dangerous weapon in the hands of those who know how to use it. Makbef manages to convince the public that he is defending their interests in a speech where he announces his decision to appropriate the national wealth. The transgression of politically and socially accepted values is punished through laughter. '*Mak*', in Creole, is the abbreviation for '*makro*', 'pimp' – at one point Makbef, being too busy indulging in sexual exploits, asks Sooklal in an innuendo to sleep with his wife. '*Bef*' not only means 'bull' but also connotes physical and intellectual lethargy. The connotations of his name also highlight the treacherous gap between his status as political leader and the hideousness of his private characteristics.

With the growing confidence in the potential of Creole as dramatic language, the promotion of the national language and literature no longer entails a rejection of English and French cultures. On the other hand, the theatre in Creole seeks inspiration from both local and foreign cultures, transcending – but not shunning – a Mauritian reality to address a universal quality. The contextuality of performance – 'the propensity of performance to achieve different meanings/readings according to the context in which it occurs' (Kershaw 1992: 33) and especially this opening up to a multi-cultural dialogue are two key elements which will be further exploited in Virahsawmy's chef-d'oeuvre, *Zozef ek so palto larkansiel.*

Zozef: *Creole as a symbol of a multi-cultural identity*

Zozef ek so palto larkansiel (1984) a translation/adaptation of Andrew Lloyd Webber and Tim Rice's *Joseph and his Technicolour Dreamcoat* is the first musical comedy in Creole. With more than 40 performances within the first few months of its production, *Zozef* is the most popular play in the history of theatre in Mauritius.

Although the words and the music are borrowed, the adaptation in terms of content, symbol and form is ingeniously creative and strongly rooted in Mauritian culture. The socio-cultural complexion of the audience, its sense of community and – paradoxically – its search for it, provide the context for the adaptation of the performance. The theme of the musical is symbolic, the brothers gathered around the coat of Joseph represent the different communities around the Mauritian national flag. Instead of the technicolour dreamcoat we have a rainbow which becomes the symbol of the multi-ethnicity of Mauritius, a symbol of unity in diversity. The Mauritian nation, constituted of migrant communities, does not have a common pre-colonial identity to recover; the concept of a nation stands instead at the cross-roads of various Eastern and Western influences, it is something in the process of being forged, out of a mixture of cultures. The performance integrates the use of dramatic elements from both traditional and modern popular performances, from across time and continents. Lloyd Webber's music is arranged for various local instruments, with strong elements of the sega – both a dance and a musical art form of African origins marginalized in the past – as well as Indian music and dance.

Zozef proves to be especially effective in translating abstract elements of culture and values into concrete means, immediately recognizable by the audience. The imaginative capacity to construct 'potential worlds' (Kershaw 1992: 21) is illustrated through the successful connection made between the content, the form and the audience.

The enormous success of *Zozef* shows that it appealed to the aspirations of a society in search of its identity. In this search, Creole itself – the lingua franca that cuts across social, religious and ethnic barriers – becomes the symbol of identity in a post-colonial multi-cultural context. Virahsawmy uses the Creole language to consolidate the notion of a Creolized national identity.

Theatrical efficacy – the potential influence, however minute, that theatre may have on the general historical evolution of wider social and political realities (Kershaw 1992: 1) – cannot always be tested or measured, but *Zozef* had a strong enough impact to provoke an eminent journalist to write his first ever article in Creole in the most prestigious French weekly. Alain Gordon-Gentil (1981), explains that after realizing the dramatic and poetic potential of Creole, he decided, as a symbolic gesture, to write his article in the language. He describes *Zozef* as '*ène couronnement pou la langue créole*', 'a crowning achievement for Creole' (Gordon-Gentil 1981). The production was an important landmark not only within the realm of Mauritian theatre, but a landmark in Mauritian culture itself.

The success of the two most popular plays in Creole, *Zeneral Makbef* and *Zozef,* relies on the exploitation and the celebration of a language that was being discovered by the Mauritian public and the relationships that Virahsawmy builds between theatrical and non-theatrical texts produced by the local community, in the form of folklore, song, dance. Virahsawmy's theatre illustrates that while an intense sense of place and time allows theatre to be oppositional and relevant to the audience, it need not reduce the appeal of the performance to a minority or limit the performance to a local source.

Toufann: an intertextual Tempest

The creative potential of cross-cultural contact was further developed in *Toufann* (1991), a rewriting of Shakespeare's *The Tempest. Toufann* operates on several levels of intertextuality, first of all within the Shakespearean plays themselves. In Virahsawmy's play, Prospero's daughter is 'Kordelia', Gonzalo becomes 'Poloniouss', Alonso is 'Lerwa Lir', Sebastian is 'Edmon' and, most interestingly, Antonio is turned into a self-conscious 'Yago'. Towards the resolution of the play, Virahsawmy presents a Yago who is fed up with being considered a villain by literary critics. He says:

> **Yago** *Mo esperé ki bann kritchik literèr konpran ki mo pa mové net.*

> **Yago** I hope that the literary critics will understand that I am not completely evil.
> (21)

The cultural productions that stem from the 'unexpected transfers' (Pavis 1992: 2) of translation or adaptations, across time and space, are fascinating. The title '*toufann*' is a bhojpuri[7] word for 'cyclone', a familiar hazard in Mauritius. Trinculo and Stephano become 'Kaspalto' and 'Dammaro', with stereotypical Mauritian names, connoting a drunkard and a drug addict respectively. Prospero's island is one of high-tech computers, and Aryel, his creation, is a robot. Virahsawmy engages in an increasingly 'toufannesque' dialogue with Shakespeare. When Ferdjinan tries to give Aryel a hug, the latter has his 'chips' perturbed and he runs the risk of 'perdji kontrol', 'losing control'. Ferdjinan explains that an accident in the past did irretrievable damage to certain parts of his anatomy. He says:

Ferdjinan   *Dezir ou plezir sexiel pa interes mwa*
　　　　　Dan Aryel mo trouv enn konpavon. Se tou ... Dan
　　　　　Zot lozik sa pa posib ... Dan mo lozik, Li normal.

Ferdjinan   I am not interested in sexual desire or pleasure
　　　　　In Aryel I see a companion. That's all ... In
　　　　　your logic that's not possible ... In mine,
　　　　　It is normal. (22)

Instead of Ferdjinan, it is Kaliban who marries Prospero's daughter and becomes king Kaliban, an intelligent, attractive young '*métis*', of mixed white and black race, defies the boundaries that communities create between what is included and what is excluded. The re-appropriation of Kaliban is engineered to debunk the prejudices against 'half-castes', and to overthrow the master–slave relationship that has, in various ways and under different forms, been part of the history of Mauritius. When Prospero loses his temper at Kordelia's decision to marry Kaliban, the following exchange takes place:

Prospero   Sa...sa...sa...b...b...ba...
Kordelia   Shut up papa! *Si to djir sa mo la, mo aret koz ar twa ziska mo mor.*

Prospero   This...this...this...b...b...bas
Kordelia   Shut up Dad! If you say that word, I will not speak to you till I die. (22)

Kordelia stops him from saying the word 'bastard' and challenges his arguments about the superiority of *royal* blood by asserting her belief in *human* blood.
　　Through theatre, Virahsawmy makes Creole the meeting point of world cultural currents which promotes the importance of that language and illustrates Virahsawmy's vision of a future Mauritius based on the acceptance of the already existent biological and cultural miscegenation. Theatrical adaptation, which encourages the building of bridges and promotes the exchange of ideas and experience, is a particularly effective tool for his main preoccupations.

Theatre and the emergence of a literary language

Since 1990, Virahsawmy has channelled his dramatic career into translations/adaptations. His other more 'conventional' translations of Shakespeare include, *Trazedji Makbess* (1997, Macbeth), not to be confused with the satirical play

Makbef (1981), *Enn ta Senn dan Vid* (1995, Much Ado about Nothing) and *Zil Sezar* (1987, Julius Caesar). These dramatic translations allow the playwight to work simultaneously on promoting the status of the language as well as its corpus – the linguistic features of the language. The need to 'elasticate' the language of a target play, in translation, so as to remain true to the experience drawn from the source play while also enabling the translation to carry a broader meaning in the target language (Gooch 1996: 15), takes on wider dimensions with Creole. This 'elasticating' involves a real linguistic engineering, including the extension of the vocabulary, the forging of different registers by forcing the language to function in fields in which it is not yet comfortable.

Virahsawmy sees the translation/adaptation of plays into Creole as an important step in the standardization of the language. While it is true that the Mauritian public is still reluctant to read whole texts in Creole and that publishing in Creole is not profitable, Virahsawmy has persevered in promoting Creole as an indispensable instrument in the development of Mauritius. From using Creole as a means of dramatic communication, Virahsawmy has redirected his dramatic career so as to use theatre as a means of developing a literary norm.

Conclusion

The very choice of Creole as dramatic language has caused the disappearance of an elitist conception of the audience. The theatre in Creole emerges as a challenge to a combination of dominant values, from those of political, linguistic and cultural imperialism to capitalism. By recuperating a language and its culture, it gives a voice to the silenced and threatened communities. Starting off from protest theatre, the dramatic art explores different avenues. Favory seeks to develop a popular theatre that involves audience participation while, with Virahsawmy, the stage becomes a space for a collective revaluation of the cultural identity, inculcating a sense of confidence in the multi-cultural. Virahsawmy's efforts to ensure that neither the language nor the theatre settles into an intellectual ghetto, leads to some fascinating examples of intertextuality. More recent developments in Mauritian theatre in Creole, especially in the realm of translation/adaptation, have proved that the future might lie in a confrontation with the heterogeneous in cultural as well as literary trends. Virahsawmy's translations/adaptations of Shakespeare into Creole certainly indicate that this theatre is initiating a dialogue between its language and other languages, between its own imaginative and symbolic space and those of other cultures. Through dramatic translation, the theatre opens up to other cultures and at the same time stretches the linguistic fields of Creole. Virahsawmy's focus on a literary and linguistic orientation also sets his creative work within the framework of a possible standardization of the language. Theatre thus becomes an important and influential area where the official status of languages, or lack of it, is being confronted by concrete practice.

NOTES

1 Virahsawmy is still the most active playwright, putting equal emphasis on performance and publication. In 26 years he has had over twenty plays published and/or performed. His plays reflect his wide-ranging preoccupations with political, cultural and linguistic issues.
2 Favory's emphasis is on performance, and *Tras* is his only play published. *Tras* received wide local media coverage and was also selected to be performed at the *Festival de Nancy* in 1983.
3 Asgarally has published several plays in English but *Ratsitatane* is his only play in Creole. As the first historical play in Creole the latter made an important contribution to the ackowledgement of the language. It was also translated and peformed in English in Perth, Australia in the context of the *Festival international de la mer* in 1984.
4 A Réunionese artisanal co-operative, under the direction of Firmin Lacpatia, specializing in the publishing and diffusion of literature in Creole.
5 As pointed out earlier, in real life English and French have the monopoly of institutional linguistic diffusion in Mauritius.
6 Mauritian Creole is often referred to as 'Kreol' to mark its specificity in relation to other Creoles. Also, in the main orthographic systems used so far (Virahsawmy and Ledikasyon pu Travayer) 'c' does not feature as a consonant.
7 Bhojpuri is the most widely-spoken language of Indian origin in Mauritius. Now mostly confined to rural areas.

BIBLIOGRAPHY

PRIMARY TEXTS
Asgarally, Azize,1983, *Ratsitatane* (Port-Louis: Hart Printing).
Favory, Henry, 1983, *Tras* (Mauritius: Royal Printing).
Virahsawmy, Dev, 1977, *Li* (Rose-Hill: Bukié Banané).
— 1981, *Zeneral Makbef* (Rose-Hill: Bukié Banané,).
— 1984, *Dokter Nipat* (Rose-Hill: Bukié Banané,).
— 1984, *Zozef ek so palto larkansiel* (Audio-cassette).
— 1985, *Abs Lemanifik* (Rose-Hill: Bukié Banané).
— 1987, *Zil Sezar* (Rose-Hill: Bukié Banané).
— 1991, *Toufann* (Rose-Hill: Bukié Banané).
— 1995, *Enn ta Senn dan Vid* (Port-Louis: LPT).
— 1996, *Galileo Gonaz* (Port-Louis: LPT).
— 1997, *Trazedji Makbess* (Port-Louis: LPT).

SECONDARY TEXTS
Asgarally, Issa, 1995, *Literature et révolte* (Le Flambuoyant).
Benoit, Pierre, 1981, ' *"Li"*, *couronneé à l'etranger est toujours interdite à Maurice*', *Week-end*, 4 October): 8.
Banham, Martin and Eldred Durosimi Jones, 1988, '...tinap ober we leck giant' . African Celebrations of Shakespeare', in Chew, Shirley and Alistair Stead, eds, *Translating Life: Studies in Transpositional Aesthetics*, 1999 (Liverpool: Liverpool University Press).
Boal, Augusto,1979, *Theatre of the Oppressed* (London: Pluto Press).
Calvet, Louis-Jean, 1974, *Linguistique et Colonialisme* (Paris: Payot).
Chelin, Antoine,1954, *Le théâtre à l'île Maurice, son origine et son développement* (Port Louis: The Mauritius Printing Ltd).
Conteh-Morgan, John, 1994, *Theatre and Drama in Francophone Africa. A Critical Introduction* (Cambridge: Cambridge University Press).
Decotter, André, 1983, *Le Plaza un demi-siècle de vie théâtrale* (Mauritius: Précigraph Ltd).
Epskamp, Kees, P., 1989, *Theatre in Search of Social Change* (The Hague: CESO Paperback).
Gainor, Ellen J., 1995, *Imperialism and Theatre: Essays on World Theatre, Drama and Performance* (London: Routledge).

Gooch, Steve, 1996, 'Fatal Attraction' in David Johnston, ed., *Stages of Translation* (Bath: Absolute Classics) 13–21.

Gordon-Gentil, Alain, 1981, 'Théâtre plein dépi quinze jours: ki fère?' *Week-End*, 7 June: 11.

Johnston, David, ed., 1996, *Stages of Translation* (Bath, Absolute Classics).

Kershaw, Baz, 1992, *The Politics of Performance: Radical Theatre as Cultural Intervention* (London: Routledge).

Labonne, Daniel, 1984, 'The new role of theatre in Mauritius', *Theatre International*, 11/12: 49–53.

Le Page, Robert and Tabouret Keller, Andrée, 1985, *Acts of Identity: Creole-Based Approaches to Language and Ethnicity* (Cambridge: Cambridge University Press).

McGrath, John, 1981, *A Good Night Out – Popular Theatre: audience, class and form* (London: Eyre Methuen).

Morgan, Marcyliena, ed., 1994, *Language and the Social Construction of Identity in Creole Situations* (California: Center for Afro-American Studies Publications).

Pavis, Patrice, 1992, *Theatre at the Crossroads of Culture* (London: Routledge).

Peacock, Keith, 1984, 'The play-text, theatrical dynamics and the status interaction', *Theatre Research International*, 9: 39–49.

Ramharai, Vicram, 1990, *La Littérature mauricienne d'expression créole: essai d'analyse socio-culturelle* (Port-Louis: Editions Les Mascareignes).

Renaud, Pierre and Gaëtan Raynal, 1972, *Histoire et Légendes d'un théâtre* (Port-Louis: The Mauritius Printing Ltd).

Salhi, Kamal, ed., 1988, *African Theatre for Development* (Exeter: Intellect Books).

Scaglione, Aldo, 1984, *The Emergence of National Languages* (Ravenna: Longo Editore).

Stein, Peter, 1982, *Connaissance et emploi des langues à Lîle Maurice* (Hambourg: Helmut Buske Verlag, Kreolische Bibliotek, Band 2).

Virahsawmy, Dev, 1995, 'Mauritius', in Banham, Martin, ed., *The Cambridge Guide to Theatre* (Cambridge: University of Cambridge Press): 693–4.

Telling the Lion's Tale
Making theatre in Eritrea

ALI CAMPBELL, CHRISTINE MATZTKE, GERRI MORIARTY,
RENNY O'SHEA, JANE PLASTOW
& students of the Tigre/Bilen theatre training course

> 'Until the lion has a voice, the tales of the hunt will be only those of the hunter'
> (Eritrean proverb)

JP[1] When you have worked on, researched and written about a subject over a period of time, it becomes a danger that you no longer see what is going on with the freshness of first vision. Theatre in Eritrea is something which occupies a large part of my time and being, but when I was asked to produce this article it seemed that rather than rehashing what I have written in reports and project proposals the work might come more richly off the page if I asked my collaborators on the 1997 training project to describe what they — as newcomers to the project — saw. We then agreed that it would also be important to hear the voices of the trainees who experienced the project. This article then is a medley of those voices. I have simply written in the connecting passages that hold the narrative together.

The Eritrea Community-based Theatre Project has been in existence since 1995 and has so far run three major training programmes; an initial basic skills course for 57 Tigrinya-speaking trainees over three months in 1995, a pilot, one-month, Theatre-in-Education programme for 17 teachers in 1996, and our most recent and ambitious development in the summer of 1997, a basic skills course for twenty Tigre and Bilen students, and an advanced 'training-the-trainers' project for twelve Tigrinya-speakers, to enable them to work with villagers on creating their own community theatre.

I set the project up at the request of the Eritrean government following an initial chance meeting in 1992, shortly after Eritrea had won her 30-year liberation struggle against Ethiopia. That war had left the country devastated, with nearly a third of the population of 3.7 million living as refugees abroad, some 70,000 fighters dead and an unknown civilian casualty toll. Before the war, indigenous cultures had been suppressed in favour of Ethiopian Amhara language and performance forms.[2] Many young people had never learnt their traditional stories or the meaning of their dances and songs.

The Eritrean People's Liberation Front had tried to nurture Eritrean cultures, performing the music and dance of all nine of Eritrea's language groups in its cultural troupes,[3] but new ideas from other parts of the world about dynamic theatre in the widest, performative sense of the word had not reached Eritrea. Traditional performance was separated by an insuperable gulf from dialogue-dominated drama as introduced by first Italian and then English colonizers between 1890 and 1952.[4]

This article will try to reveal through a number of voices how the work in 1997 felt from the inside, the kind of impact it made on some of those involved and the mistakes and methodologies with which we all worked and from which we all learnt.

Before I hand over to some of those other voices I would just like to explore why this project might be working in Eritrea. Firstly and most importantly there is a government, and particularly a Bureau of Cultural Affairs under the leadership of Solomon Tsehaye, which has consistently supported the work, has not sought to censor what students want to say, and has embraced the idea of a bottom-up cultural movement which seeks to empower and celebrate the culture and lives of the mass of the people. We have also been lucky enough to gain support from funders such as Oxfam, The Rockefeller Foundation and The British Council who have again not sought to impose an agenda on our work, but have trusted us to encourage participants to let what is important to be said emerge through the process of training and rehearsal. It seems to me crucial that those of us lucky enough to work in Eritrea all know that we are not teachers or ideologues, but facilitators who hopefully provide a toolbag of techniques and ways into working which participants can then use to fashion their own performances.

Moreover we all know that we are working to make ourselves redundant as quickly as possible. The project aims to offer training in both basic skills and in how to pass on those skills to community groups in all Eritrea's main ethnic groups. This will take time, but the essential idea has been to work constantly towards handing power and control to participants as soon as possible, and to create a sustainable network of theatre groups in Eritrea which can mutually support each other.

Before the 1997 project we already knew this kind of theatre could work, because the core Tigrinya group of 16 course graduates had undertaken a two-month tour in 1996 with plays about land reform and issues of dowry and virginity. Audiences of up to 7,000 had sat on stony hillsides to watch the performers, lit only by two powerful lights, which often flickered when the hot-wiring that connected them to our portable generator was trampled on or kicked. The group had travelled on local buses and sometimes by camel to reach remote communities, but everywhere audiences participated with gusto. The children wanted to learn how to make such plays and we heard that months afterwards the songs from the shows were still being sung and the issues raised were still being discussed.

This encouraging news carried us into the on-going experiment of the 1997 training programme.

Questions to students (1)
What did you learn from the course?

Mesmer: I know that actions speak louder than words.
Romadan: Self-confidence.
Idris (Keren): I learned different things from the discussions we had in groups –
for example, about women's rights.

Ali Campbell is a massively experienced community and theatre-in-
education practitioner who has worked extensively in the UK as well as in
Europe, South America and Africa. He is an avowed exponent of Boalian techniques – although he has many other approaches to making theatre that he can,
and in Eritrea perforce did, bring to the fore. Ali was in charge of our 'training
the trainers' project, living for a month in the village of Sala'a Daro.

The Bees and the Flies

AC It is August, 1997. My students and I are sitting in our 'theatre': a circle of
stones and planks we have joyfully placed in the centre of the compound where
we work. We have made a good start. We are going to live here in the village
and just listen to people as theoretically they come to trust us more and open up
about what the development issues really are as opposed to what officialdom
deems them to be.

Back and forth our discussions range from the development issues that will
inform the content of our work to the theatrical styles and stratagems that will
equip us with effective performance forms. A legacy of the Italian occupation,
together with the grand, rotting Opera House in Asmara, is the almost exclusively held belief that proper theatre is script-based and usually written by dead,
white European men. I'm not talking about villagers here, who have their own
ideas about song and storytelling, but about the 12 members of our company,
all of whom have undergone training in a range of theatre techniques at an
earlier stage of this project, but who, despite their quite sophisticated, urban
backgrounds and expectations, don't really take improvisation seriously,
whatever the subject, unless it revolves around lots of men talking and usually
fighting whilst the women build imaginary cooking fires, get beaten and
scream when things get tough.

It's hard to find an issue around development that isn't a women's issue. We
have already brainstormed some of the things we feel as a group we might
explore through theatre (what *kind* of theatre remains open!) and in the safety
of our compound all the kinds of issues we are ready for have been duly listed
and roughed out as scenarios for Forum Theatre, which is one of the forms I
feel we ought to try when it is our turn to occupy the communal space by the
church tonight. Here is the list:

WATER PROBLEMS
NO PRIMARY SCHOOL
ELECTRICITY
INFIBULATION
OPPRESSION OF WOMEN
UNDER-AGE MARRIAGE
DIVORCE
TRANSPORTATION PROBLEMS
NO CLINIC
GENERATION GAP
BETRAYAL/DISHONESTY/MONEY
CARE OF OLD PEOPLE
SANITATION
FAMILY ARGUMENTS
EXPLOITATION OF CHILDREN
ORPHANAGE
VIRGINITY PROBLEMS
CUTTING INFILIA

How politically sound and educationally correct these intentions now sound. As always Mother Africa shows me how things really are. Nowhere else have I learned so much, and so thoroughly, through humbling failure. Up the hill we march to the meeting place by the huge, ostentatious church: a patriarchal palace among medieval dwellings, and paid for by the people who live in them. The audience gathers slowly, and even the way they do this should be sign enough to someone really looking at what's happening (as opposed to focusing on their delightfully symmetrical plans) that there is a pattern to traditional life which an hour of audience participation can't hope to alter. First, the children, ragged, beaming, happy and cautious, always looking for cues from elders. Then the women: hiding their faces behind their customary white muslin veils, shyly perching at a distance on the rocky wall of their own little enclosure, off to one side. Then the young men, pretending not to be too interested but making sure they're close enough to see everything without there being any danger of being made to *do* anything ... this much they share with their age-group the world over. And last the elders and the priests.

This is their place, and they control what is being said in it: the outcome of discussions and meetings here is pulled into their sphere as if by gravity. I, who always watch the audience when we do Forum, looking for their relationship with the piece and for the signs of what is contentious, should be able to tell after all these years that a theatre space and the way it is laid out and occupied are already a great part of the script, but there is no way of telling just how much the very presence of this venerable score of robed ancients will influence everything that happens here.

On with the show, which opens with our 'Trojan Horse' gambit: the children. Up to 200 of these enchanting, vivacious survivors have been working with some of the team, and these so far have been the happiest, most energized sessions. Today we have an excellent traditional tale about a man who comes to market with some iron to sell. He leaves it on trust with a certain shopkeeper, but when he returns to claim his metal the shopkeeper tells him that the rats have eaten it. In revenge, the man steals the shopkeeper's baby. When his distraught wife asks what has happened to the child, the man says that an eagle has eaten it. General hilarity from the audience.

Our baby Forum goes well: the audience are invited to be the judges of the case, and several adolescents come out and try to solve the case. I can see from my vantage point the broad semi-circle of audience animated and hugely engaged in their different ways. What will they do with the 'serious scene'?

We have built up this piece to deal with issues around family planning, including arguments for fewer children (because of health and education resources, etc.) versus more (security in old age, labour for reconstruction), all laid out wittily and with considerable humour.

One by one the faces of the priests clamp shut.

It doesn't matter that our avoidance of the doctrinaire is impeccable: the priests already know the answers to all this stuff, and to lay out alternatives or, to invite their enactment by the people is at best a waste of time and at worst – naturally – heresy. The Joker, whose role it is to facilitate audience intervention, does one of the sorriest mimes of getting blood from a stone it has ever been my torment to witness, and I've seen a lot. The women don't just not speak: they vanish. I don't mean they move but they vanish all the same, eyes downcast and mouths covered, voiceless, meek, passive.

At last a voice is heard. A priest stands up, ceremonial staff in hand, and all heads turn. I don't need to know what his Tigrinya means: the Old Testament demeanour says it all. This is the word of God, and God, too is an angry old man with a day's *Suwa*[5] supping behind him and the authority of 16 centuries behind that. And God says: YOU WILL GO FORTH AND MULTIPLY.

Curtain.

So what's it to be then? We have a whole season of plays worked out, all now defunct except for the children's work, which is blooming. We have those wonderful stories, and what's more the women telling them seem to be having some sort of quiet meeting, in a different house every night, where they keep telling more to the three women in our group: Maharat, Elilta and Sennait.

I think back, rather wistfully, to our very first night in the village when each of the students was adopted by a 'mother' in the true generosity of all Africa, and billeted in a traditional house with the idea of generally absorbing village life. On the whole this has worked.

Down we all sat, surrounded by the children. 'Welcome to Sala'a Daro' began one of the deceptively picturesque elders, 'which as you all know was named thus because of the great height and generous shade of its oaks. As you know, our nomadic forefathers first settled here for the sake of the oaks.' (Translated literally 'Sa-la-Daro')

'That's not right!' piped up another ancient. 'Everyone knows our ancestors weren't common nomads. We have always been here, and the oaks shielded our eyes from the dazzle of the mid-day sun on the natural dam across the valley. So we stayed, for the sake of the oaks.

'Nonsense!' retorts a third. 'There was a great famine and the fruit of the Daro served as bread.'

Meanwhile, an old woman is telling Maharat the REAL story: 'A woman saw an angel in one of these trees, and the angel told her this would be a good place for all the people to live.'

And when we get down to the bar, full of excitement at this generous (but not issue-based enough) sharing, Samuel tells the children's version of the story: that once there was a tree full of devils that stopped anyone from living here, but St Thaddeus came and banished them, and now we live here for the sake of THAT oak, not the boring grown-up ones.

How I could have failed to see the entire script of a perfect community play, handed to me on a plate on my very first day, remains a rich source of humility as I write this now. Maybe we were so sure that one kind of theatre means Development and another means Entertainment, that we couldn't see over the mental wall we had built between them. I will never know. But where the church walls of present-day Sala'a Daro cannot be breached those mental walls will always come tumbling down if we give ourselves a chance.

A community play rehearsed with all the groups in the village who had a version of the story of Sala'a Daro to tell. A play rehearsed with these groups separately and put together at the last minute. Upsetting no-one, because not actually raising in its overt, spoken content, issues no-one is ready or willing – yet – to open up in a mixed group in public. Better still: a promenade performance, moving from group to group and tree to tree as each tells a part of the story. A play which celebrates diverse stories of the very origins of the community through a form – promenade – that multiplies points of view, leaving the audience to be swayed as they will, and engages them in the most basic and inclusive participation you could hope for: walking.

Days of rehearsal in ever larger segregated groups later, we are three days from the end of our stay and three weeks into the project, and we know we have created a fabulous monster. For these unforgettable last days in the village, the whole story takes shape. Fifty women swathe themselves in the huge bales of white muslin I bought; decorate a tree; make ceremonial popcorn with which to shower the audience; choose harvest hymns and blessings to go with their dances. Two hundred children turn binliners into capes and wings, make little horns from the burrs of thorn bushes, paint their faces with toothpaste stripes and fashion claws from twigs and rubber bands. Is this development theatre in a village where half the children don't make it to five? Is the sheer naughtiness of devising a truly nasty song, the deliciousness of preparing a huge scarifying surprise and getting ready to terrify grown-ups a kind of empowerment? Is happiness, in that context, development? In the second poorest country in the world, are outrageous and joyous memories, in between herding sheep and drawing water, a kind of wealth? I hope so. We have no shortage of development issues to justify all this fun in the wonderful scene devised by the young men, who although reluctant at first end up delivering a Busby Berkeley routine with matching straw hats and Real Men's cudgels with which they make a series of images of construction, reforestation and all the clinic and school-building you could wish for ... and it isn't silly. It is strong, and poignant, and only a little bit camp round the edges.

And we did it, on a fine hot day in August 1997! All the world was there, and it was dusty and chaotic, and my friend Renny said that never, ever, had she felt such pure excitement in a promenade: the sheer newness and iconoclasm of running from one scene to another, in a huge crowd, and not just sitting where all the official stories are usually told!

And joy of joy, the cream on the cake: the priests! Half an hour late, drunk to a man, festooned in magnificent robes, beating drums, parading icons, shaded with great brocaded parasols and all walking the wrong way! Just as the first scene came to an end (starring one quite sober priest whom we frog-marched out of the raging wake when his friends weren't looking) they hove into view: marching albeit unsteadily to a strong, dominant rhythm, heading past us and away, completely cluelessly, wonderfully adrift, as, with only a second's hesitation, the entire population of Sala'a Daro took in their finery, looked over their shoulders as the angel tree unfurled great pinions of white and blossomed with popcorn and blessing and song and left the priests. After all, you can see priests any time. But a tree full of angels is a once only thing.

Why 'The Bees and the Flies' of my title? Daniel, one of the best listeners in our group (which we ended up calling the Bees and the Flies) was told this traditional Tigrinya story one night after lights out by his adopted father:

> Once upon a time, long, long ago, the flies had a kingdom just as the bees do today. But they were always in such a hurry, flying this way and that, and never noticing what each other was doing or could do. And so they went about their crazy business until one day in the rush they killed their King. You didn't know flies had a King? Exactly. That's why they don't.
>
> But the Bees were wise. Oh, they were busy, but each at the task that suited their skills: the nurses, the workers, the builders, the soldiers and of course the Queen. And whatever you make of their way of doing things, let me ask you, who makes the honey – the bees or the flies?

Iyob told the tale, then, to a couple of thousand people; accompanied by traditional instruments with the women ululating and showering us with popcorn. All the versions of the story were valid in the end. There wasn't a moral as such, but a moment of silence, a song to the 70,000 matyrs of the liberation war, and a tree-planting where my present of a baby Daro was held aloft by a beautiful old priest, in one moment of wonder and respect, meshed together and sang the harmony the women wove around us. This is, from my point of view, the story of what Sala'a Daro really means. I hope I'm asked back there again, and I'll make no end of plans, but please, if you meet me before I go, don't ask me what I'm going to do there.

Ask the Bees and the Flies.

Rehearsing with some of the children's group, Sala'a Daro

Questions to students (2)
Do you think the course has changed you as an individual? If so, how?

Idris (She'eb): It helped me to ask about my own traditions and to learn. Also how to work with girls.
Idris (Keren): Courage. In other performances, when I got on the stage I was sweating, but now, no.
Mesmer: Before I came to this course, though I had an ambition to act, it was not so great as it is now. It changed my voice. It changed my relations with people, especially with the other actors.

JP Gerri Moriarty and Renny O'Shea take up the story. Both women are experienced community arts workers who have taught in a wide variety of situations and nations, although for both this project was an African 'first' Gerri and Renny ran the two-month training for Tigre and Bilen artists in Keren, Eritrea's second city, working with a group of enormously enthusiastic people. Most had had lives severely disrupted by war, many had had only primary level education, and nearly all thought theatre meant something far from their traditional arts which involved a lot of talking, building a theatre, and above all making sure you hung up some curtains![6]

RO & GM Day 1
In the Community Association hall, benches are laid out in formal rows. The

Rehearsing with the young women, Sala'a Daro.

students stand to attention to greet us – do we look as nervous to them as they do to us? They tell us of their experience of theatre so far. Mohammed Z comes from Nakfa. He attended an EPLF school where he took part in performances and when he went to the Sudan in 1989 he continued performing songs and drama. There is no on-going drama group in Nakfa – two or three days before a celebration they are told to get a show together. Mohammed A comes from Agordat – his group meet regularly and pay a birr each per week. One of their recent plays was about a child who was due to be initiated with tribal scars and who tried to flee to the mountains to escape scarring. The students explain what they want from us to develop confidence, and techniques for working with people as leaders, to find out the basics of theatre – 'to build a house, we need foundations'. And so we 'tutors' begin to learn about this culture, about the students, about Eritrea. The learning quickly deepens as we begin practical work – for example, the students create sculpted images of important moments in their lives. A boy sleeps under a tree with his camel; busy electricians crowd around a machine that needs repair; children pore over their school books; tanks roll over dead bodies.

Insert (The heat is unbearable. I have a bad headache. The first time this happens, I am convinced I have malaria. Now I know I have a bad headache.)

Day 12

Today, three of the students are running a warm-up for the whole class. They offer a mixture of theatre games and vocal exercises we have taught them, an

Eritrean children's game, a South African chant. They have planned it well and lead confidently; afterwards we discuss what worked well and what could be improved. We continue with sessions of yoga and voice exercises. These are paying off – the iron-tense shoulders have relaxed, movements are gentler and more flexible, voices are richer, fuller, more confident. We are also working to encourage flexible and imaginative minds – today we are using a continuum exercise. This begins with a contentious statement. For example: 'All men should take their turn at cooking', and we argue our views, moving position if we are swayed by the argument and counter-argument. 'God created man and woman equally, but cooking is women's speciality' says one group. 'God created man and woman equally, they both eat and they both have hands' says another. An audience gathers at the open classroom window and joins in the debate. 'Why are we doing this?' asks one student. Because community drama is not agit-prop, it explores conflict, it celebrates difference. The illuminated face of a farmer at prayer, the wary look of a nomad woman as she leads her donkey, the smile of a kind teacher talking to little children, the watchful eyes of the man who sells plastic sandals in the market appear in exercises and improvisations, as we learn to watch, to think and to communicate with more precision.

Insert (Goodies arrive by car from Asmara. We've been dreaming of the delights of cheese and chocolate, but the greatest pleasure comes from finding rubber gloves and disinfectant.)

Day 14

To take a risk is to lose something.

Not to take a risk is to lose everything.

We rise at 5.30 with the cockerels, meet the group as the sun rises over the mountains, walk along a dried-up river bed out of town. The rains have been falling for a month, but it will be another month yet before the water flows.

Hot. Shady rocks by a green pool. We watch goats and herons and a horse – and a man who dives naked into the water. Muffled giggles. Fatna disappears under her shawl screeching with laughter. We move on....

Hotter. Up a hillside strewn with boulders. Why did they fall there? What have they seen? We sit, eyes closed, and imagine the story from the first fires at the world's beginning, through ice and forest, to wars – Italians, British, Ethiopians making their mark on the land. We walk, eyes still closed, to our own places – on boulders, under a cactus, at the top of a rocky slope and sing to each other. Greetings. *Assalaam aleikum.* Big voices ringing round the valley. The song of the boulders.

Hottest. Through the dust back to our cool schoolroom. Inside we breathe cold stone floor and shady air. Breathe into our hearts, heads, bellies, breathe out the sound they make. Sing the sounds of our whole bodies.

Two lines of chairs. Two lines of silent people gazing into each other's eyes. Still. Finding it so difficult. Holding each other's eyes, speaking into the stillness saying profound, beautiful, ugly, frightening things with our gaze. Thirty minutes pass. We stop. A long sigh.

A few instructions from the teachers and our translator, our voice, have been the day's only words. No-one has spoken for six hours.

Next day we will start by drawing, covering the floor with our day, then work on the same floor until it's smudged and unrecognizable.

Next day Hiabu will tell us about how his day became a meditation and memorial to his friends killed in the war.

Next day we will try to talk about our day's journey which we have shared and not shared with each other and realize it is beyond words.

There is no word for 'magic' in Tigre.

Insert (A cease-fire has been declared in Northern Ireland. What is happening? Why is it happening? I have had no letters from home. I want to cry.)[7]

Day 25

We are making two shows. It has been interesting dividing the group, trying to achieve a balance of skills, of sages and space cadets. The stories and themes come from the students' lives and experiences – we are overwhelmed with material. The first group's play concerns a young woman torn between her family and her right to make her own life. We are exploring some huge themes, some rarely publicly expressed; the gap between town and country, young and old, men and women, tradition and progress, those who stayed in Eritrea during the war and those who left. Everyone has stories, everyone is scarred, the war is all around us still. There are landmines in the mountains. The road to Keren is littered with tanks rusting in the gullies beneath new bridges built over the bombed remains of old ones. And still you can smell people's hope.

Insert (A baking hot day. There is now no gas, no water and no electricity.)

Day 32

'Homecoming' – the second group's play – has an episodic structure, telling the stories of three people returning to live in their villages after the war. Yesterday the cast missed out an entire scene, causing narrative confusion all round, but today the sequence seems to be in place and my anxiety levels have decreased. The orphan, faced with his grandfather's refusal to let him continue with his schooling, sings:

> Where does my father lie?
> Did he fall in the Gamhare, did he die in Nakfa?
> Which of you can give me news of my father,
> You who are the friends of the martyrs?
> When I overcome the problems I face
> I will keep all my father's promises.
> Grandfather, leave your hard work, ploughing and keeping sheep
> I have begun my education to learn.
> Let me learn to fulfil your son's place.
> Which of you can give me news of my father?
> Tell me, where does my father lie?

Suddenly, the building where we are rehearsing is filled with armed soldiers

Rehearsing with the young men's group, Sala'a Daro

and policemen. The male members of the cast and all the other young men are rounded up in lorries and driven away to the police station. This makes most conventional dress rehearsal disasters seem like minor inconveniences. Eventually all are released, having proved successfully that they have completed their military service, but not before our anxiety levels have gone through the roof.

Insert (On the road to Asmara, a soldier steps out in front of the car, holding up his hand. I execute an emergency stop. He only wants to hitch a lift. That's not what you think when it happens to you in North Belfast.)

Day 35
Is it going to rain? Will we have to cancel the performance? Same old questions as at home. Local people are confident that the clouds will pass. The directors give notes from last night's shows; the actors are not listening but the children of Haile Mental are fascinated. The drumming and singing warm-up attracts the adults. More and more people crowd onto the football field, 2,000 at least. There has never been a theatre performance in Haile Mental before.

The actors have been growing in confidence, and they know this is the last time that we will see them perform – they know this is a gift they can give us. The audience catches the heightened mood.

As the young woman describes her circumcision there is a hush. When she says 'No' to an arranged marriage there is a gasp and then an intense whispered debate. In the next show we watch faces change in the crowd as the audience discovers that the character they have laughed at as the 'village idiot' is an

'The Angel Tree', the women's group of the community play in performance, Sala'a Daro

ex-fighter traumatized by his experiences of the war. As he tells of his dreams some of the audience stick birr notes on his forehead and in his pockets – a great compliment. After his first performance, Hamid, one of the youngest students said, 'I was very nervous in front of all those people. And then I looked and saw that I was from that community and I was telling the stories of that community. And that is what gave me the courage to perform.'

We would like to have time to rework the pieces, based on what has happened in performance, we would like to have time to evaluate properly with the students, but time has run out. There will a break of a few weeks, then the cast will tour the plays all over Eritrea.

Questions to students (3)
Can this kind of theatre be beneficial in Eritrea?

Fatna: Since it is a traditional way of acting, people watch it relaxed, they can understand it simply. As to what I noticed from the performances, it was helpful, because all the people were discussing the concept of theatre. They were saying these are real problems and all the people should hear how to solve them.
Hamid (Keren): In this community theatre, the audience are the whole family, so it can help Eritrea a lot to progress.

JP The final element in the training project was research-based. If you are trying to make syncretic theatre, bringing together indigenous performance forms with modern, progressive modes of drama, it seems necessary to at least try to gain an understanding of those indigenous forms. In many African countries extensive research has already been carried out into such forms and master performers are not hard to get hold of. But in Eritrea the long years of colonization, enforced Amharization, displacement and war mean that many, and particularly the younger people we usually work with, have scanty knowledge of their traditional dances, songs and stories; and know even less of their history and significance.

The EPLF had been well aware of this problem and had utilized traditional performance forms in their variety performances as well as undertaking some research into Eritrea's indigenous cultures. But this information has often not been collated systematically and is all in Tigrinya. In 1995 we had begun by researching Eritrean drama history, both civilian and revolutionary.[8] Now we wanted to begin to try to understand Tigre and Bilen performance cultures, both to enhance our performance work and in order to bring these cultures to a wider audience.

In two months, with one researcher and two Eritrean assistants, it was never going to be possible to do more than scratch the surface, but we have come away with sufficient material for a video on dance forms, and for articles on the dances[9] and on how Tigre and Bilen youth have been trying to make their own theatre in the post-liberation period. It is at least a beginning. Here, our workaholic researcher, Christine Matzke, tells what it felt like trying to grapple with her enormous brief – despite amoebic dysentery and a violent reaction to the anti-malarial drug, Larium.

Trying to Find the Stepping Stones

CM We are sitting outside a bar in Hagaz, a small town about half an hour's drive west of Keren, sipping hot, spicy tea. 'We' are eight elders from Hagaz, Mohamed Salih Ismail (one of two Eritrean research trainees), Awate, a local guide and friend, and me – the project research assistant. I have been told that the people of Hagaz make the best tea in Eritrea and it tastes true; the flavours of the sugar and spices blend to a delicious aroma which helps revive our spirits after a two-hour marathon interview. All of us – interviewees, interviewer and translator – look exhausted and want to relax.

It is the last week of the Eritrea Community-based Theatre Project 1997 and we have almost come to the end of our work. That is, time forces us to conclude, even though the gaps and holes seem to be getting larger by the minute. Our questions are willingly answered, but as our information grows contradictions also appear, producing a fruitful tension which we are now unable to explore further. There is also a nagging awareness that our research has been only partial; that it has focused on written documents, interviews and student performances, without there being the time to experience Tigre and

Bilen culture in its living context. Yet we also know that we have come a long way since we started our work in Asmara and that we have collected an awful lot of information.

Wherever we have been – Asmara, Keren, Hagaz or Mensura – people have encouraged our work, wanted their culture to be recorded, wanted to be able to share experiences with different communities and to let other people know about the wealth of their cultures. Much knowledge was buried under the traumas of war, exile and return to Eritrea, but there is incredible willingness and patience to dig it up again, to facilitate our research because of the importance of their culture to people's own lives and to the identities of their communities. Our informants have been constructively critical of our rather theoretical approach, and this only makes me long to have more time to live and work with these people in order to learn more.

Mohamed, Tesfazghi Ukubazghi (the second research trainee), and I began our work in Asmara at the Research and Information Centre (RICE), shuttling between its small, damp reading room and the spacious offices of The British Council: going through documents possibly relevant to our work, translating passages, practising interview techniques and conducting our first interviews. The scope of the enquiry was initially impossibly large, and had to be narrowed down in order to pursue one or two areas in reasonable depth. Together with Jane, we decided to focus on dance, as it was a major interest for the Keren theatre training project, and to document the students' previous experiences of theatre and drama.

It was only when we moved to Keren, after some three weeks, that the work truly began to make sense. Through close interaction with the students, in workshop, video and interview sessions, pieces slowly fell into place. The opportunity of recording the regional Bilen performance troupe practising for the annual Expo cultural festival in the capital was also extremely helpful.

We will not be able to complete the picture – culture is far too dynamic for that – but sometimes we see a dance we have previously only read about, or we find a story that correlates to a song, such as the one about Omar wad Bashakir, who became a goatherd in order to stay close to the woman he loved, since his poverty barred him from marrying her. This was a story not far removed from reality for some of our informants.

It has been the enthusiasm of the students that has carried us as a research group. But the support and debate with other members of the team, Gerri, Renny and Jane, has been thought-provoking and encouraging. For me, the work is a process of give and take, of communal teaching and learning between students, informants and team members alike, which has brought together the practical and academic sides of the work.

When once again I was despairing about the wealth of material we have no time to tackle, Gerri remarked that we should be conscious of the fact that we have had time only to find the stepping stones. And this, I think, we have achieved; others can continue to build the performing arts in Eritrea.

JP As I write this epilogue in June 1998, the future for our work in Eritrea is unclear. We should have been preparing for a further training programme working with 40 teachers, and a Tigrinya and a Tigre theatre group should have been working full time. We had secured funding to keep the work going and expanding for the next three years, and the Minister of Culture was keen for the project to develop. However, a few weeks ago underlying tensions between Ethiopia and Eritrea exploded into war over border demarcations. All foreigners have been advised to leave the country and all flights have been suspended. Many of our actors have been mobilized for the war.

International arbitration efforts are underway, but it is difficult to find out up-to-date news as the western media is as uninterested as ever in a dispute between two of the worlds' poorest nations.

We hope the insanity of full-scale war can be avoided, that Eritrea's reconstruction can continue and that the project will be able to resume speedily. But for now we can only wait.

NOTES

1 The names of the writers throughout the article have been indicated by the use of initials. Hence **JP** = Jane Plastow, **AC** = Ali Campbell, **GM** = Gerri Moriarty, **RO** = Renny O'Shea, **CM** = Christine Matzke.

2 The Amhara were the dominant Ethiopian ethnic group which sought to impose their language and culture over all the peoples of the Ethiopian Empire. For further information on Ethiopian cultural imperialism see Jane Plastow, 1996, *African Theatre and Politics, The Evolution of Theatre in Ethiopia, Tanzania and Zimbabwe. A Comparative Study* (Rodopi: Amsterdam).

3 For further information about the EPLF Cultural Troupes see Paul Warwick, 1997, 'Theatre and the Eritrean struggle for freedom: the cultural troupes of the People's Liberation Front', *New Theatre Quarterly*, 51 (August): 221–30.

4 The Italians colonized Eritrea from 1890 to 1941, and they created its present borders. The British took over during the Second World War under a UN mandate until Eritrea was annexed to Ethiopia by the UN in 1952. The notion of dialogue-based drama as opposed to music and dance-based performance culture was introduced by the colonizers, and the two forms had always been seen as separate in Eritrea.

5 *Suwa* is the local home-brewed beer. The priests drank it copiously and often.

6 Drama as performed in Eritrea by both amateur groups and EPLF Cultural Troupes always modelled itself on the naturalistic stage as imported from Europe. Hence, during the liberation struggle, Cultural Troupes carried around portable stages, and always put up curtains. When we first worked with our trainees they could not imagine how you could put on a show without at least a front-of-house curtain.

7 Gerri was particularly concerned at this time as she comes from Northern Ireland. However, general umbrage was taken if the group were called English in Eritrea. Renny is of Irish extraction, Christine is German, Ali is Scottish, my son, who accompanied us, is half Tanzanian, which left only the nanny and myself as English.

8 See Jane Plastow, 1997, 'Theatre of conflict in the Eritrean liberation struggle,' *New Theatre Quarterly*, 50 (May): 144–54, and Paul Warwick, 1997, 'Theatre and the Eritrean Struggle', also in *New Theatre Quarterly*, 51 (May): 221–30.

9 See Christine Matzke, 'Trying to find the stepping-stones: writing Tigre and Bilen dancing in Eritrea. An impressionistic choreography', *South African Theatre Journal*, forthcoming.

(The authors would like to acknowledge the financial support of Oxfam UK & Ireland, Christian Aid, and The British Council which made this project possible, and a grant from The British Academy which enabled the academic research to be carried out.)

Alemseged Tesfai
A playwright in service to Eritrean liberation

JANE PLASTOW

This article is based on an interview carried out with Alemseged Tesfai in November 1997. However, it also draws on earlier interviews undertaken as part of research into Eritrean theatre by 'The Eritrean Community-based Theatre Project' in 1995, and on conversations with the playwright over the past six years.

When I asked Alemseged Tesfai, in 1996, if he would be prepared to help polish up a rough translation of his play, *Eli Kal'a Quinat* (*The Other War*), from his native Tigrinya for publication and possible performance in English, it was the first time I had had the considerable pleasure of jolting his usual, apparently imperturbable, *savoir faire*. I suddenly saw what this burly, self-confident man in his fifties might have been like as a young man in the early 1970s, when he first came to London and hung out with the hippies around Leicester Square for some days or, more seriously, when he made the decision to leave post-graduate studies in America to join the Eritrean liberation forces. 'Do you think anyone would be really interested in this?' he asked, and I swear he was nearly blushing. It is a good feeling to be able to excite and give pleasure to such a man, and it was especially good when the plan came to fruition, and thanks to the efforts of the West Yorkshire Playhouse in Leeds we were able to mount a studio production of this most famous of Eritrean plays, at which Alemseged and many other eminent Eritreans were present.

Yet Alemseged Tesfai became a playwright almost by chance, and still sees his playwriting activities as a mere utilitarian response to the demands of the Eritrean liberation struggle; a struggle which, as for so many Eritreans, has been the defining factor in his life.

It is impossible to write about Alemseged (Eritreans always use their given name, the second name being a patronymic not a surname) without also writing about Eritrea's 30-year war for liberation from Ethiopian colonialism. Alemseged was born in the Eritrean village of Addi Quala in 1944, when the British had taken over the country from the Italians who first invaded, and indeed defined the country by that invasion, in 1890. For the time Alemseged's father was an educated man. Tesfai had reached the fourth grade, the highest educational level allowed to Eritreans by the Italians. He was a government employee and, unusually for the time, ensured that all his children were given a modern education. Until he was eight, Alemseged lived just inside Ethiopia in the historic town of Adwa, but because of scarce educational opportunities he then spent his school years between the Eritrean capital of Asmara and the Ethiopian capital, Addis Ababa. In 1952 the United Nations had given in to Ethiopian pressure to federate Eritrea to Ethiopia and many elite Eritreans consequently travelled to Addis Ababa for education and work.

The federated status of Eritrea never fitted in with the Ethiopian emperor, Haile Selassie's, absolutist style of rule. Throughout the following decade, he systematically undermined independent institutions until in 1962 the weakened Eritrean assembly, packed with the emperor's yes-men, voted through an act of union with Ethiopia. A minuscule armed liberation movement began as early as 1961. When he finished school Alemseged found himself faced with a demand to join Ethiopia's conscript army, an army from which he already felt profoundly alienated. For a year he simply avoided conscription until he managed to get a job with Ethiopia's prestigious airline. Then aged twenty, in 1964, he enrolled at Addis Ababa University, initially studying political science then changing to law.

On graduation Alemseged was employed as a legal assistant by the Ethiopian Ministry of Finance, and it was during his time with the Ministry that he had the experience which planted the seed for the play which many years later emerged as *The Other War*. In 1970 Alemseged's senior officer, the Minister of State for Finance, took his young assistant on a trip to southern Ethiopia. They ended up in Jijiga, the administrative centre for the Ogaden which is inhabited by ethnic Somalis, and which was then, as for many years later, waging an irredentist war.

Alemseged tells the story. 'I don't know if they knew I was Eritrean, or if they just didn't care. My Minister was talking to the military commander of the area and they discussed how it was impossible to control the area by conventional military means. So they were encouraging young Amhara soldiers to marry or to force Somali women to have children with them. By this means the commander explained that in the long term the children would become Ethiopian and the Somalis would lose their identity. As an Eritrean this action deeply horrified me. Years later I saw they were doing something of the same thing in Eritrea, and this became the starting point for thinking about the play that became *The Other War*.'

Alemseged only worked for the Ministry of Finance for a year before he went to America to begin post-graduate studies in law. However, by the mid-1970s the hit-and-run groups of the 1960s had grown into a fully fledged Eritrean guerrilla army, and in 1975 Alemseged's nationalist beliefs impelled him to return to home to join the Eritrean People's Liberation Front (the EPLF).

At that time the EPLF and Eritrea's other liberation force the ELF, or Eritrean Liberation Force, looked well on the way to winning their war. Ethiopia controlled little outside the capital and victory looked imminent. However, in 1978 the USSR backed a huge military offensive by the Ethiopians and from being in almost total control of their country the Eritreans were pushed back in 'the strategic retreat' to the high mountains in the very north of their land, the area known as Sahel.

Life in the mountains was very hard. Because of Ethiopian MiG fighters it was unsafe to go outside during the daytime. Almost all activities had to be carried out at night and in the daytime everyone had to retreat to underground shelters hacked out of the mountains. For years the fighters ate little but lentils and sorghum, never saw a proper road, and maintained trench lines stretching hundreds of miles across the mountains. The Ethiopians, with the biggest army in black Africa, backed up with enormous Soviet support, unleashed a series of offensives involving hundreds of thousands of troops, and routinely used napalm, torture and starvation tactics to defeat the Eritreans who received no international aid. Moreover in 1980–1 the two Eritrean liberation fronts fought a murderous war against one another which resulted in final victory for the more socialist-progressive EPLF.

During this time Alemseged, like everyone else, trained as a combatant. But because there were so few educated Eritreans he was quickly assigned to a succession of jobs ranging from war-reporting, to the developing of educational curricula for children in liberated areas, and the development of cultural and literary activities. The retreat of 1979 was used by the EPLF as an opportunity to restructure their organization. This was relatively easy to do because for the first time most of the fighters were in the same area. It was also crucial to the EPLF's philosophy which argued that the war was not just a military struggle, but a struggle to free Eritrea from repressive feudal culture and the stranglehold of reactionary religious forces, both Muslim and Christian.

In an overwhelmingly peasant nation a man of Alemseged's education was extraordinarily rare, and this – whilst in no way denying his considerable intellectual acumen – helps explain why his career has involved so many and such varied high-level posts. In the late 1970s Alemseged Tesfai was assigned to the EPLF educational department. For a while he was a headmaster of a secondary school before becoming involved in developing educational curricula. Then in 1981, to his own considerable surprise, he was assigned to the Division of Culture, with particular responsibility for developing Eritrean theatre and literature.

The EPLF had set up a cultural department in 1975, but this went through a major restructuring in 1979 when for the first time cultural development officers such as Alemseged were appointed, and cultural performance troupes were much encouraged. At Arag, behind the front lines, the cultural officers first had to dig out their premises so that they could work with some measure of safety. It was an unusual task for artists and one that took five months, cutting into Eritrean hillsides to dig not only shelters, but also offices and even a rehearsal hall. The authorities were greatly concerned that Eritrean culture had been devalued during the Ethiopian occupation, that traditional cultural forms were being lost and that there was minimal printed or performance material in Eritrean languages.

For Alemseged this hard, simple life had its compensations. His job involved writing, and he could give significant amounts of time to study and literature. The EPLF collected what library materials it could, and Alemseged spent time reading this material before writing the first two Eritrean textbooks on literature and drama. He also started writing plays.

I asked Alemseged what had been his inspiration for writing plays – not a line followed by many lawyers and freedom fighters. He said his mother had been the first source of interest in the arts. 'She was not educated, but she told us many stories.' To prepare himself he had read whatever material was available in Arag; a few textbooks on theatre techniques and a little Shakespeare, Soyinka, Ngugi and J.B. Priestley. 'This opened my eyes to Western theatre, but I had always, since I was a boy, loved going to the theatre and particularly the cinema … and I think you could say that was what gave me the greatest inspiration.'

Alemseged's plays are in a naturalistic, almost Ibsenesque mould, and this is hardly surprising since his influences had been overwhelmingly Western. In both Eritrea and Ethiopia the modern theatre tradition has been heavily playwright and dialogue-dominated. This was true of much early African theatre as a result of colonial domination but in both Ethiopia and Eritrea, for reasons of language, geography and, especially in Eritrea, being effectively cut off from much of the rest of the continent because of the war, the syncretic forms combining traditional culture with progressive Western cultural forms so common to other parts of Africa, failed to emerge. Alemseged himself knew this was a possible limitation to his work as he explains:

'I knew in my mind that if Eritrean theatre was to develop it needed to go back to Eritrean culture and folklore, deep into the thoughts and actions of the population and develop from there. But I didn't have that kind of capacity, there were physical limitations at that time.'

Alemseged has written three plays, all between 1981 and 1984. The first was *Luul*, in which the eponymous heroine is a factory worker who conscientizes her fellow workers and operates as an underground EPLF comrade. *Anqtzi* (*Meningitis*) was inspired by an outbreak of that disease and described in heroic terms the work of barefoot EPLF doctors as they fought to control the epidemic. Both texts are obviously primarily agit-prop on behalf of the struggle, as is, on one level, *The Other War*. What is most obvious about Alemseged's kind of propaganda however, is that his heroes are not the front-line fighters, but those working to support the struggle behind the scenes. Alemseged told me that he chose not to write about front-line situations because there was not enough conflict! He was referring, of course, to the unity amongst the EPLF fighters, rather than to their relations with the enemy. It is also interesting, and in contrast to an accusation which has been levelled at many African male writers, that the focus of Alemseged's interest is so often women; women who are not mere sexual or maternal objects, but active, politically, socially and domestically engaged subjects of the drama.

I already knew that women formed one-third of Eritrea's fighting force and that improving women's status was seen as a key part of the EPLF's social revolutionary programme, but I wanted to ask Alemseged how conscious a decision it was to emphasize the role of women in his drama, particularly in *The Other War*.

'Of course partly this is to do with the plot of the play, but it was also by design. Women in Eritrea are given much respect, they are the carriers of tradition. During the struggle they were the carriers of hope and light, and of course they participated so strongly in the struggle in the field and outside....

Mothers are especially revered in Eritrea, they carried the brunt of everything, so we are very conscious of mother homage and many songs were made about mothers.' (The gains women made during the struggle are now under threat from traditional social mores, but that is another story.)

The playwright had himself married a fighter during the struggle, in a simple ceremony similar to that related in *The Other War*. When I probed him further as to the source of this play, he told me how his wife, stationed at a distant part of the front, had asked him to visit a woman refugee she knew. This woman had a daughter who had married for love – an Ethiopian. However, the mother had found living with her new son-in-law intolerable. She had consequently fled to the liberated areas, taking her three purely Eritrean grandchildren from her daughter's earlier marriage, and leaving the children of the Ethiopian. This story then, with the political background from Alemseged's 1970 experience in the Ogaden, became the essence of his play, with the interesting twist that in *The Other War*, Letiyesus, the mother, is persuaded to take also her half Ethiopian grandson. As Alemseged explained: 'I made the young child an object of contention. He became a symbol of either oppression or freedom.'

The Other War was written with particular actors in mind, because Alemseged was writing for and directing the members of the Central Cultural Troupe. This troupe – one of many including brigade, women's, children's, disabled and even prisoner-of-war performance groups – was made up of fighters who put on variety shows for the fighters and for people in liberated areas. These shows would last for around four hours, and their central emphasis was song and dance, both traditional and revolutionary. Plays were new to many in the audience and developed from short skits or pieces of agit-prop to texts like *The Other War*, which runs for nearly an hour. *The Other War* toured for a year in 1985–6 to the various fronts as part of a larger variety style show, to liberated areas in the west of Eritrea and, after a major Ethiopian offensive in the west, perforce to the Sudan where nearly a million Eritreans had taken refuge from the war. Unlike many writer/directors of brigade cultural troupes Alemseged did not accompany the group as he still had administrative and development work to attend to. For some of the time while the play was on tour, the playwright was back in the front line, when yet another Ethiopian offensive meant that all the able-bodied were needed to fight.

Alemseged knew his plays were popular during the struggle. It was, however, only when *The Other War* was videoed that he was publicly credited as its creator since the EPLF viewed all its work as collective, and strongly resisted any possible build-up of personality cults in relation to its leaders. Alemseged has not written another play since 1984. In 1986 he was appointed to run the whole Cultural Division. But after less than a year he was assigned to other jobs and play-writing became just another thing he had done as part of his war work.

Like many others in Eritrea – particularly those who fought with the liberation fronts – Alemseged could tell many stories of the horrors of war, of his own traumatic experiences, and of guilt about living on when so many of one's friends have died. Like nearly all other fighters he very rarely chooses to speak of such matters; at least to the outside world. It is not the done thing in Eritrea to speak of one's own experiences in any way which might be construed as the least bit boastful or for the purpose of eliciting sympathy. The collective ethos meant that individual suffering was accepted as the expected price of communal victory. The dead, 'the martyrs' – some 70,000 Eritrean fighters – are glorified; the living speak of the solidarity of the Front, of major events and of the general life of the fighters, but only reluctantly of their individual roles.

I first met Alemseged in 1992 when he was in charge of finding new directions for Eritrean culture. He wanted Eritreans to have the chance to know and become involved in a whole range of cultural activities and indeed to have the chance to experience many kinds of theatre. He encouraged me to initiate community theatre in Eritrea, but he also invited opera companies, playwrights and directors to visit and undertake projects in the new nation.

'There was one thing that we wanted to maintain and that was that theatre and arts should belong to the people. We wanted to expose the Eritrean people to different things and then let them choose what they would like to do. We felt that arts in general – I was responsible for all not just theatre – should be set free.'

Alemseged was only in charge of the arts division for a year after independence before he was called on to lead the Land Commission. As in so many African countries land ownership is a massively important issue, and in Eritrea land had been held under complex and differing systems which favoured the old feudal elites. Art was abandoned as the Commission wrestled with questions of how to reallocate land on an equitable basis, including allowing women land rights for the first time and working out how to deal fairly with the peasantry, the quarter of the population which had been displaced during the war, and the returning fighters. As always, Alemseged seemed to wear his responsibilities not lightly, but easily, as befitted a man who is undoubtedly one of the inner circle of government; the friend of ministers, regional governors, senior justices and ambassadors.

After land, reconciliation. Alemseged liaised with government and foreign aid organizations in an initiative called The War Torn Societies Project. This project was part of a wider United Nations research programme dealing with how to reintegrate and assist the establishment of post-conflict societies. Alemseged was responsible for producing a preliminary report in 1996 on issues of governance in Eritrea. I had only known Alemseged Tesfai as an urbane enthusiast for the arts, and increasingly as a friend, so I was interested to find that he was seen as a hard man by many of the staff of foreign NGOs, and as one who was deeply suspicious as to whether they really had anything worthwhile to offer Eritrea.

Following on from the necessity of war-time, Eritrea has embraced the philosophy of self-help combined with a free-market approach to trade and industry, but Alemseged, like many senior policy makers is, I think, deeply wary of the agendas of foreign aid organizations which have, to date, been barely tolerated as a short-term source of assistance in regenerating the country. Alemseged is a nationalist, who is at present engaged in the first, state-sponsored writing of an Eritrean interpretation of the period from 1941 to 1962 which was the crucial background to the liberation struggle. He believes that Eritreans have an ancient history of broad co-operation across ethnic and religious differences which must be fostered. Foreigners have historically taken little notice of Eritrean voices or needs, and like many others Alemseged is not prepared to have his country and its struggle hijacked by foreigners and their views. This does not mean xenophobia. When responding to criticisms of his apparent hatred of the Ethiopian, Assafa, in *The Other War*, Alemseged passionately explained that he was not targeting inter-racial love. 'Mutual love between individuals, whatever their origin is, is not a concern of this play. The problem arises when love and sex are made to be instruments of social domination and repression.' I do not think it would be far-fetched to apply some of the same analysis to Alemseged's attitude to the outside world in relation to Eritrea. Friendship, cultural exchange and disinterested assistance are not problems, but Eritrea has had enough of being manipulated by the outside world. She wants to take her place as a grown-up country making her own decisions and possible mistakes – without nannies or imposed agendas from abroad.

Alemseged Tesfai lives in a small, albeit by Eritrean standards, very comfortable villa in the extraordinarily charming, Italianate capital, Asmara, with his wife and small son – like many long-term fighters he has come late to parenthood. He cannot walk more than a few yards down the palm-tree fringed main streets of the capital without being greeted by other ex-fighters, and he is firmly part of the ruling PFDJ – the People's Front for Democracy and Justice – the EPLF turned civilian. He is also a rare thing in Eritrea, a published author. His novel, which translates as *The Son of Hadderab*, deals with a bandit or *shifta*, who becomes transformed by his engagement with the struggle, is crippled in the fighting and ends up as a farmer. More recently a collection of short stories, plays and recollections, *Two Weeks in the Trenches* won its author the 1997 Raimok prize, a major national award.

Alemseged is never likely to be short of work, and he is committed to helping to give Eritrea a voice through his writing, both fictional and academic. Whether he writes more plays is another question. 'I don't know', he said to me when I interviewed him for this article. 'I had not thought of it. But with this interest maybe if an idea comes to me, I will try to write another play one day.'

REFERENCES

Plastow, Jane, 1997, 'Theatre of conflict in the Eritrean liberation struggle', *New Theatre Quarterly*, 50 (May): 144–54.
Plastow, Jane, 1998, 'Uses and abuses of Theatre for Development. A case study focusing on the relationship between political struggle and development theatre in the Ethiopia-Eritrea war, 1961–91', in Kamal Salhi (ed.) *African Theatre for Development* (Exeter: Intellect Books): 97–113.
Tesfai, Alemseged, *The Other War* (English translation 1998 by Paul Warwick, Samson Gebreghzier and Alemseged Tesfai) in Martin Banham and Jane Plastow (eds), *Contemporary African Plays* (London: Methuen).
Warwick, Paul, 1997, 'Eritrean theatre in the liberation struggle', *New Theatre Quarterly*, 51 (May): 221–30.

Performance Studio Workshop
Igboelerin East

CHUCK MIKE & members of the PSW

[The Performance Studio Workshop (PSW)[1] is a Lagos-based laboratory for alternative communication, social development, community empowerment and the perpetuation of mutual understanding between peoples through culture and performance art.' We print below extracts from PSW's 1996/7 Report, which includes a record of work in a Yoruba community. We are grateful to Chuck Mike and his colleagues at PSW for permission to reproduce and edit their material.]

In 1996 PSW had conducted highly successful work in the Yoruba village of Oluwole (see Jumai Ewu's contribution elsewhere for an update on Oluwole). Buoyed by this experience a PSW team set off to another Yoruba community in Igboelerin East, with a 'Theatre Outreach Workshop'. The story is continued in their own words:[2]

Towards Self-development, Actualization and Empowerment: Theatre Outreach Workshop with the people of Igboelerin East

Previous experiences of the Minor perspective explored the utility of an entrée into the target communities. 'A(bout) with Aids' was the title of the 1995 entry skit into Epeme. In Oluwole the entrée was 'Ikpiko', a play on female genital mutilation (FGM). This reporting year, 'Oyela, the Drum that Beats a Change' (formerly called 'Whose Choice is it Anyway?'), a sketch also on FGM, was created and performed by the joint team of PSW 1996/97 Apprentice and the TFD (Theatre for Development) Cell of the University of Ibadan, Department of Theatre Arts, as an opening skit in Olosunde.

The material evolved from a one-week creative orientation session in Lagos. Day One was used to acquaint the Cell with improvisational techniques. As expected, it was a novel experience for the undergraduates who were more attuned to the formal theatre practice of 'script to stage'. For two days the performers soaked themselves in the world of the material, learning and discussing circumcision as practised by the people of Igboelerin East. Four days were given to the creation of the material from a story-line conceived by the group. The creation was left strictly to the group but was supervised from time to time by the Director and Programme Officer for the integrity of its content. (The framework for the TFD Cell groups' eventual working autonomy had been set at the outset of its initial training over a year before.)

It was in the best interest of the project that participants also became familiar with research methodology before going into the community. The most important component of the research was data collection. To this end, a comprehensive tutorial was held on the last day of the workshop by the Studio's IEC officer. The 'researchers' were introduced to techniques of community liaison, information retrieval, how to carry out community surveys and participatory research. Strongly emphasized was the need to have an objective and balanced attitude to whatever new information they received in the process of fact building. This was to become an essential part of their work over the next couple of weeks.

Community Profile: Igboelerin East

Igboelerin East is made up of some 70 communities. Most of them are hamlets and villages of about 150 people. The first of these communities is about 10 km of earth road from Lagelu Local Government Secretariat. The villages are similar in appearance with mud houses and zinc roofs. The compounds are clean except for goat dung while the perpetrators of this hazard doze lazily under huge bamboo trees enjoying the cool afternoon breeze. But for the chattering of playing children and the almost inaudible thuds of mortars and grinding stones, the quietness of these villages make them almost serene … a far cry from the bustling urban centre some 20 to 30 minutes' drive away. Albeit, the creaking of local grinders and the tolling of church bells in other villages are tell-tale signs of life behind the thick bushes.

The villages of Igboelerin East share a common genealogy and ancestry. Their occupants are kinsmen and often intermarry. The basic occupation of the men is farming while the women are petty traders and farmers. Five villages or more share a common health centre, school and church. With the exception of Oyedeji, there is a noticeable absence of small-scale businesses such as chemists or provision stores. The dominant religion is Christianity, though there are Muslims. As with most Yoruba communities, immediate traditional power resides in the persons of the Baale. The small village of Olosunde where our tale begins – and ends – is divided by politics surrounding its traditional ruler.

DRAMATIS PERSONAE (WORKSHOP PARTICIPANTS)

For Igboelerin East	Petty traders
The Baale	Men
The 'Opposition'	Women
The Catechist	Children
School teachers	
Youth Corpers	*For Oluwole & Environs*
Elders	The Baale
Farmers	Wife to the Baale

For *Lagelu Local Government*
Primary Health Care Co-ordinator
Primary Health Care Officers (4)
Community Development Officers (3)
Education Officer (1)

For *Inter-African Committee on Harmful Traditional Practices (IAC)*
Programme Officer (1)

For *Association for Reproductive & Family Health (ARFH)*
Programme Officers (4)

For *University of Ibadan, Department of Theatre Arts*
Lecturer (1)
Students (TFD Cell) (5)

For *the Performance Studio Workshop*
Director
Programme Officer
Production & Training Assistant
Technical Assistant
IEC Officer
Apprentices (3)

Special Guest Appearance
Chairman, Lagelu Local Government

Act I: 'Outside In'

Prologue

By 9:00 am on 15 October 1996, guests from Lagos and Ibadan made up of representatives of funding organizations, local NGOs and members of the Ibadan Area Task Force on FGM had converged at the Lagelu Local Government Secretariat, Iyana-Offa, to be conveyed to Olosunde, the venue of the Opening Ceremony.

Olosunde village is situated about 22 km off the Ibadan-Iwo Expressway along a winding earth road. A small settlement of Yoruba-speaking people, the population of the village is less than 200 including children. Surrounding it are other mostly smaller villages all making up Igboelerin East. The largest of these villages is Oyedeji with a population of over 500 people – larger of course than Olosunde.

The choice of Olosunde community for the Opening Ceremony was dictated primarily by the Local Government chairman. During a recce of communities in the area by PSW's Programme Officer, several other communities were identified which might have been suitable for the experiment. However, when the chairman 'suggested' Olosunde ... *it would have been deemed foolhardy to disagree with the suggestion if the project was to be approved.*

Olosunde, like Oluwole and the majority of the villages under Lagelu LG, had similar development – or rather underdevelopment – problems: lack of electricity, potable water, and health-care facilities, bad roads, etc. Other problems emerged in the course of the workshop.

Guests arrived at Olosunde community at 11:45 am – an hour and 40 minutes behind schedule. As the convoy of six vehicles drew to a stop, reactions spewed from the invited guests: '*What a journey! I thought we were never going to get here.*' '*How did you find this place?*' '*Na wa for you theatre people o, you always manage to find the remotest of places. Who would ever have thought there were villages behind all those bushes.'* Behind their cool façade, the visitors must have been a little disturbed during what seemed like a never-ending journey. Perhaps they thought their guide had misguided them.

The crowd from all the villages had begun to disperse, having waited for a long time and finally given up hope that their visitors would come. They soon began to return, however, when they saw the vehicles and strangers alighting from them. Villages swarmed out of their homes as the church bell began to toll informing them of the visitors' arrival. The Baale of Olosunde appeared, a quiet, insignificant looking man followed by other village leaders. After briefly introducing himself and his cohorts, he welcomed the guests on behalf of Olosunde and the other communities. Without much ado, the programme commenced.

Act I, Scene I: Opening Ceremony

Mini Dramatic Information Blitz on Female Genital Mutilation
The Opening Ceremony, which also doubled as a 'Mini Dramatic Information Blitz on FGM', took off a few minutes after noon inside the St Paul's Anglican Church, Olosunde. The introduction of village dignitaries was made in Yoruba by Mrs F. O. Agbaje, a local government health officer. Representing the Chairman, she expressed his apologies for not being able to attend the occasion and conveyed hopes for a fruitful ceremony. Amongst the invited guests present were Ford Foundation's Representative and Programme Officer, Mr Fateh Azzam, and his wife, Professor Bolanle Awe, Country Co-ordinator MacArthur Foundation, Mrs Funsho Orenuga, Programme Officer Inter-African Committee (IAC), Mrs Ladipo of the Association for Reproductive and Family Health, the Baale of Oluwole, Mr George Olapade and his wife, and a host of others.

In stumbling Yoruba, PSW's Programme Officer (PO) briefly explained the purpose of the gathering. She said that the day's event marked the beginning of interaction between visitors and the villages present. The PO stated that the team would, over the next week, visit each of the villages around Olosunde, learning more about them and sharing with them experiences PSW had gained over the years, experiences which might be beneficial to them and the development of their villages. She reiterated that contrary to popular belief, PSW and the invited guests were not politicians, neither were they developers with elaborate goals. All that the team had brought to share was an abundance of good will and experience.

The Dramatic Information Blitz was focused on three areas of concern: the physical, sociological and legal implications of FGM on the lives of women and girls. It was important that for any enlightenment to take place, answers had to be provided for the million and one questions that drifted across the people's minds but might never be asked. Such answers had to be ones they understood and believed in … answers which did not threaten their culture.

Mrs Orenuga of IAC started the first of the discussions. 'Female

Circumcision (FC) as a Harmful Cultural Practice'. Her emphasis was on the mis-beliefs centred around female circumcision amongst the Yorubas from a medical perspective. With the help of an anatomical model (a plastic model of the female genital organs), she explained how it was medically impossible for the baby's head to touch the clitoris during child-birth. She further clarified that FC makes labour more painful than necessary. In closing, Mrs Orenuga stated that contrary to Yoruba belief promiscuity could only be checked by good up-bringing and not by FC.

Mrs Ladipo of the Association of Reproductive and Family Health, Ibadan, spoke next. Her focus was on the sociological and psychological implications of FGM on women and girls. It was obvious that Mrs Lapido had a wealth of experience in community health services as she took her position before the audience dancing and singing. In her account, she emphasized that tradition in itself is not bad. Noting that there were good cultural practices which should be upheld, she observed that there were other practices which destroy life and should be questioned. She emphasized the importance of children to the Yorubas and added that FGM was a threat to the life of the female child and complicated the processes of child-birth. Stressing that society often ostracizes barren women, she spoke at length about self-confidence which all women should have but many do not possess due to the many degrees of pain inflicted on them in the name of tradition. At the end of her delivery, Mrs Lapido implored the audience to desist from such harmful practices as FGM. She led the villagers in a folk-song which asked them to hold on to good practices and reject negative ones.

Though entertained, members of the audience were becoming impatient, anxious to express *their* views on all they'd heard so far. The women, who were in the minority, were noticeably silent while questions were asked by the men. A few of the men seemed convinced by the arguments tendered so far but others remained unconvinced. They were also unwilling to listen to more on the subject. The women's response was difficult to analyse. It seemed as though they were afraid to even hope that a change would ever occur.

By the time Ms Lana started on the 'rights angle' of the programme, the God-given and convention-supported rights of women to a healthy, normal and long life, the audience was visibly tired. People began to walk out when impatiently an elder man retorted: '*We have heard all you have said from the beginning and we will stop FC. If there is more besides this matter please go on, if not, let us go.*' All this time the women still sat quietly.

The church, which according to the vicar attracted only about 100 on Sundays, was occupied by over 450 at the Opening Ceremony. Sixty-five per cent of this number were men between the ages of 36 and 67. The remaining 35 per cent was made up of women and children.

The second segment of the programme opened with the performance of *Oyela, the Drum that Beats a Change*, a piece jointly created by the PSW Apprentice and TFD Cell teams. The 35-minute skit was introduced with drumming. The crowd which was beginning to disperse during the talk on rights soon trooped back out of curiosity. As the players made their way to the stage through the audience, children cheered and laughed at their costumes. As is characteristic of Studio Outreach performances, players were costumed in fragmented costumes consisting of a basic uniform over which they donned items such as caps, ties, wrappers and head-ties which depict their many character transitions. This kind of costuming was apparently new to the audience and was deemed quite amusing.

The Skit

Oyela opened with the naming ceremony of a new baby girl born to a rural couple after several years of childlessness. Well-wishers and friends teemed in to congratulate the couple and partake of the ceremonial bounty. As evening approached, the new father's friend approached him and asked when the traditional rites were to begin seeing that the day was almost over. The father responded by saying that they were awaiting the Baba Olola (circumcisor). No sooner had he spoken than the subject of the discussion walked in. Baba Olola was welcomed by both parents and friends. He asked if all was set for the ritual: pepper, oil, kola, etc. The parents responded in the affirmative and Baba set to work, sharpening his razor. Just then, a young university student arrived. Greeting everyone, it became apparent that he was the younger brother of the new mother. Having heard of his sister's good fortune, Oluwole had come to rejoice with her. He beckoned to his sister to come aside as he had a request to make of her. She replied that he should be patient for a few minutes as they were in the process of performing an important traditional ritual. The young man, puzzled, questioned the nature of the ritual and was told that the circumcision was about to begin. Oluwole (the student) was inflamed and asked his sister if she was ignorant of the announcements on the radio by the Ministry of Health warning against the circumcision of girls and women. She said she had heard – but it was tradition and it had to be done. An argument soon ensued between the father, Oluwole and Baba Olola. Baba advanced all the reasons why the circumcision of girls was practised amongst the Yorubas. Principal amongst them were to curtail a woman's sexual desires and curb promiscuity, to ensure easy child-birth and prevent barrenness. To further buttress his point, he narrated the Yoruba fable of a King who went away to war. By the time he returned, his wives, assuming him dead, had become involved with other men. The situation distressed the king greatly and he sought counsel from the oracle of Ifa. Ifa responded that between the thighs of a women protrudes a small mass of flesh; to curtail her sexual urges, this 'evil' object must be cut off! Since that time, therefore, the ancestors have excised the female clitoris. Hmmm...!

Oluwole tendered his counter-logic by explaining the risks involved in circumcision. These included the possibility of infections like tetanus and AIDS. He explained how AIDS could be contracted through infected blood by the use of unsterilized blades. He also expatiated on the issue of promiscuity by using the Ijebus (a Yoruba tribe) as example. The Ijebus according to research do not practise FC yet the rate of promiscuity amongst their females is no higher than the rest of the Yoruba groups. Neither are their women more often barren. He educated the Olola, and by extension the audience, on the complications arising from FC. To emphasize his point, he narrated the story of a couple who had wanted a child for over 12 years. Eventually blessed with a baby girl, they went as custom demanded to the Ololo's place to circumcise her. After the 'operation', the bleeding could not be controlled and the girl eventually died.

Oluwole's story was the final stroke that broke the camel's back! The new mother and her friends immediately protested against the operation and the father had to seek the audience's counsel on what to do. On one hand was tradition which must be upheld, on another was the health and life of his newborn child. He asked men and women, boys and girls in the audience what he should do. It was unanimously shouted that he must not circumcise his daughter. The new father turned to Olola and apologized for wasting his time but said he no longer wished to have his baby girl circumcised. Baba Olola too was convinced by the many arguments and vowed that from thenceforth he would not circumcise any more female children or women. In the presence of the audience, he broke his razor to pieces, packed up his equipment and left. The play ended with song.

Mo dupe mo bi mo tutun o	I am grateful, I have a new baby
Araye	people hear
Mo dupe mo bi mo tutun a	I am grateful, I have a new baby
Araye	people hear again
Mo dupe mo bi mo tutun	I am grateful I have a new baby
Ema ba mi ya labe	please do not circumcise her
Mo dupe	I am glad
Mo dupe mo bi mo tutun o	I am glad for my new baby
E ma ba mi ya labe ko ri	Please do not circumcise her
O pe!	I warn!

The audience joined in the song, clapping in appreciation of the performance. The song continued while the players scattered through the 'auditorium' to conduct interviews with women, men and children in the audience.

The interviews went on for about 20 minutes and the performers distributed handbills on FGM. The handbills were printed in Yoruba and captioned '*Ma da abe fun Omo obirin mo. Asa ilera ti ko dara ni*' ('Stop Female Circumcision. It is an unhealthy practice'). By this time, guests from Lagos and other faraway places began to leave. The Baale of Oluwole was called upon to give a report of developments in the community since the intervention of the Studio earlier in May. He briefly described the May Outreach and expressed his community's appreciation of PSW's work. He implored the people of Olosunde to openly receive the team. Reiterating the gist of the PDO's opening remarks, he said PSW had not come to occupy their land or steal away their property, but instead had come to share experiences with them for their future gains. He pointed out that he had never visited Olosunde in spite of the fact that the communities were close by. It seems he had not met the Baale of Olosunde before that day. He expressed his joy and appreciation once again to the PSW for fostering the link which he promised to follow up.

To elaborate on FGM activities in Oluwole, Mrs Olapade, the Baale's wife was called forward. In her account, she elucidated that following the Outreach campaign on FGM there had been no re-occurrence of the practice in her community. Over the issue of TBA (Traditional Birth Attendant) training, however, the LG (Local Government) was yet to announce commencement. Thus far though, some women in the communities had signed up for the training – ready for the time it would commence.

To round off activities for the Opening Ceremony, the Baale of Olosunde gave a vote of thanks and, on behalf of Olosunde and all its surrounding villages, wished the team a fruitful Outreach. Before the team departed, the director presented the Baale with a bottle of Schnapps.

Act I, Scene 2

Ejioku
After the Opening Ceremony, the Outreach team of 14 persons led by the Studio Director retreated to Ejioku, their temporary abode for the 'outside-in'. The accommodation was the Local Government Guest House volunteered to them by the LG Secretary. In the evening, a post-mortem of the day's activity was conducted.

Some of the findings from the research conducted during the opening were new and quite interesting. For example, a woman was questioned about whether, after seeing the play, she would still consent to circumcising her female children. She replied that she had two daughters, one was circumcised the other was not. As they both grew, she noticed that her uncircumcised daughter was brighter and more self-confident than the circumcised one. Though she told no one, she believed this to be a result of circumcision and promised not to allow it to happen to her grand-daughters. A 16-year-old secondary school boy had been asked what he thought of the campaign against FGM. His response was that he believed the campaign was timely. When probed on his response, he responded that he had several girl friends and from experience believed that uncircumcised girls perform better sexually than their circumcised counterparts.

There was a general consensus amongst the team that the message had been well received by the audience. There was a particular man who seemed unreceptive to the campaign, and it was decided that the team seek him out in the course of the Outreach to hold further dialogue with him. The profile of Olosunde as gathered during the interviews was shared with the house to familiarize participants with the community in which they would be working over the next two weeks. The performance was analysed and notes were taken for the correction of flaws in subsequent performances. It had been a long day and participants were worn out. The Director called for an early night and the team dispersed with anxieties about what the coming days would bring. It was early yet to discern what kind of people these were!

Act I, Scene 3

As usual, the day began with house cleaning followed by breakfast. The serious activities of the day began with a plenary session. The Director gave the framework for subsequent activities and delegated duties to all participants for the duration of the workshop. The University Theatre Arts Lecturer was undergoing his second outing with PSW and was to assist in project co-ordination which in his words was 'a baptism of fire'. The Programme Officer indicated the specific activities for the day and for the rest of the week. The first week, beginning that day, was to constitute Phase One of the workshop – the 'outside-in'. Twenty-one villages were to be visited in guerrilla theatre style with the performance of *Oyela*. This was to be followed by post-performance follow-up (interviews with inhabitants) of each of the communities on FGM practice – if present in the village – and other developmental problems the communities might be facing. The ultimate objective of the Outreach, besides sensitizing the people on FGM, was to seek a possible location for the 'homestead' experience. Four communities were scheduled for investigation each day.

The first port of call for the first day was the LG Secretariat to request a guide from the Community Development sector. It was expected that, by virtue of their work, Community Development Officers (CDOs) would be conversant with the geography of the communities under Igboelerin East. This made them the best possible guides for the team. Besides, experience has shown that communities were often more receptive if they believed the project had their LG's backing. Mrs Adekanbi was appointed as the team's guide for the duration of the workshop.

The group arrived at Oyedeji about 4:00 pm singing and dancing. This drew villagers out from inside their homes. On inquiry, the group was directed to Baale's home. Incidentally, the Baale lived in two homes in two villages! On this occasion, he was in his other home. His deputy received the group in his place. Dr Lanre Bamidele, on behalf of the group, thanked the chief and the villagers and explained the Studio's mission. The objective of the visit was to perform for the villagers a short skit, after which the locals would be required to answer a few questions. The elders initially were elusive, stressing the absence of the Baale, an indication that, therefore, they could not permit any performance. At this point, Dr Bamidale informed them that PSW was not a stranger to the environment having collaborated with other villages and with the LG Chairman in the past. He also noted that one of the daughters of the village was a member of the team. As soon as her name was mentioned, there was evident recognition and an elder retorted that they should have been told that to begin with. The deputy chief gave his consent for the performance to take place. Again as custom demands, Dr Bamidele on behalf of the crew presented a bottle of Schnapps. With the permission of the elders, performers changed into their costume fragments and, in 'pied-piper' fashion, drummed and danced around the village, luring audiences to the village square.

The approximate number of audience members at Oyedeji was 300, consisting of women, men and children. The performance was staged in the open-air to the enjoyment of all. In the post-performance discussion most of the questions were centred on culture. '*Since circumcision often was handed over through lineage what would happen to those to whom their forefathers had handed over the practice but who refused to continue it? Was male circumcision also harmful? What "cure" was there for those who had been circumcised?*' The questions were answered to the best of the performers' abilities. Where they felt inadequate, the villagers were directed to the Research/IEC Officer or the Assistance Project Co-Ordinator. The villagers also had the opportunity to answer questions from the performers. The majority agreed that after seeing the play, they believed FGM was harmful and should be stopped. Some admitted to having heard about the campaign to stop female circumcision on the radio several times but the reason for the campaign were never made as clear as in the play. As a village, they pledged to stop the circumcision of girls. Handbills were distributed and pasted on the door of the village chemist. The second in command to the Baale said there was no circumcisor in the village. He said the circumcisor came only on the market day and from another village. They assured the Director that they would report back to him about what they had learned. The market was on the following day.

The Outreach team returned to Ejioku and tallied up their findings. There was unanimous agreement that the village was obviously backward in development. Unfortunately, the villagers did not seem to realize this. Research findings revealed that the basic developmental problems facing the village could be prioritized as: lack of a functioning health facility, high school drop-out rate, absence of low-scale industries, lethargic attitude of inhabitants, and, perhaps, an unstable or ineffective leadership structure. Of all the other villages around Olosunde, Oyedeji was the only beneficiary of the road grading project. Yet, in spite of this development trend, there was an obvious absence of any kind of business such as tailoring and hair-dressing in the village. Instead the people were at peace in their abject poverty, taking pride in being the biggest village in the community. On the other hand, perhaps, the fact that the Baale seemed to have his loyalty divided between two villages accounted for the condition of the village and for the attitude of its inhabitants. Whatever the case, the insalubrious state of the village ruled it out as an option for the live-in experience.

To take advantage of the large audience turn-out that the market would provide, a skit on 'Imoto to' (cleanliness) was created and performed at the Oyedeji market the next day. The skit addressed the unsanitary state of the village and showed how, as a result, people were susceptible to sickness and diseases. it also indicated that, with the absence of hospitals or health care centres, the consequences could be fatal. The business of the market did not afford maximum participation or concentration as was anticipated. The arrival of buses in the square where the skit was being performed was a persistent intrusion on the performance. Nonetheless, post-performance interviews with traders and buyers revealed that, even though it seemed the performance was not seen by all, its message had filtered through the market and the majority could narrate sequence by sequence what the skit was about. There was an average of 500 people in the market during the day.

The next five days took a similar pattern, however. '*Oyela*' was the entry skit. The bus hired for the Outreach team arrived at the team's Ejioku base every morning at 8:00 am to transport them to Igboelerin community, about 25 km away. Because of the muddy earth road, the bus would sometimes get stuck and participants were forced to alight to push the vehicle. Very often crew members reached their destination covered in mud. On arrival at the villages, the crew paid courtesy visits to the Baales, who were in many instances aware of the team's imminent arrival. After preliminary courtesies, and with the permission of the Baales, the pied-piper approach was used to draw villagers to the community square, church ground, school field, or wherever a performance was found more convenient. It was commonly an open arena. After the performance, villagers engaged in group or individual interviews with the performers for about 25 minutes before the team moved on to the next leg of the journey.

The villages were close by and the team often walked from one to the next. Some, however, were not as near, though from the villagers' perception, all the villages were '*ni tosi be yen*' ('just around the corner'). Around the corner could well be a good one and a half to two km away! The reception accorded to the performers differed also from village to village. In smaller communities like Morola and Alatere there were exceptionally warm welcomes. Children and elders alike at the end of the performances expressed their gratitude to the group for thinking to come to them. They offered gifts of fruits, cocoa, etc., as a sign of their appreciation. In Olufowokan, however, the group was literally chased out of the village. Smaller children were warned to stay indoors because 'kidnappers' were around! All attempts by the Community Development Officer to speak to them met with hostile resistance and the team had to leave … some discouraged and upset.

But for these brief moments of disappointment the experience was interesting. Each evening at Ejioku, new information was gathered and shared. Despite the proximity of the villages to one to another and the appearance that they were spiritually one harmonious community, we perceived that there were differences and political conflicts below the surface. This was to become a major obstacle during the 'Homestead' experience.

The developmental problems of each community were somewhat similar, differing largely in how they were prioritized. For example, while the people of Bankeso, Lakinde and Olalere (the total population of all three communities amounting to about 180) lamented the lack of a health-care centre within reasonable distance from their village, Oyedeji, which had such a facility – though not functioning – complained of the government's insensitivity to their electrification appeals. Other villages had problems that included lack of schools and bad roads. On FGM, however, the performances were well received and the people promised to stop female circumcision.

At the end of six days, 21 communities had been covered, one more than the targeted number. The final community (Bankole) was included at the last minute by virtue of its closeness to Isagade. The population of the villages ranged between 20 and 450 while the approximate number in the audiences at each performance was between 20 and 235. At the post-mortem concluding Phase One of the Outreach, Olosunde was unanimously agreed to be the location for the 'Homestead' experience. The rationale for this was that the community appeared to be central to activities in Igboelerin East. The team had also been offered living space for the second phase of the workshop at Bolorun-duro Villa, within the village. It was assumed that if Olosunde was receptive to the programme, chances were that other villages would emulate them.

Act II: Homestead

On the morning of Monday 21 October 1996, workshop participants departed from Ejioku. The bus arrived at 9:30 am to convey participants to Olosunde village for the second phase of the Minor Theatre Outreach Workshop. En route, they stopped at the Local Government Secretariat to notify the Chairman of the commencement of Phase Two of the project.

The group arrived in Olosunde before noon. The accommodation was partially tiled. Raw cement was visible. There was no roof but a ceiling made of tin did exist. No pipe-borne water was available. There was no electricity, bathing or toilet facilities. There was a well about 500 m away. The interior walls were unplastered yet a fence surrounded the house. The structure was flanked on all sides, except on the front, by bush. Opposite our home for the next few days sat an abandoned health clinic project. Was this a sign?

Once settled, a plenary was called to allocate duties and map out an itinerary for the next five days. Workshop participants were divided into four groups. Group A was to focus on health and hygiene practices within the village. Members of the group over the next two days were to discuss with the villagers ways of improving their health status – especially of the women and children. Group B was allotted to education. They would visit the secondary and primary schools in Olosunde. The third group, C, was for women in development and was to investigate problems facing women in Olosunde and to collaborate with them on ways for improvements. Group D was to focus on men in leadership. Each group was carefully selected with an awareness of gender balance. It was important that in setting up these working groups, women and men were represented for the benefit of the villagers who already had misconceived notions of the role of women.

On subsequent days, the group dispersed in the mornings to their different appointments and met together in the evening to analyse findings. At the end of three days, Group A's report showed that Olosunde had no health care providing facility within the vicinity. Pregnant women very often had to be rushed to Ejioku – a distance of about 20 km. Though there was a fully operational facility in Alaboro (about 20 minutes' walk from Olosunde), the villagers rarely used it because of its registration fee of N35.00 which they found too expensive. The team also examined the unfinished structure meant to be used as a mini-clinic but, because of the politics of land surrounding it, the structure had remained uncompleted over a period of five years. Other health concerns that evolved from the group's research was the high number of deaths in the village, especially in the immediate past. The villagers attributed this to superstitious beliefs such as witchcraft and 'juju'. At the time of the Outreach, the village was in mourning for a prominent son of the village believed 'to have been killed by the wicked eyes of witches because his star was shining bright'.

Group B's findings on education showed that at the time of the experiment, students were not at school because the majority of pupils had not paid their fees. This was the case in both the secondary and primary schools. According to Group B's research most of the parents in the village sent their children to the schools in Oyedeji and in the township. The reason given was that there were no teachers in their own school. Further to this, youth corpers who were sent to serve there often changed their postings. The few teachers interviewed disclosed that parents were often slack in paying their wards' fees and since the government had ceased paying teachers' salaries for some time, the only avenue to raise money was to ensure that parents paid up. Staff records revealed 20 teachers but only seven of those turned up for classes. The group took a tour of the secondary school and spoke with the students. It was impossible to hold conversations with SS3 students (the highest class) in English because they did not understand. In one of the classes visited, a member of Group B asked for a volunteer to read what was written on the blackboard. Not a single student could read. It made one wonder what language the teachers taught in. How does one teach supply and demand in Yoruba? Even if that could be taught, how does one explain current and light in physics using Yoruba as the language of communication?

The school buildings were almost collapsing. In one of the classrooms, a whole section of the floor had caved in leaving a gaping hole in the ground. Though the average classroom had about 25 students, there were only a few chairs or desks (six at the most) in each class. Some classes had no desks at all and students had to stand.

Discoveries in the primary school were not very different. Two classes often had to share one classroom. The teachers in early education appeared more committed than their higher school counterparts, but most of them resided outside of the village and the school had no text books. The PTA, in spite of numerous appeals by the teachers, was not forthcoming in remedying the problem. According to one of the teachers, the parents in Olosunde had a lack-adaisical attitude to education. Whilst understanding that things were tough, they believed that even when the situation was much better, very often the last thing parents would invest in was their children's education.

From Group C's research on women and development, it was obvious that if ever the saying 'women are their own enemies' was true, Olosunde was living testament to the assertion. First the research group discovered that, unlike other communities, there were no women's groups in Olosunde. Neither were there co-operatives of any kind among the women. The closest semblance to this was a joint co-operative made up of men and women from neighbouring communities. Members of this group contributed money monthly (ranging from N20.00 to N40.00) for social events. On investigation, it was discovered that there were no trained traditional birth attendants amongst the women and they had never heard of the voluntary health workers.

In fact, the process of drawing responses from the women was extremely difficult. All were reluctant to put forward 'names', even for something as prestigious as being a government-recognized TBA. On one occasion a woman lamented that she had been cursed and abused by her female counterparts at the market place for mentioning a friend's name as birth attendant. The said friend accused her of having evil intent. The women of Olosunde according to the group's findings were basically farmers. A few of them traded in small items such as salt, dry fish, and *eko*. At all times when the group requested to follow them to their farms they diplomatically turned them down saying their farms were far away. There was very little sign of development or intention to develop amongst these women.

Group D, like C, found out very little to work with during their research. For the most part of their fact finding, the men were out of the village at their farms. Several meetings were arranged with the Baale to call the men together for a discussion but none of these meetings took place. The obvious conclusion was that the Baale was a very weak leader who did not enjoy the respect of his people. Added to this was the issue of being the 'unrightful' heir to the 'throne'. Most villagers believed that the position of Baale should have been occupied by another. However, the politics of the village and that of the local government enabled the incumbent Baale to be 'enthroned' ... *and upon all this ... his performance was naught to speak of.* The men, like their wives, had no groups or societies. According to the Catechist of the church, the men did very little for the development of the village except marry many wives. He pointed out areas of development where the men folk could have made their impact felt through the building of roads or a new well. He concluded that the younger boys had no examples and this explained their nonchalant attitudes to education and development.

Each group, with its assigned sector of the community, spent the next couple of days attempting dialogue towards solutions to the seeming problems. Great energy was spent encouraging action from people. Many general meetings were scheduled but not one was held. The Outreach team working to the pulse of the villagers was given several appointments. The team always reported at the meeting venues yet the villagers never did. When encountered the next day by members of the group they would smile and exchange greetings but no word passed as to why they did not show up at the meeting.

By this time, the Outreach group was becoming despondent. Nothing seemed to be working. As a ploy to reach the people, the Baale's wife was approached to assist in preparation of the team's meals while they were out in the field. She promised to gather villagers together the next day. No meeting was called and the Baale's wife did not turn up to cook. Gentle persuasion, cajoling, and promises to bring the Local Government in followed. Nothing was working! The situation was worsened by bites from sandflies which had disfigured the participants' skin. Some had fallen ill with malaria and the TFD Cell members were becoming further dispirited because the activity had overlapped with the beginning of school year. They were anxious to get back for the coming semester.

Esther, a youth worker, suggested we talk to the 'opposition', Mr Majegbogbe. According to her, he might be of use in getting people to co-operate. Mr Majegbogbe was, we later found out, in contention for the position of Baale but had been edged out by political forces. Apparently he had some clout in the village as it was also discovered that he had been the rallying point for the incomplete health structure which had fallen foul of accusations of impropriety. This, coupled with the distance to other villages involved, brought the project to a standstill. Mr Majegbogbe's house occupied a small space bordering the edge of Olosunde but still within its confines. He referred to it as 'the village of Majegbogbe'. However, he too was of little help in mobilizing the villagers.

New strategies were devised every evening but without the input and contributions of the villagers the essence of the exercise which was self-development was futile. To cheer themselves up, after dinner participants brought out their percussion instruments under the moonlight to dance and sing. This soon brought in the youth who joined in the merriment. With the belief that the attention of the youth had been caught, male participants began to engage them in dialogue. As soon as the youngsters realized that the matter was taking a serious trend, they bade the team good night and left. The catechist had been right.

By the sixth day *in situ*, the situation had become desperate. There was an unvoiced feeling of failure among the team. This called for drastic measures. On the pretext of going into town to procure foodstuffs, the PDO stopped at the Lagelu secretariat in Iyana-Offa to inform the officers of the situation in Olosunde and how unco-operative the villagers had been so far. Fortunately, she met the Chairman. Unknown to the workshop group, the villagers had also been to see him after the Opening Ceremony. According to them, they felt it was important for them to inform the Chairman that 'his visitors' were corrupting their children. They continued by saying that the visitors (Outreach team) were demonstrating to the children the process of love-making. (This reference was made to the anatomical model used by Mrs Orenuga to support her arguments on FGM.) The villagers complained about FGM being the focus of attention when there were other pressing problems within their community.

Fortunately, Mrs Agbaje, who represented the Chairman at the Opening Ceremony, was present. She gave a full account to the Chairman of the events at the ceremony. After much persuasion the Chairman obliged the team leader and visited Olosunde community. The joy and happiness on the faces of the depressed participants when they saw the Chairman cannot be described. For a moment the PDO became a heroine. The Chairman and his entourage were taken to the living quarters of the participants at the Bolorunduro Villa. He expressed shock at the conditions under which the team was living and commended them for their endurance. The villagers, on sighting the Chairman's car, trooped out of their homes and before long a small group had gathered. The Chairman rebuked the villagers for their attitude. (The Baale was not present.) He stressed the importance of development to any community and expressed his confusion as to why the people had not embraced a rare opportunity. He added that the team members came from well-to-do homes and that they really did not have to stay in the village under such conditions if they were not interested in the village's development.

The Chairman's attention was called to the abandoned hospital structure and other developmental problems facing the village. He promised a donation of N50,000 from the Local Government to complete the building before the end of November and pledged that the LG would post a health officer there as soon as the structure was finished. He stressed, however, that these would be done only on the condition that the people played their part and did not rest on their oars waiting for the government. Before he departed, the Chairman gave the participants N500 as a personal token. He promised to be present at the Closing Ceremony the next day.

If successes were to be measured daily, that was the happiest day in the lives of the participants since the commencement of the project. The team fixed an 8:00 pm meeting with the villagers to begin work on the creation of skits. After thorough analysis of the village and its problems, the group decided to focus on two main areas: a) men and health, b) women in development. The villagers did not turn up. The group worked late into the night by themselves.

The Skits

The first skit opened with two men from two different villages arguing about where a meeting should be held; each felt that the meeting should be held in his village by virtue of seniority. The argument progressed for a while and was interrupted by a third villager who wanted to know what the noise was about. He was informed of the impending meeting and their inability to agree on the venue. Man III was irritated by the air of levity and admonished both men, saying that people like them were the reason for lack of progress and for poor co-operation that existed amongst communities in Igboelerin. He cited the example of the abandoned medical project and how the clinic remained uncompleted after several years. As if on cue, an elder of the village walked in during the discussion with another young man and after listening to the issue at hand, he was incensed saying that his father had given them the land to build the hospital on; had he known the land would be so misused, he would have used it for farming. The young man, obviously disappointed by the attitude of these elders, intervened. He drew the men's attention to the usefulness of the hospital and how their lack of co-operation had robbed them for so long of what could have been an asset to them. He reminded them of a pregnant woman who died because she was not able to get medical attention on time. The men, seeing the sense in the young man's speech, agreed amongst themselves to come together and resume work on the hospital project. Not knowing how or where to start however, they turned to the men in the audience for suggestions.

The second skit opened with a village scene: women in their different households working. An appointed levy collector walked to the first woman and requested her contributions for the *aso-ebi* (uniform) the women wished to buy for the *ileya* (Eid-el-Fitri) festival. After much noise, the woman paid the levy collector and bade her goodbye. At her second and third stops, the levy collector was told by the woman that they could not pay the money because of the poor sales of palm-oil that season. The women complained that instead of looking for a solution to their problems the levy collector was asking them to pay for *aso-ebi*. The collector said that, since she was just a woman, a palm-oil miller, and also affected by the current trend in palm-oil sales, she could not proffer any solutions. What they could do, however, was call a meeting of all women and together they would seek a solution to their problem. At this point the skit was rehearsed to stop and accommodate suggestions from women in the audience.

The dialogue of the skits were culled from actual conversations between the villagers and the performers. Characters were caricatures of people met and spoken with in the course of investigations.

Closing Ceremony

The ceremony took place on the 30 October 1996. The turn-out of the villagers was the largest since the workshop began. It was ironic that in spite of being a weekend, villagers who ordinarily would not have the time, gathered for the closing. It almost seemed as though they were all present – to see the team leave. After opening prayers by the catechist, the Community Development Officer, representing the LG Chairman, declared the ceremony open. The skits were performed. The audience found the piece hilarious, and *were* sensitized by their messages. Reactions from the audience indicated that they were concerned about the issues raised.

The people, especially the children, were excited when they heard recognizable names. The use of some of their names by the players, the utilization of some personal articles like head-ties and scarves brought the skits closer to home. The playlets paused, as rehearsed, to entertain suggestions from the audience on the issues raised and, though the villagers had not been part of the creation, they merged smoothly into their roles. The men gathered together and decided to begin work on the hospital. They assessed outstanding work on the structure and agreed that what was left to do was the construction of windows and doors. After completing these, they would levy themselves to equip the place with drugs using assistance from the LG. With the women, they said, they would contribute N50 a week towards the completion of the work. After the second performance, the women unanimously agreed to contribute N20 every three weeks to buy themselves a milling machine that would service all the villages involved in the project. They selected two representatives for TBA training and promised to attend the TBA meetings henceforth. One woman also enlisted for the VHW (Voluntary Health Worker) training. On the issue of economic independence, they agreed to go for courses at the LG Secretariat on how to make local soap and candles, which they could sell to supplement incomes. At this point the school teacher interjected and pleaded with parents to pay their children's school fees. He added that most of the villagers insist on sending their children to schools outside Igboelerin thereby developing other areas and leaving their immediate communities underdeveloped. To conclude he thanked the team on behalf of the villages and hoped that they would be back soon to see how far the villagers had moved concerning their development. The ceremony ended with singing and dancing and taking of photographs. Though the PSW team tried to look sad about leaving, they could not curtail their singing and rejoicing as they drove out of the village back to their Ejioku base.

At Ejioku, a post-mortem of the week's activities was conducted. In summary, from the laziness and lethargy perceived there, not much was expected from the villagers. The group's impression of Olosunde was of a petty-minded people who would hold on to minor conflicts at the cost of their development. The group expressed their regret at not having carried out the Homestead workshop in Bankole Village instead. Individual reports were compiled by the Documentation Officer. The following day, the team members set off for their different destinations. The UI team were glad to resume their registration and the PSW team headed for Lagos.

Follow-up in Olosunde

In April 1997, six months after the workshop, the Production and Training Assistant together with the Technical Assistant paid a follow-up visit to Olosunde. To their disappointment, though not unexpectedly, no changes had taken place. The abandoned hospital structure was still at the point it was left, the latrine toilet which the team had started on Bolorunduro villa was yet to be completed. The only steps taken since October was that the women had started attending the TBA meetings but this had stopped due to circumstances they could not elucidate. There was no information as to why nothing had been done. There are, however, reports from the LGA Health Officers that a decline in FGM is prevalent. According to them, as reported by the villagers, many had heard the propaganda to stop circumcision but did not understand the thinking behind the programme. The Outreach brought answers to their questions.

NOTES

1. PSW can be contacted at J. K. Randle Hall, 5 King George V Rd, Onikan, Lagos. Tel: 00 234 1 263 7478, Fax: 00 234 1 263 1158.
2. We have extracted from PSW's report an example of work which produced problems and frustrations. As previously indicated, this needs to be put in the context of other work reported by PSW which was clearly enormously successful and positive. We admire the honesty and tenacity displayed by the PSW team in this report and the way in which they encourage even the most negative experiences to be an essential part of the learning and working process.

Art as Tool, Weapon or Shield?
Arts for Development Seminar, Harare

DAVID KERR

This is a very personal account of a seminar on Arts and Development held in Harare between 4 and 8 March, 1997. My point of entry is to compare the seminar with other conferences and workshops which I attended in the late 1970s and early 1980s during the first flush of Southern Africa's Theatre for Development movement. In the intervening period I had refrained from attending international theatre seminars, so the contrast between my experiences might provide a useful indicator of the extent to which the Theatre for Development methodology/ideology has been established, and in what way it has changed. Naturally, these are also modified by alterations in my own theory and practice during the intervening years.

This is not the place to attempt a genealogy of Arts for Development, a task which would require tracing the various indigenous adaptations African cultures have made to the didactic elements within their own art forms. It would also entail describing the attempts made by colonial educators to mobilize African communities through a variety of imposed or transformed, indigenous arts.

Instead, I offer a much narrower historical framework – the 'conferencization' of arts for development in Southern Africa, interpreted from a very personal standpoint. For the sake of brevity I shall refer to the early Arts for Development seminars as 'pioneers', in order to contrast them with the Harare seminar. No normative value is intended by this choice of word.

Perhaps the most influential workshop for launching the Theatre for Development movement was the one held at Chalimbana about 30 km east of Lusaka in Zambia in 1979. This provided a venue for the marriage between two types of activist – adult educators and social workers on one side (particularly the Botswana-based Laedza Batanani team of Ross Kidd, Martin Byram and Martha Maplanka) and the university-based artists with their roots in travelling theatre (such as Mapopa Mtonga, Dickson Mwansa and myself from Zambia, the Zimbabwean Stephen Chifunyise, and Tanzanians Amandina Lihamba and Eberhard Chambulikazi). The workshop linked the mobilization and social analysis skills of the adult educators to the drama and choreography skills of the theatre workers.

The Chalimbana workshop's main achievement was to develop the methodology initiated by the Laedza Batanani team:

1. Research into a community's problems;
2. Using a workshopped technique to create a play contextualizing those problems;
3. Presenting the play to the community;
4. Using the post-performance discussion as the basis for initiating action to solve the problems.

This methodology, with several variations, spread rapidly throughout Southern Africa (Swaziland, Lesotho, and Malawi, in addition to Botswana, Zambia, Tanzania and Zimbabwe).

The Chalimbana workshop, however, had several constraints, recognized even at the time. The main defects were:

1. The shortage of participants who spoke the language of the local Chalimbana village (the 'guinea pigs' of the experiment). Most of the Zambian participants spoke Nyanja, a widely understood lingua franca, but almost nobody spoke the minority Lenje language which was the first language of the local villagers.
2. The lack of genuine involvement by the local villages in the post-performance discussion;
3. The lack of meaningful follow-up programmes by the workshop organizers in addressing problems (such as illiteracy and poor roads) raised by the plays.

Theatre workers addressed these deficiencies at various international and regional workshops during the ensuing years, not only in Southern Africa, but in other regions too. The Malya project in Tanzania, the Kamiriithu experience in Kenya, the Morewa workshop in Zimbabwe and the Marotholi Travelling Theatre of Lesotho were all experiments which attempted to increase the participation of rural villagers, so they could build indigenous art forms as tools for social development or weapons in the class war.

The choice of metaphor here is important. Much of the debate in the pioneer workshops and seminars was about the extent to which theatre should be seen as a shield against colonial and neo-colonial indoctrination, or, even more controversially, as a weapon of class struggle. The metaphors need to be put into a historical context. The Chalimbana conference took place during the last and most aggressive phase of the Chimurenga war in Zimbabwe, and just a few months after Ngugi wa Thiong'o's release from the detention earned by his involvement in the Kamiriithu theatre.

There was a strong current among both academic and non-academic theatre workers of privileging art as a weapon/shield which could be used for the protection/mobilization of workers and peasants. There was also a strong interest in building a South/South network of popular/socialist artists in order to 'delink' African culture from Northern metropolitan control. This view emerged with particular strength at the 1982 Koitta workshop (Bangladesh), which brought together theatre workers from Asia, Africa, Latin America and the Caribbean. Among other activities the workshop helped launch the International Popular Theatre Alliance (IPTA), intended to provide a vehicle for South/South popular theatre networking.

At the 1984 Morewa workshop and conference (Zimbabwe), a pan-continental organization, UAPA (Union of African Performing Artists) was launched with considerable fanfare. The history of IPTA and UAPA is well-known. IPTA, which was intended to have a rotating leadership, did manage to publish two issues of a newsletter from Lusaka, and it also mobilized, with some success, for the release of theatre workers detained for their political beliefs (one Philipino and four Malawians). Its demise, however, was fairly inevitable, given the funding crisis associated with scandals which rocked UAPA in the mid-1980s. The worst of these was a very public struggle for power between the chairman and secretary general, and an even more disgraceful theft by a senior committee member of funds intended to establish a school for the performing arts in Harare.

It was this betrayal of radical energy and solidarity which, more than anything else, made many popular theatre workers in Africa retreat from net-working. In my own case, I concentrated on very local, unprestigious theatre work in support of Malawian village-based primary health care. It was with a once-bitten-twice-shy trepidation, therefore, that I attended the 1997 Arts for Development seminar in Harare, which many delegates, like myself, felt to be haunted by the ghost of UAPA.

The differences between the Harare seminar and the pioneering workshops were quite marked. There was a small rump of grizzled veterans, which included Stephen and Tisa Chifunyise, Mapopa Mtonga, Dickson Mwansa, Ngugi wa Mirii and myself. In addition, there was an extraordinarily varied assembly which included three South Africans, four Mozambicans, four Malawians, one Kenyan, several Britons and, of course, many Zimbabweans. As well as stage drama activists, there were fine and graphic artists, musicians, dancers, arts administrators and TV soap opera producers. Among these were young artists who had made their name in the late 1980s, such as the dynamic Zimbabwean, Cont Mhlanga of Amakhosi and Jayne Lungu of Television Zambia's *Play Circle*.

The large size of the British contingent was due to the sponsorship of the conference which was by the British Council. This in itself was a remarkable development. During the late 1970s and early 1980s the main sponsor for arts and development projects were the Scandinavian NGOs and donors such as the International Theatre Institute, the Gulbenkian Foundation and the International Council for Adult Education. In the eyes of many popular theatre workers at that time, the British Council, with its support for tours of the Royal Shakespeare Company or itinerant classical pianists, became associated with elitist 'neo-colonial' art. Several veterans at the seminar were not quite sure if the British Council's new interest in Arts for Development represented a genuine realignment towards popular culture, or an attempt to appropriate a radical movement.

The British group themselves was very varied. There was an eminent theatre academic, Martin Banham, who provided an amiable, avuncular chair for the meeting. There were several enthusiastic and conscientious arts administrators, such as Julia Rose, John Martin and Keith Lawrence and there were academics with wide experience of mobilization theatre, such as Jane Plastow (Zimbabwe and Eritrea) and Alex Mavrocordatos (Mali). Two of the British delegates were connected to post-graduation courses in Arts for Development at British universities, John Elsom at the City University, London, and Alex Mavrocordatos at King Alfred's College, Winchester. These courses seemed to be filling a gap left by the doomed UAPA Arts college in Harare.

The South African contingent, though small, made a major impact, especially as two of the delegates, Lebo Ramofoko, a television producer, and educator Masitha Hoeane, were perhaps the most articulate participants at the seminar. During the pioneer workshops, South African inputs were provided by ANC delegates, but, for security reasons, tended to be very low-key. Many of us expected the 1994 democratic elections to provide a radical shot-in-the-arm to the Arts for Development activities, similar to Zimbabwe's 1980 independence.

The actual situation is rather more complex. Scepticism about Arts for Development crystalized quite early in South Africa owing to the Sarafina II debacle (see p. 121, eds). Many South African community art activists feel that Mbongeni Ngema's handling of Sarafina II has provided severe obstacles to the use of arts for development purposes (especially in the field of AIDS awareness). My impression from contacts with South African community theatre workers is that they would rather concentrate on small-scale community analysis and local skills development. This is needed in order for artists to break down the simplifications associated with 'theatre for struggle' and move towards the greater complexity required by a 'theatre of reconstruction'. For that reason, many South African community theatre workers seem unwilling to participate in high profile regional or continental processes of networking, even if that means having to 'reinvent the wheel' of arts for development strategies.

No such parochialism could be associated with the South African delegates to the Harare Seminar. Masitha Hoeane proved an eloquent, impromptu, keynote speaker on development, emphasizing its reliance on human rather than material resources, and the need to encourage humane disciplines. Lebo Ramafoko presented an energetic and enthusiastic case for artists to use the mass media of radio and television in order to reach wide audiences. Her experience of incorporating health education messages into a South African Broadcasting Corporation soap opera (*Soul City*) differed markedly from that of most veterans at the seminar.

During the pioneer workshops the participants tended to represent face-to-face arts of theatre, music and dance. There was a feeling that the macro-media of radio, television and commercial popular music had a built-in cultural imperialism, due to the colonial origins of these media in most of Africa, and to the way technological imperatives create a dependency on Western programming formats. This feeling led to a perhaps rather romantic concentration on face-to-face arts and an almost puritanical neglect of mediated arts.

At the Harare seminar, the role of mediated arts for development was one of the most hotly debated issues. Cont Mhlanga presented a model for breaking down the cultural imperialist tendencies of the media. He described the way Amakhosi in Bulawayo used their existing cultural facilities to encourage alternative distribution of locally made programmes, documentaries, features and music through video and audio cassette hire. Zambian cabaret singer, Maureen Lilanda described the way commercial music could be used to break down gender stereotypes. Tisa Chifunyisa addressed the perennial problem of feedback in mediated art forms. She described the 'Sara' project in Zimbabwe, which used a variety of media – posters, radio jingles, face-to-face drama and TV/radio drama in order to attack prejudices against girls' education in Zimbabwe. The face-to-face media were able to provide a context for feedback missing from the mediated performances.

The most radical case for using the media for developmentally oriented arts came from John Elsom who suggested that technological innovations in the field of satellite communications and video recording facilities made the whole concept of media imperialism obsolete. He suggested that the cheapness and fluidity of the new millennial media would make it impossible for the Northern metropoles to sustain their dominance of media systems. He envisaged a positive climate for Third World filmmakers, musicians and actors to fulfil the insatiable appetite for cultural diversity in the global village. I found myself playing devil's advocate to this vision, adopting a stronger media imperialism position than I would ideally have wanted to. I argued that the vigour and subtlety of capitalism was strong enough and still sufficiently rooted in the Northern metropoles to frustrate any egalitarian tendencies in the new technologies. The seminar could find no common voice on this issue.

A related, but much less hotly contested issue was that of the relationship between popular theatre and arts theatre. During the pioneer workshops it became conventional wisdom to distinguish between a people's theatre (in African languages, using indigenous forms/stagecraft, and with themes geared to the 'masses') and 'elitist or 'art' theatre (in colonial languages using Western forms/stagecraft and bourgeois themes). This was a useful distinction at a time when many African national theatre associations were dominated by expatriate clubs and needed to decolonize themselves through the assertion of Afrocentric theatre modes.

At the Harare seminar the Mozambican delegation provided a useful corrective to this conventional binarism. Perhaps owing to the more popular position of Portuguese in Mozambique, compared to English in anglophone Africa, the Mozambican theatre workers, Candida Bila, Joao Chaque, Carlos Mende and Lucreca Paco, found it difficult to sustain distinctions between popular and elite theatre. They felt that conscientization of urban audiences (not excluding the bourgeoisie) was just as important as that of peasants and workers. Moreover, the skills and material resources associated with or generated by urban art theatre could be transferred to efforts in popular theatre.

Another important difference between the Harare seminar and the pioneer workshops was the role of arts other than drama. Participants in Harare not only looked at drama but also media entertainment, fine and applied arts, music, dance, and arts administration. In the pioneer workshops all these were considered, but tended to be subordinated to drama (for example, the way artistic skills were channelled into puppetry at the Chalimbana workshop). The Harare seminar explored the interdependence of the arts and the way they could support each other.

Underlying all these discussions was the wider issue of patronage. This crystalized around two closely related sub-issues:

1. The extent to which 'outsiders' could make contributions to community development programmes;
2. The role of NGOs (especially those funded by Northern agencies).

Some of the Zimbabwean delegates including Cont Mhlanga and ethnomusicologist, Dumi Maraire, took a quite strong 'indigenist' line, suggesting that only artists who were part of a local community could offer genuine and self-reliant support for development without imposing alien values or creating dependency on external resources. Not surprisingly, many of those whose work was in communities other than their own argued that the fluidity of modern migration patterns and the hybridity of even the most remote and rural cultures made the whole paradigm of 'insider' and 'outsider' meaningless. The latter group, perhaps because it was more numerous, seemed to win the day.

The issue of patronage was brought into sharp relief since the seminar was hosted by a single sponsor, the British Council. One whole session looked at the role of donor organizations, especially NGOs, as vehicles or patrons for arts for development strategies, particularly with respect to networking and the provision of training. Representatives from one government agency (ODA, Britain) and three NGOs (NORAD, Action Aid and Plan International) gave brief presentations.

The Arts for Development activists working in the field, agreed that some agencies (e.g. NORAD) were far more sympathetic to art as a tool for transformation than others (e.g. ODA). Despite these differences the participants still felt able to raise common issues. The most serious of these was sustainability – how do NGOs encourage communities to become self-reliant and to avoid becoming dependent on external support?

It was in the lack of any meaningful response to this question that I found the most remarkable difference between the Harare seminar and the pioneer workshops. In the early 1980s, even if Arts for Development workers accepted NGO funding for seminars, they felt this was a temporary measure until indigenous South-based infrastructures and alliances became established. There was a strong spirit of repudiating the 'neo-colonialism' of NGO funding. At the Harare seminar it was only Ngugi Wa Mirii, veteran of the Kamiriithu experience, who used strong anti-imperialist rhetoric. He described NGOs as 'shock absorbers' of capitalism, mitigating the worst social effects of G7 domination of the Third World, without doing anything to change the structural imbalances in global economic systems.

That outburst produced a rather embarrassed silence, especially as many delegates wanted to encourage the British Council to support various projects. Most of the arts activists knew that they had been depending on donor funding for over twenty years, and to bite the feeding hand was not only imprudent, but also hypocritical. When African theatre workers attempted an autonomous alliance, greedy individuals destroyed it, while the honest and conscientious majority were too busy or naive to prevent the destruction of UAPA. Given that failure, networking organized by Northern-based agencies such as the Human Rights Forum or even the British Council, seemed better than no networking at all.

As I flew back to Gaborone on my British Council-sponsored ticket, I tried to come to terms with the changes which the last fifteen years had brought. The barometer of the Harare seminar certainly seemed more finely calibrated than that of the pioneer seminars. The emphasis on media and other popular arts reflects popular culture much more accurately than the old 'Theatre for Development' paradigm. The incorporation of South Africa and Mozambique into the regional arts community provides more complexity in the relationship between national arts traditions and the policies/practice of cultural workers. The experience of earlier failed workshops has given a salutary sobriety to cultural workers' relationship with rural people's organizations. This implies a more mature and patient appreciation of the need for institution-building.

The biggest change of all is the ambigious and less abrasive attitudes of cultural workers towards Northern funding for arts activities and training. This is no doubt based on a more realistic evaluation of North/South economic relationships than the rather simplistic polarities advocated during the pioneer workshops. Metaphorically, the weapons and shields of the early 1980s have been turned into ploughshares – tools of development, in recognition that the slogans of the liberation struggle are now too simple for the post-liberation tasks of reconstruction.

Yet … I think it is more than mere nostalgia which makes me feel some regret for the idealism and loin-girding optimism of those early workshops. Wa Mirii's comments on the neo-colonialism of NGOs, however tactless, need an answer. The control of the G7 countries over the Third World, and particularly Africa, has become even tighter with the collapse of the Soviet bloc and the widespread imposition of structural adjustment programmes. Many NGOs are doing very valuable work in reducing the social harm created by SAP programmes on people's health, education, agriculture, housing, employment prospects or water supplies. One cannot help feeling however, that they are merely putting bandages on wounds which should never have been made in the first place.

At present, since almost all arts for development work is sponsored by NGOs with specific amelioration goals, it tends to be directed towards 'bandaging' strategies – namely plays, songs, dances, posters, radio jingles or soap operas advising people how to improve their lives within fairly narrow sectoral domains.

The major task of cultural workers still lies ahead – to create institutional solidarity and art forms with a holistic perspective, which can mobilize African communities to struggle against an iniquitous world system. The weapons and shields manufactured in the pioneer period of arts for development were undoubtedly crude (for example, in their relative neglect of gender issues), but the struggle for which they were designed is far from over.

I believe that the institutionalized instrumentality of arts for development as currently practised in Southern Africa needs to be transformed in ways which can help communities understand the macro-economic inequalities at the root of their major problems. In that task, there is still a need for art as weapon and shield, however improved and refashioned those artifacts may need to be.

Arts & Development II
Furthering the agenda, Ibadan

In his *Pedagogy of the Oppressed*, Paulo Freire asserts that development is not something that is given but evolves through the collective action and reflection of all members of the society.[1] The statement is apt for the main thrust of this article which reviews a workshop at the International Institute of Tropical Agriculture (IITA), Ibadan, Nigeria, 16–20 February 1998. It was convened by the British Council in collaboration with the Performance Studio Workshop (PSW) and the Nigerian Popular Theatre Alliance (NPTA) with assistance from the United States Information Service.[2] It attracted participants from South Africa, Botswana, Zimbabwe, Kenya, Ghana, Cameroon, the UK, the USA, and the host country Nigeria.

The workshop's title, 'Arts and Development II: Prospectives through Theatre (Furthering the Agenda)', reflected its intention to follow up on two previous international workshops: Harare (Zimbabwe) March 1997, 'Arts and Development' and Epeme-Lagos (Nigeria) March 1995, 'Theatre for Development: Revisiting the Agenda'. The aim was achieved through a conscious effort to revisit and develop issues raised at the earlier workshops facilitated by the presence of participants from both workshops and through a flexible programme that responded to the needs of those present. As a result, deliberations often took the form of cross-referencing between the three workshops, a factor that will be reflected in this paper.

For me Ibadan '98 was unique because it demonstrated the growing interest in Theatre for Development (TfD) as a discipline and the awareness that its future lies in the broadening of its cultural activity through collaboration between the various cultural media and development processes. This was evident in the range of participants drawn from theatre, television, film, radio and journalism. This development has as much to do with the shifting nature of the practice and its training programmes as it has to wider social changes.

Interestingly also the workshop combined reflective discussion sessions with some practical activities that included an ice-breaking, context-setting performance by PSW's performance outfit and, more significantly, visits to two local communities. Generally TfD workshops are criticised for their physical exclusion of primary constituent members. Participants tend to be practitioners and other allied professionals with no representation from the various projects to which they refer. That the absence of communities is more visible when workshops take place in relatively posh venues where the issues being addressed appear to be light years away was a point made early at the workshop. According to those present, Harare '97 took place in 'a very up-market hotel' and in Ibadan, we were at the IITA where participants were comfortably accommodated amidst beautiful, green and lush scenery. That this might constitute a contradiction made some feel uncomfortable The argument was that if one wanted to move and influence the 'real' world one had to operate in the context of that 'real' world in order to be taken seriously.[3] Yet in Nigeria as in most other African countries where decadent opulence exists side by side with abject poverty the 'real' world is never that far away no matter how hard one tries to shut it out. One only needed to walk a few hundred yards to the gates of the IITA to be confronted by the reality lived by millions of Nigerians.

Another reality is that the IITA has much in common with TfD and the workshop, in its goals if not wholly in its approach. It is an internationally funded non-profit agricultural research training institute formally established in 1967 by the then Federal Military Government of Nigeria and supported by the Consultative Group on International Agricultural Research (CGIAR). It also has historical links with the Ford and Rockefeller Foundations. With a campus sited on 2,400 acres of land donated by the Federal Government, the Institute's aim is 'to help fight hunger and alleviate poverty in sub-Saharan Africa through improved and sustainable agricultural production'.[4]

This developmental goal is shared by TfD and certainly the subject of productive and sustainable agriculture echoes most communities' desires located as they are in predominantly agricultural economies. However, as far as I was aware there was no representation from the IITA at the workshop. Such absence highlights the relevance and continued fight for the recognition and acknowledgement of the symbiotic relationship between material and human development which TfD advocates. It is also one that would reinforce the call for closer collaboration between TfD and development agencies.

TfD stresses collective action and reflection and this is evident in its practical processes. Certainly, practitioners need the time and space to reflect away from actual community contexts in which they work. A workshop provides an ideal opportunity to combine reflection with action. It is also one of several possible approaches to networking. Whether or not networking is necessary is a question often raised because practitioners are uncertain about whether it contradicts what their activities should be concerned with, that is, getting on with facilitating development in communities.

Ibadan '98 attempted to take on board these issues. Simply put, networking is about making contact with and maintaining connections between people with an interest in the practice. It is also about disseminating information and receiving feedback, sharing concerns, ideas and examples of good practice, debating issues, celebrating 'successes' and generally coordinating the activities of the practice. Ibadan '98 acknowledged that there are several interdependent dimensions to networking. There is that which needs to take place between practitioners and their constituent communities; between practitioners themselves; between practitioners and development agencies,and between practitioners and government/funding organizations.

As every practitioner knows the success of any TfD project depends largely on the effectiveness of contacts and lines of communication established between practitioners and communities before, during and after a particular intervention. Primarily the objective of TfD is to encourage community participation and dialogue in development whereby community participation in theatre becomes symbolic of and catalytic to its participation in development. Community participation on various levels is essential, and the extent of its presence is a key index of TfD's success. During Ibadan '98 visits were paid to two communities, Oluwole and Ketepe, which provided 'laboratories', introducing newcomers to the practicalities of TfD and throwing up issues, particularly related to community participation, for discussion.

Oluwole

Located some five kilometres off the Ibadan-Iwo road, Oluwole has a population of about two hundred and is predominantly Christian. The main occupation is farming with palm-kernel, cassava and yams as the major crops. There is a small palm-oil industry.

During 1996, PSW presented a sketch about Female Genital Mutilation (FGM) in the village, and this was followed by five days residence in the community during which facilitators became aware of local concerns and political features. These included the lack of infrastructural development, and the role being played by a progressive Baale.

A warm reception for the workshop visitors was arranged by the villagers who gave up part of their working day to ensure its success. It was obvious that PSW had earned the community's trust and the warm relationship between the two groups was extended to the visitors. With the initial greetings and introductions over, it was time to receive some feedback on the village's progress since PSW last intervened. This happened in a whole group, open forum. It was followed by visits in small groups guided by the villagers to different sites to view the projects being undertaken. It emerged that the community had made progress on some fronts. FGM was no longer practised and the message for its eradication was being spread to surrounding villages. We asked about what effect this would have on marriage prospects for women and the men replied that it would not harm their prospects. Some participants wondered if it had been truly eradicated or just simply driven underground. There was no basis for such skepticism although there was still room for further action on this subject. The villagers had also formed a co-operative and had levied themselves to start a co-operative farm cultivating cassava, vegetables, and maize as an income-generating venture to finance some of its projects such as the oil-milling machine and the building of public lavatories. Not much money had so far been realized and there was still some way to go. Based on its motto of 'if you step I will step' (meaning 'if you take action the other will respond') derived from TfD's principle of self-reliance, PSW's director proposed that workshop participants made individual contributions towards the community's funds.

Although there seemed to be an understanding on the part of the villagers that TfD's role was to stimulate action on all sides of developmental processes there was still a general dependence on outside agencies such as the local government. This was noticeable with regard to the issue of sinking a well to deal with the village's water problem, an action that was yet to be taken. Similarly, the community had not gone very far in addressing its need for public lavatories although a start had been made.

Back at the workshop base, there was an informal feedback session in which participants gave their impressions of the visit. There was a positive feeling about the community's efforts and its relationship with PSW. But the point was also made that the community might be trying to confront too many projects at the same time and there was the danger that morale might be affected by trying to do too much and not succeeding. This was refuted as there were obvious links between the different projects. For example, the income-generating projects were necessary to enable other projects to take off and be sustained. However, it was agreed that adopting a strategy of combining 'simple' achievable projects with difficult long-term ones so that at any give time there could be successes as well as 'works in progress' was not such a bad idea.

On the procedure of the visit, it was suggested that speaking to villagers in smaller groups or on a one-to-one basis would have been much more effective than a whole village gathering where opinion leaders could easily set the agenda. From experience, PSW was able to argue that, practical difficulties apart, where structures are in place that a community seems happy with it is important that outsiders do not go and deliberately rock the boat by initiating different responses in different people. Outsiders do not live in the community and do not therefore understand its politics. There may be individuals with their own agendas therefore one has to be careful how one instigates dialogue and co-operation in communities. It was clear that the Baale of Oluwole had the trust of his people. There was also Iyalaje, the oldest woman in the village, who was respected and whose opinion on village matters counted. In a typical farming community it is common to assume that men would hold dominant power. But judging from our reception at the village it was apparent that at least on occasions such as this the women are visible and heard. Both male and female, young and old felt able to participate in the visit and their hospitality, which included sharing of songs and dances as well as offers of food, and involved women, children and men.

Ketepe

Ketepe is a much smaller community than Oluwole, with a population of about fifty which for some unexplained reason is predominantly made up of elders, women and children. Its close proximity to Ibadan may mean that its able-bodied young men have gone into the city to live and work. It is predominantly a Muslim community with a mosque situated at its centre. Its chief industry is soap-making with farming at subsistence level.

Contact between PSW and the community had taken place at the initial level of research. Issues affecting the community included the electrification of the village, the supply of pipe-borne water and the construction of a shelter for its soap factory. Just before our visit, PSW had called on the community a number of times to acquaint it with the purpose of our visit. We were in turn informed about the procedure of the visit. As this would be taking place at the very early stages of an intervention programme we were to keep an open mind. It would start with a presentation of kolanuts and Schnapps to the Baale, followed by PSW's performance on FGM. This would be following closely the Oluwole model and no doubt PSW hoped that it would be just as successful.

On this occasion, due to the number of visitors involved vis-à-vis the number of villagers, the risk of 'cultural invasion' was real and we were warned to play down what we had to say lest we intimidated the villagers. That discussion should be as analytical as possible although we were not sure what form this would take, whether individual or whole group. What was certain was that, as in Oluwole, non-Yoruba speakers would need to be accompanied by speakers of the language who would act as interpreters. We would then return to the workshop base to continue the analysis at the same time as devising short skits based on information gathered and on our experiences of the visit. The skits would be taken back to the village at some stage of the workshop and presented there for discussion and analysis. These seemed simple enough although there was real apprehension about how it would work given that, though three days had passed since the start of the workshop, participants were in practical terms still relative strangers to one another and even more so to the community. However, the euphoria of the Oluwole visit the day before was still very much evident and so the party set off fairly confidently.

The visit produced its own real life drama that would equal any presented by PSW. The first set of participants to arrive at the village were surprised to find that, unlike Oluwole, there was no-one waiting to meet them. They huddled in a group under the large, shady tree at the centre of the village, the venue for most of its meetings. Trying to appear as friendly as possible some paid the soap factory a visit to greet the workers. Since the factory was an open space located near the entrance to the village, the party could not fail to see the women busy at their tasks as they drove in. We wondered what could be happening as we awaited the arrival of the others.

Not long after they arrived, we learnt that the villagers were not ready to engage with us for a number of reasons. Although PSW had been working in close consultation with the Baale, he had very little control over his village which consisted predominantly of women. Due to the significance of the soap factory to the economy of the village, real power lay in the hands of the women. They would not be drawn to meet us because they claimed they could not afford the time. If we had a performance for them, we should take it to the site of the factory so that they could continue with their tasks while we performed. Given the large, open, wood fires and the narrow spaces between individual sheds this was impractical and unsafe. It emerged that the village was in fact an over-researched environment that had been visited by several agencies and its experiences of such visits had been negative. The villagers claimed they had been too trusting and open with visitors in the past. That they had responded with the expected hospitality and generosity and had allowed themselves and their village to be photographed for purposes they claimed to be unsure about. The result had been broken promises about bringing development to the village and a sense of betrayal. They also said they were unclear about PSW's motives. Given the number of visits made earlier to the village by PSW, this surprised us. What was clear was that, being very much virgin work, trust between the two parties was yet to be fully established. Perhaps time had not been given for this to happen before we 'invaded' the village. This would have its drawbacks in terms of any future relationship between the community and PSW unless it was addressed. Time was also needed to get to know and understand the village's politics. For example, in trying to explain the villagers' attitude the Baale had asked: '*If people are not happy, how can they dance?*' To which the women, speaking through their spokesperson countered: '*Who said we are not happy?*' That, surely revealed divisions within the village. Again when it was suggested that we moved the performance to a nearby village which had shown a willingness to receive it we were informed that the move would give rise to further tensions between the two villages that might take several years to resolve. Another contradiction was the soap factory that was initially presented as a co-operative actually functioned on an individual basis. The community that was lukewarm in its reception was incidentally to profit from the visit by selling soap to its visitors at an inflated price.

That there were problems in the village was one issue, but another was how to deal with the crisis. Should we simply pack up and leave? More than anything the visit revealed a number of pitfalls in community intervention: practitioners need skills in conflict resolution and an arsenal of strategies and counter-strategies to deal with sensitive relationship problems.

One of PSW's strategies that worked on this occasion was that where one cannot negotiate one had to confront. At first this appeared to be rather too risky. But it worked due to PSW's understanding of the community's culture. It adopted the defensive role of the wronged party and accused the villagers of not dealing openly and honestly. In this community, as in many Nigerian communities, no matter how angry one is one must never turn one's anger on unsuspecting visitors. It was insulting to visit their past experiences on a group of visitors that had nothing to do with the source of their anger. The confrontation also worked because there was a certain degree of untruth from the Baale and the community.

Eventually the misunderstanding was partially cleared up. An audience with a few representatives from the factory including their spokesperson, and visitors from the neighbouring village and school children was able to gather under the tree to hear what the facilitators had to say through the FGM performance.

Audience participation: the Baale becomes involved in the debate, Ketepe

This part of the visit worked very well because the skit was flexible and the performers skilled enough to incorporate the conflict that had just occurred between villagers and visitors. It also involved local participation, both physical and vocal, so that the performance became a means of dialogue and resolution of the immediate conflict. Thus what seemed a pretty hopeless situation at the start was turned around in the end.

The visit ended on a positive note with better understanding on both sides and a promise of a warmer welcome when PSW returned to follow up on the visit.

Discussion of the visits revealed that Oluwole and Ketepe provided different learning experiences for participants. A warm, trusting relationship between facilitators and communities is an index to success and it takes time for this to develop. Community research is also important to understand its politics, culture and needs, and the practice has to be flexible enough to respond to its mood. TfD needs to be clear about what its aims are and about facilitators' expectations vis-à-vis communities' expectations in order to evaluate outcomes. It obviously cannot do everything for everybody. And while follow-up work is necessary there has to come a time when follow-up has to stop in order to allow communities to grow. It is tempting to over-protect by constant enquiry.

A spokesperson for the Ketepe village women is engaged in a scene

Workshops provide a context for demonstrating the extent to which practitioners are willing to constantly assess themselves, their commitment, agendas and ways of working. Often workshops become the forum for raising issues arising from and affecting the practice. Epeme '95 itself had been convened to bring practitioners together to discuss and clarify what the discipline is about and to figure out a common identity. Almost every discussion about TfD has to confront this issue. While it is difficult to come up with a single, universally accepted definition practitioners are agreed that it is about putting theatre in the service of development and that development itself is primarily about people and involves both material and human aspects. Terms such as *Theatre of the Oppressed, Grassroots Theatre* or even *Community Theatre* tend to suggest a theatre meant for a particular group of people rather than one that serves a particular purpose. Such labels not only sound patronizing but are in fact exclusive. It is no wonder, therefore, that while seeking to address the needs of marginalized communities, the discipline has neglected to address those in government without whose support long-term solutions to developmental problems are impossible. The need to address both fronts simultaneously and to extend the notion of the discipline both horizontally and vertically led to the adoption of the name TfD at the end of Epeme '95.

The issue was revisited at Harare '97 which also focused on collaboration between the arts in general and the importance of development strategies within the arts. It is indisputable that effectively used theatre has a vital role to play in development and is usable at any and every stage of a development programme. It is also clearly only one among several possible artistic tools. The goal is to increase awareness of the role that the arts can play as a collective in development rather than viewing them in any compartmentalized way. That African theatre generally combines music, dance, song, poetry, drama and many more forms is a known fact. The point is to begin to be more conscious of the identity of each of these disciplines and their power and influence in development work. This is important if intervention is to be linked to the cultural forms of communities rather than impose a form on them.

Ibadan '98 continued the discussion on collaboration between the arts that preoccupied those who attended Harare '97. As in Harare there were representations and case studies from theatre, music, radio, film, journalism, and television. As Ladi Ladebo a film-maker from Nigeria said in his presentation, the arts are interdependent as far as their role in development is concerned and no form or medium can on its own provide all the answers. It is high time, he suggested, that the arts began to work together rather than compete against one another like crabs in a basket.[5] The issue, therefore, goes beyond practitioners working in different fields to reinforcing, supporting, promoting and extending the work of one another. The mass media have the ability to reach a much wider audience than theatre. Although their approach to communication is not face-to-face and can undermine participation, feedback and evaluation, processes central to TfD, they can effectively support theatre's work and vice versa. In addition to the examples already cited one can mention Nigerian television series of the early 1980s such as *Cockcrow at Dawn* and *Kasagi* which reinforced the government's Green Revolution and Operation Feed the Nation programmes.

A multi-media, multi-pronged approach to a particular development issue draws attention to it, reinforces its impact and effectiveness. It also ensures wider access to and choice of information, ensures that this is presented in an entertaining way and is certainly an effective way of attracting and utilizing funds.

The issue of funding TfD leads to the necessity of networking with governments and other development organizations who have direct responsibility for shaping and implementing policies that affect development, and networking with funding organizations including large businesses. There was a general feeling that TfD suffers from a dependency syndrome: there is a high degree of dependence on funding agencies and this contradicts its principle of self-reliance. The problem increases when it is clear that donor funds always come with strings attached. Funders have their own agendas both stated and hidden, which at the end of the day have to be met. Usually they target specific issues which may not necessarily be a community's most pressing need. Examples of donors flexible enough to allow a quick and immediate response to communities' needs are few and far between. Case studies were cited at Ibadan where practitioners have had to target issues identified by funders irrespective of what communities' needs were. While at times it was possible to work around this problem by broadening the base of analysis and linking issues together, there were times when the choice was between practitioners compromising their principles or not being funded at all. Other cases involved instances when donor funds were packaged in the form of high interest loans which undermined individuals' and communities' capacity to develop, leaving them in debt and far worse off than they were before any intervention took place. On the whole it was clear that funding agencies were not often in the best position to assess communities' needs nor even to identify those with the right skills to facilitate the meeting of these needs.

However, funding agencies are a necessary part of the practice and it is impossible to ignore their benefits. It was suggested that the problem was more of approach and assessing how practitioners perceived themselves and their work. Practitioners need to be more assertive and investigate ways of marketing and delivering their services so that governments, big businesses and donor agencies can see clearly the benefits of dealing with them, and in effect sponsoring the arts. Because self-reliance is a skill that has to be learnt, artists in the first instance need to be trained to go out and compete rather than to be beggars in the field. The existing situation in which trained artists have to rely on patronage rather than their skills in order to survive or have to take on jobs unrelated to their training and for which they have no skills has to be turned around. Situations in which graduates are churned out in their thousands each year with no jobs or no ability to create jobs for themselves point to gaps in arts education. There is a need to expand existing curricula to include among other subjects marketing, fund-raising, administration and research.

Also advocated was a more structured way of networking with governments and agencies. Practitioners need to streamline the way they carry out their operations through the establishment of high profiled, unified bodies at provincial, national, regional and continental levels. They also need to be clear about what they can do and are prepared to take on, and to sensitize funders to these. This may require close consultation with communities in putting together a catalogue of issues that demand attention, and identifying practitioners with the skills to facilitate intervention.

On the one hand, the growing popularity of TfD among developmental organizations and artists in general was perceived as positive and desirable. On the other hand, there was awareness that if care is not taken it can easily be appropriated for purposes other than those for which it is intended. It is necessary to check what is, in the last five years, beginning to look like a bandwagon effect in order to protect the credibility and integrity of the practice and of genuine practitioners. A national or even regional register was proposed at Harare and revisited at Ibadan. The register would not only serve as a means of monitoring quality but also would provide developmental organizations and governments with a useful and credible list of practitioners. The register could go further to include information about national, regional, and continental development issues that practitioners feel could benefit from TfD/arts intervention programmes.

Harare had highlighted how networking on a trans-African level has been less effective than between Africa and the West. This assumed that networking already existed on a national basis but this is not necessarily the case. Nigeria and Zimbabwe, which have national organizations, are exceptions rather than the rule. Brief and bitter references to the failure of the short-lived Union of African Performing Artists (UAPA) were made at workshops and in a few publications. However, until the facts are fully documented it will be difficult for lessons to be learnt. The establishment of provincial, national, regional and continental organizations is vital to effective networking.

Improving contact via e-mail was proposed at both Harare and at Ibadan. Although this was perceived to be a more comprehensive and immediate means of disseminating information (than publications for example), it can only complement workshops which emphasize human contact. A query was raised on both occasions as to whether there ought to be funded posts of co-ordinator(s) charged with the responsibility of, among other things, facilitating networking between practitioners, funders and institutions engaged in training. The British Council had offered to support such a post in the first instance if an agreement could be reached. Debates around this issue focused on the responsibilities of such a post, who the person(s) should be accountable to and what the criteria for appointment should be. There was a strong feeling that the post should not suggest a replacement of national or regional organizations being proposed and that the person(s) must be resident in Africa and accountable first and foremost to the proposed union of practitioners.[6]

As in previous workshops Ibadan '98 attempted to revisit some of the contradictions identified in the practice. They included TfD's strong base in academic institutions whilst its primary constituencies lay outside; its dominance by middle-class, male facilitators and the most appropriate language for the practice. On this last issue there was agreement that the notion of language includes both the verbal and the non-verbal and that it must be accessible, a language that includes rather than excludes. The dominance of gender-specific language within the discipline is an issue that needs to be addressed side by side with other gender-related issues.

In countries where dozens of languages co-exist and where each community is culturally unique it is possible for facilitators to find themselves working in communities whose language they do not speak. It may also be difficult to be accessible and at the same time reach a large audience. In many cases one is sacrificed for the other. Reliance on international languages such as English and French or even on translations and interpretations when available can create difficulties. The use of an interpreter or translator can undermine having one's voice heard, representing one's self.[7]

TfD is an aural practice although the written word may have its place, for example, where literacy is one of the problems being tackled, or where the documentation of a particular project takes a literary as opposed to an audio/visual approach.[8] However, there was a general uneasiness where literary drama, even of a political nature, is equated with TfD. Some felt that to even develop a TfD performance from a written synopsis tends to create unnecessary barriers, limit creativity and raise unhelpful questions about ownership. But then the general interest of participants in seeing Femi Osofisan's most recent production which was then in rehearsal at the University of Ibadan suggested that literary, political theatre is perceived as complementary to TfD and that there are a few things that each form could learn from the other.

NOTES

1. Paulo Freire, 1972, *Pedagogy of the Oppressed* (Harmondsworth: Penguin). See also Paulo Freire, 1973, *Education for Critical Consciousness* (Dulles: Continuum).
2. The Performance Studio Workshop (PSW) is described in its brochure as a non-profit theatre established in 1988, with Chuck Mike as its Director. It is 'a laboratory for alternative communication, social development and the perpetuation of mutual understanding between peoples through culture and performance art'. The Nigerian Popular Theatre Alliance (NPTA) formed in 1989 is a non-governmental voluntary alliance of theatre practitioners, performers, educationists, cultural and development workers interested in using theatre for development purposes. Its current President is Oga Steve Abah.
3. Martin Banham, Chair of the workshop in his opening report on the Harare workshop.
4. *Answers to Questions most Frequently asked about IITA*, IITA Brochure, IITA Ibadan, 1994.
5. As Ladi Ladebo explains, if you put plenty of crabs in a basket each one would want to get to the side of the basket, to get out by climbing on to the backs of others. But the one whose back is climbed simply grabs hold of the legs of the climber as if to say: *you take me along with you or there will be trouble*.
6. Ngugi wa Mirii, 1996, *Funding of Arts and Culture in Zimbabwe*, Policy Dialogue Series, SAPEM (April). In this article wa Mirii draws attention to the dangers of imposing 'experts' as part of aid development packages, particularly experts who live far away from the activities that they are supposed to be overseeing.
7. Ladi Ladebo drew attention to the editing of *The Thrift Collector*, a 39-episode, half-hour series on population development made for the United Nations Population Fund (UNFP) in which the original performers' voices had to be edited and replaced by professional actors in order to make them sound more acceptable.
8. For example, Ngugi wa Thiong'o and Ngugi wa Mirii, 1982, *I will Marry When I Want* (Heinemann) documents the Kamiriithu project. It is interesting that the play not only reflects Kamiriithu's history, issues and their analysis raised in literacy groups and in villagers' autobiographies, but also served as follow-on reading in literacy classes. It even helped to generate funds for the centre's other activities.

Fifteen Years Between
Benue & Katsina Workshops, Nigeria

FRANCES HARDING

In reflecting on a Theatre-for-Development[1] workshop of 15 years ago in Benue State, Nigeria, it is not difficult to see the limitations imposed by its rigorous approach – the unsympathetic workshop preparations, the collection of information referred to as 'data' and its subsequent analysis, selection and transformation into a drama. In spite of these reservations, its open agenda marked it out as something of an ideal experience. It is a mark of its strength that it can stand the test of time and be held up as a yardstick against which to consider later efforts. Here, I compare this tightly structured workshop with the relaxed and confident experience of a more recent one in Katsina State, further north in Nigeria. In the former, local performance forms flanked a central dialogue drama; in the recent one, local performance forms provided the central feature of the performance and incorporated a dialogue drama. Whereas the Benue Workshop took place over two weeks, such a luxury of duration has become a rarity today. The Benue Workshop resulted in detailed collaboration and analysis and a series of performances in which most sectors of the communities were represented. The later one in Katsina relied on the experience of the participants to identify relevant information more rapidly and from it to create a performance within a much shorter space of time. If there was any 'casualty' in this, the later workshop, it was the women with whom some of us worked within the confines of their homes. We did not have the time to explore the possibility of having them create a dialogue performance for their own entertainment although we hope to be able to do so in the near future. It emphasized for me the importance of having different spectatorships for different performers – most especially along gender lines – but we need also to think along lines of status, occupation and age.

The Benue Workshop

The Benue Theatre-for-Development Workshop (the 'Workshop') took place in the last few days of 1982 and into the first days of 1983 in four villages in Benue State, central Nigeria. It was funded substantially by the state

99

government on the initiative of Dr Iyorwuese Hagher, a graduate of Ahmadu Bello University and then Director of the State Council for Arts and Culture.

Most of those who made up the 70 or so workshop participants were inexperienced in the participatory theatre process and its techniques. There were a dozen or so extension workers with backgrounds in local government, education and the churches, but the majority of the participants were either students at a local Education College who were attending as a compulsory part of their Theatre Arts course even although it cut into their Christmas holidays, or else were part of the newly formed in-house company of the Benue State Arts Council.

The Workshop lasted two weeks and was divided into two phases: the initial phase of three days was designed as a preparatory one and the second took place over ten days in the 'host' villages where the processes of drama-building based on continuing research and discussion developed.

On the first morning, there was a formal opening by the State Minister for Social Development, Sports and Culture, and then further addresses by distinguished members of the platform party. The platform party then retired. This was the cue for the work of the Workshop to begin.

The underlying principle of Theatre-for-Development is the theory of education posited by Paulo Freire in which the notion of a 'narrative stance' adopted by an 'educator' confronting a passive 'audience' of learners is rejected in favour of a shared participatory approach to learning in which members of a group learn from each other. Each individual brings different knowledge to a group and by exchanging it, acquires more knowledge and a greater understanding of how the parts create the whole.

This basic principle needed to be reflected in the practice of the Workshop and the need for the theory to be translated into practice soon became apparent. At the time, there were few handbooks suggesting activities which would explore, articulate and strengthen this principle, and the initial exercises were conventional rather than radical. At the time, it was felt that there was no time to develop appropriate exercises along the lines of what have come to be called 'trust' games, but the limitation was also due to inexperience. It is difficult for educators/activists trained in an authoritative style to discard it rapidly and equally difficult for students/learners accustomed to deferring to authority to assume a more challenging stance.

Some exercises in gender equality and inter-ethnic relationships would have been particularly useful.

The First Phase

In this first session, individuals from each of the different ethnolinguistic groups present were asked to sing a short song and the rest of us were to learn the chorus. This was successfully done in four languages: Igala, Idoma, Tiv and Igbo. There was some discussion about the ways in which this skill could be used in new situations – for example an old and familiar song could be used in a completely new context thus giving it new impetus and meaning deriving largely from the context; an old melody with new words, or familiar words to a new melody were also suggested as ways of making an impact without moving outside of the already existing repertoire of song. New songs and new melodies were also avenues open to those who could utilize them.

After this rather formal session on song and music, the next was on dance. This too adopted a fairly rigid approach in which the session leader demonstrated a dance and the rest of us copied it.

At this point, we were divided into three groups and each group had to produce/create a short dance and perform it to the rest of the Workshop. It is helpful to consider in some detail one of the dances devised at this stage and to consider the criticisms made of it.

The dance piece was based on the experience of grass-cutting and how the workers grow tired. The performers choreographed the movements of the grass-cutting and began to dance with rhythmic movement and activity. This created a satisfying sense of common purpose and common skills. Eventually however, the cutters grow tired before the task is done and each gradually ceases to cut. At this point in the dance, one of the dancers comes into the centre of the group to exhort and encourage them to go on, but the workers are unable to do more and the dancer carries on alone.

Criticism followed each of the performed pieces and the criticism of this piece was largely technical (there was a great deal of dance skill within the groups) so that factors such as a lack of co-ordination of the dance steps were cited. Others felt that the performers were not sufficiently representing the characters of tired workers! Yet others, however, tried to get at more theoretical issues by suggesting that the device of using one 'worker' to entertain the others was not group work and that this glorified both the individual worker and the individual performer unjustifiably. These points could have led to interesting discussions in which the relationship of local practice, the demands of entertainment and their relative importance in Theatre-for-Development were explored. This was not taken up, however, and the performers were not given the chance to explore those dimensions in which social issues amalgamate with and emerge from performance.

On the following day, the first session was devoted to 'drama'. This session followed the pattern of the two earlier sessions in which the whole company was divided into groups and each group presented a 'performance' to the others. Themes such as 'Surprised to see me'?' and 'Getting fertiliser from the store' were selected and assigned to each group. These themes appeared to have the potential to develop into discussion material linked to the proposed workshops in the villages, but, as with the dance and song sessions, no link through discussion was made at this stage.

This was the last practical session. There had been little in them to stimulate or develop a participatory approach either between leaders of the sessions and the participant-students, or in anticipation and most importantly, between them and the villagers.

Some concern had already been expressed among the Workshop co-ordinators at how the young student members of the Workshop would react in the villages. Whilst not 'misbehaving' at all, they were exuberant and excited most of the time and there was concern that once in the villages they would not approach the purpose of the workshop seriously enough. Some of the organizers decided therefore that all the students should have a gymnastic style training session each morning. A militaristic type programme was pursued for half an hour of each day at 6 am. Whilst this may have had a calming (suppressive?) effect on some of the young people, it also signified the antithesis of much that the workshop stood for in terms of equality, shared purpose and an exchange of understanding.

The final group session took place on the third morning prior to our going out into the villages. This was given over entirely to the theory of development theatre and was led by Oga Abah. He placed the present Workshop against a background of similar projects throughout the Third World and particularly in the countries of Africa. He drew attention to the repressive practice of educating people to assume an ascribed role in society, whether as students, peasants or workers and also in gender specific roles. The increasing disparity between rich and poor throughout the world was referred to and the need to engage with unjust social practices which supported this increase.

In reference to the immediate work in the villages, Abah pointed out that the primary objective was not just to create a drama but to create one which was based on the personal experiences of the people living there. The aim was to deepen understanding of problems in the village from the perspective of the villagers. This in turn would deepen the student/participants' understanding which they could use in future work.

Emphasis was placed on the following points:

1. The creation and maintenance of trusting interpersonal relationships between the village people and those from the Workshop;

2. The collection of accurate information on the specific problems and concerns of the village;

3. The sensitive discussion and analysis of the information so that priority issues surface;

4. The dramatization of those issues in such a way as to reflect the socio-political complexities involved in reaching a 'solution';

5. The utilization of existing performance forms so that if possible the drama of Theatre-for-Development is created as an extension of indigenous forms rather than an imposed alien form;

6. The post-performance dialogue in which opportunities arise for people of the village to discuss further;

7. Throughout all of this, continued and committed interaction with the people of the village should be maintained by Workshop participants.

In the villages: Wombu, Abagi, Ngibo and Abua

Four villages had agreed to take part in the Workshop by providing 'host' locations. In this area, all were Tiv. The Workshop was divided into four groups and each was assigned a 'resource person', a title we chose in preference to any more hierarchical nomenclature and one which was consonant with the

Freirean ideals underpinning the Workshop approach. I was invited to be one of the resource persons alongside Iortiom Mude.

The task of the 'resource persons' was to co-ordinate the activities of the group to which they were assigned and in particular, to ensure that good relations between the village people and the Workshop personnel were established and maintained — essential if any kind of trust and sharing relationship were to be built up.

They were also expected to play a leading role in stimulating discussion of the 'data', i.e. the information which the Workshop participants would gather throughout the course of their informal discussions with the villagers. In order that an analysis of some of the underlying causes of problems could be achieved, it was essential that statements were not taken or left at face value, but that further discussion led to deeper awareness.

Furthermore, in terms of creating a drama from the material which it was anticipated would be made available in preliminary discussion, the resource leaders were also expected to encourage the use of existing forms of performance as part of the process of drama-building.

The morning of the day when the participants were to set off found everyone in a mood of eager anticipation at the work that lay ahead. Few had ever tackled such a direct encounter with strangers in a way that demanded affinity and a degree of trust be set up over a very short period of time in return for very little in the way of material or other immediate reward.

In Abua village

Once in the village, each non-mother tongue speaker of Tiv was partnered with a Tiv speaker. I was with Judith Athenakaa. The village to which we had been assigned was a large one of several hundred people. Even so, when we arrived, the open space under the canopy of dark mango trees at the centre of the village was deserted. Although it was not the busiest time of year on the farm, there was always weeding to be done and some had wondered if any of the villagers would have the time to talk to us. A decision was made that some people should go firstly to greet the headman and some others wander off in different directions into the village in the hope of encountering people who would be willing to stop and chat for a while. No-one was very optimistic.

My partner and I followed a path out of the open area and between some scattered round houses which appeared to be empty of people and reached a central junction where there were houses on either side of a broad walkway. There was still no sign of people. Just then two people appeared coming towards us and we braced ourselves psychologically for a friendly, meaningful encounter! They drew nearer and turned out to be another pair of Workshop participants. They had already met people and been given the sad news that a leading citizen of the village, the local headmaster, had been killed in a road accident during the night. Hence people were not out and about as usual.

After some time, however, people started going about their business and eventually a group of men sitting under the shade of a tree asked us to come and sit with them for a while. In conversation it emerged that they were very concerned at the developments in relation to land ownership within the village. The government scheme known as 'Certificate of Occupancy' meant that individuals could own land if they paid money to the 'traditional' owners and got a certificate saying that the land was now theirs. This clashed with established land inheritance practice in which everyone has a right to farm the land owned communally by the lineage. It was this lineage land which was being sold off. The villagers had not been told by the headman who we, the Workshop participants, were and so understandably there was a good deal of wariness at the influx of ten or twelve strangers to their village.

We left the men and went to meet the headman and his wife. After we had spoken in general about the Workshop, the headman's wife began to speak about the difficulties inherent in educating young women to secondary school level or beyond. All too often, girls were threatened by sexual advances made by men, not just students, but staff also. The girls ended up pregnant and often had to end their college attendance. This possibility led many men to deny their daughters a secondary or college education.

End of Day One: Return to Base
At the end of the day, we all travelled back to the base where we were staying and exchanged notes. Within Abua village, the following problems emerged from one day's discussion:

1. The land dispute;
2. Limited availability of fertiliser for the crops at the government subsidized prices;
3. Marketing problem: this was not clear but was related to the price of produce from the farms;
4. Education: school fees are a problem; parents are reluctant to send their daughters to school; older women want to become literate;
5. Divorce: more separation than ever before; women leave for one of the towns to make some money for themselves.

Creating a Scenario
The next part of the process was to rough out one or more scenarios in which the problems which had been expressed were presented. After some discussion it was agreed that the drama would focus on one family through whose members, their relationships and their experiences, many of the problems would be articulated.

Returning to the Village, Day Two and Beyond
On the following day, we took only this outline framework with us back to the village and once there, began blocking the scenario into scenes and trying out characters and dialogues. This had an interesting effect on people. We had chosen to do it in the open area where we had first arrived in the village and although it was still not busy, several people used it as a route to their farms. Some people stopped and watched for a while and perhaps commented on

what was going on, whilst others just shook their heads in perplexity. Soon, however, a group of young men were attracted to the activity and rapidly became involved in the performance; later some older men stopped and discussed the issues that were being presented in the drama. This process of interacting at a casual, loosely-structured level went on for about four days and different people joined in for a day and left again or else returned as they pleased. Gradually, however, a central performing group of villagers formed itself along with Workshop participants and by the end of the week a drama had been built up which used the problems presented in a fictional storyline and with fictional characters. The next task was to perform it to the rest of the village.

Ten Days Later: The Performance
On the evening of the performance, all the people of the village had been informed of the intention to perform and several hundred people came to watch. Everyone waited until the village headman and his wife arrived and, once they were seated, the performance began.

The Drama
In the drama, a villager refuses to let his daughter attend school. He and his wife quarrel over this. The wife has saved money from her petty trading for the school fees but the husband says their daughter will just end up pregnant so there is no point in sending her. He instead marries her off. He insists that his wife hands over her money so that he can use it to set up his son in business in the nearby town. Just at this moment, within the drama, an announcement comes over the radio telling people that in order to encourage agricultural development, bank loans will be made available to farmers who can produce a Certificate of Occupancy on their land. Our central character, the husband, soon learns that a wealthy man from the village who now lives in town has acquired a Certificate of Occupancy on his land. In distress, the villager tries to get redress through the village head but this is unsuccessful as all authority in this matter has been taken from him under the government scheme. The right to land through purchase takes precedence over the right to land through inheritance. The headman can offer no solace. The villager takes the wrongdoer to court but loses his case.

Meanwhile the son has failed in his 'business' and has found work in the town as a cleaner. This does not bring in a lot of money, so he cannot offer his father any support. In a now desperate attempt to win an appeal court judgement in his favour, the father decides to sell his remaining produce to get funds. The middlemen exploit him and he is left destitute. The drama then returns to the initial storyline of the daughter who was refused an education. She has left her husband who seeks a return of the bridewealth from her father.

Post-performance Discussion
After the drama had reached this impasse, the performers sought the intervention and advice of the audience. It is at this stage that ideally people in the

village engage in deeper analysis of the issues raised in the performance and decide on future action. As Tar Ahura, one of the resource persons wrote in an unpublished paper:

> [The villagers] were able to see that they were surrounded by systems that collaborated to undo the poor man [sic]...They were so stung to consciousness that one [said] that the drama did not satisfy him because the middleman, the area court judge and their educated [man] with the certificate of occupancy should have been beaten up for their role in exploiting the poor.

Ahura goes on to suggest that even if the villagers could only express their sense of injustice by wishing for someone to get 'beaten up', at least they realized that they 'have the capacity to change their situations'. This fictional 'beating' would have been cathartic perhaps, but it is at this juncture that Theatre-for-Development differs from more conventional theatre in that it is seen to be *using* entertainment as a means of communication and analysis. The confrontation with reality posed by the Theatre-for-Development technique leaves the spectator poised ready for *real* action and becoming a participant-activist in the real world rather than a passive spectator in a fictional world.

Assessing and Evaluating the Workshop

Here I have only described one of the four independent workshop sessions that were going on simultaneously. Overall, there were several levels at which the Workshop can be considered to have been successful. Firstly, people engaged in a form of deliberation and debate which allowed them to articulate their problems without committing themselves to personalized criticism – or action – nor to identifying with a particular point of view. Through the processes of discussion and dramatization, people experienced the circumstances which gave rise to problems and in turn confronted the possibility of exercising some control over them.

Nevertheless, the weaknesses were there too and I want only to address those which can be thought of as 'theatrical'. The Workshop only used already existing performance forms at the most superficial level of incorporating dance as a finale to the performance. Nevertheless, even this 'weakness' points itself to another dilemma within the Theatre-for-Development genre: the Tiv people are extremely talented musicians, singer and dancers. They also have a highly developed practice of puppet and masquerade theatre called *kwagh-hir*, meaning 'something marvellous', which utilizes, amongst its many themes, several which are directly pertinent to development including: inter-generational conflict, health, exploitative practices and women's education. However the fact that there was already on the ground a sophisticated form of social critique which was not incorporated into the Theatre-for-Development was partly because the organization of *kwagh-hir* is predicated on young men's skills and, by implication, on old men's supernatural powers. To have focused the performance on *kwagh-hir* would have been to exclude non-*kwagh-hir* performers.

Utilizing existing forms of performance requires an understanding of *who* performs what. By including some, others may be excluded.

This early example of Theatre-for-Development, for all its faults in its practice, exemplifies a form where the focus of any given workshop is left almost totally open to the village participants rather then predetermined by the workshop personnel. There was at this workshop, no 'agenda' to be addressed, no 'message' to get across.

As these forms of theatre began to attract the attention of the development and government agencies however, it also began to accommodate a different string to this open-ended approach, one which Marion Frank has called 'Campaign Theatre' and is widely used as part of 'information campaigns' on specific issues especially related to health or child care. 'Campaign Theatre' seems to me an accurate title, but in Nigeria I have been told it would be taken to mean a *political* campaign and so would not be useful to them. Frank further distinguishes this from 'project-oriented' theatre whose purpose is to bring about a specific material change in a community, such as the building of a clinic.

One of the defining differences lies not simply in the content of the performance, but in the 'spectatorship'. For 'project-oriented' theatre, the audience is a specific, usually a single, community. Whereas Campaign Theatre is to be performed as often as possible in order to get a message across to as many people as possible, the locally specific plays need to be performed only as often as necessary, or even just once. Both of these are to be distinguished from the 'consciousness-raising' genre of which the Benue Workshop was a prime example and which 'does not have any immediate impact' (Frank 1995: 65).

By the 1990s this latter, open-ended 'consciousness-raising' kind of theatre is rare. It is now widely accepted that funding bodies will have some agenda albeit defined perhaps in part in conjunction with local bodies. One example of such a workshop where the agenda has been defined by the funding body and yet leaves enough room to be exploratory took place in northern Nigeria in February 1997. It is to this workshop that I next turn to provide a comparison with the Benue Workshop.

The Katsina Workshop: Seeds of Life

In Nigeria, a substantial pool of very experienced Theatre-for-Development practitioners, headed by Oga Steve Abah, had been established by the 1990s. In a recent Theatre-for-Development project funded by the British Council and held in Katsina State, the brief – to consider the effects of the encroachment of the desert on the health and lives of women and children – was open-ended enough to enable a broad-brush approach to be used. By early February of 1997, the preliminary processes of setting up the Workshop through meetings with the headman and the local government officials had already taken place. Twelve experienced workshop facilitators gathered along with local extension workers – largely women and other members of the Local Government Authority. There were both theatre and video practitioners who had already used drama and video in development, or else development workers who wanted to know how to make relevant use of drama and video in the field. There were two international visitor-participants, Afi Yakubu, a Ghanaian film director, and myself.

This project arose from the cessation of the EU funded project on foresta-tion and conservation in conjunction with the Katsina Arid Zone Programmes (KAZP) which had been set up in several neighbouring northern states and countries bordering the Sahara. The strong wind, the harmattan, blowing from the Sahara carries sand in with it, increasing the desertification of the area. Although successful, changes in the international political situation brought the programme to an early end and this had several direct effects on the lives and health of the women and children.

We worked in close co-operation with local women extension workers, headed by Maryam Musa Liadi. They all found the Theatre-for-Development technique to be one of the most rewarding ways of giving women an opportu-nity to speak, thus finding out their views and getting a message across to them.

Two villages in Katsina State, Nigeria were host locations. I concentrate on Barhim, a Muslim community of Tuareg, Fulani and Hausa people, though most refer to themselves as 'Hausa' and speak Hausa strongly inflected with Fulfulde and some Tuareg. The people had originally come from even further north but because of previous encroachment of the desert, had moved south to their present location. The name, 'Barhim' means 'Leave it alone' referring to the original settlement.

The group of facilitators divided into two. Within each group men could only work with men, but the women could opt to work either with men or women. Three of us worked with the women whose initial reserve within the walls of their home dissipated as we exchanged names and generalities. We asked if they would take some photographs of whoever they pleased. One of the younger women did so but then preferred to go and fetch her co-wife as she wanted to be in the photograph herself. The women then told us that they wanted to prepare a *tashi* for us on our arrival the following day. *Tashi* is a good-morning entertainment often used to rouse people early during ramaddan.

When we went back the next day, the women were bouyant and ready with their *tashi*. They danced in a circle, singing songs and generally enjoying them-selves. They then asked the Hausa-speaking workshop member to sing for them in exchange – which she did.

After this, it was the turn of the young girls to sing and dance. They had chosen a song-game in which one of them was dressed up in a costume repre-senting a herbalist – 'a child of the leaves' – with several coloured cloths tucked into her belt. She was placed in the middle of two rows of girls and a song and response began in which the different herbal remedies for different ailments were called out. This was the first of several indicators throughout the Workshop of the importance of local medicinal herbs.

As the girls' dances ended, the women began to discuss the importance of plants and herbs and trees in treating ailments, ensuring fertility and beautifying themselves. When we asked them to rank the trees they would like to plant they named five species or categories:

> *Dogon varo:* the neem tree – its leaves are used for cooking;
> *lele:* used to make henna for *ado* (beautifying the self);
> *zogali:* a salad vegetable;
> mango/guava, etc.: referred to collectively as 'economic trees'
> *kuka:* the baobab tree. Its dried ground leaves are mixed with water to make a gravy.

As is the practice in Theatre-for-Development, we did not begin with a fixed set of questions on the topic of the environment, but listened as the women dictated the pace and direction of the conversation so as to enable the issues which they considered important to emerge. For example, one of the women was cleaning out the inside of a long cucumber-like plant with a knife to prepare it for use as a musical instrument, the *shentu.* The seeds fell to the ground and none of the women attempted to pick them up. When asked why they did not use the seeds for planting, it turned out that they felt there was no point in planting anything as the goats strip any plant bare. There is no protective wiring available any longer since the end of the EU project. We pursued this further having seen some very handsome protective basket work shields for sale in town, but the women said that the plant, *geza* which was used to soften the straps of wood used for the baskets was no longer growing in their area. Throughout the entire time, the harmattan wind was blowing furiously, whipping wrappers and headties and hair in all directions. There was only one tree, a neem tree in the compound and one baobab just outside. Neither afforded any protection from the wind and we asked them why they did not plant any trees when the EU project was initiated. They came up with a simple answer: no-one had offered them any!

This raised the topic of firewood and the women told us that firewood was a problem because in the absence of trees to cut for firewood, they had to bring in wood from the town. Because there was no road and only soft sand, the taxis charged four or five times as much for a trip to Barhim as to other even more distant villages which had a road. The fare was N25 instead of N4. The women had calculated that it cost them on average N20 per meal. Linking the shortage of wood to the possibility of conserving it by more efficient methods of cooking, the mud stove which the extension workers wanted an opportunity to demonstrate, was then discussed. The women became interested in the stove and said they would like to see it built.

The Drama

Meanwhile, over these two days, our male colleagues had been able to meet up with several sections of the village community and some young men had become interested in the process of drama-building. They quickly offered to construct a drama about tree-planting, the need for conservation of wood and the advantages of the mud stove. They said that although they had never done any 'acting' before, 'having seen it on television', they would give it a try.

The young men put together a drama which concerned the story of a man whose wife had just given birth. After a woman has given birth, it is customary Hausa practice that her husband must provide a hot bath for her twice every day for a week afterwards. This is a serious demand on resources. Failure to do so however, is an indication of his lack of respect for his wife and a considerable humiliation for him. Stories were told of wives whose husbands had failed to provide this service and of how the women had subsequently suffered swellings and stiffness in the joints. In the drama, a woman has just given birth and her husband finds that he has not enough wood to heat the water for the twice daily baths. He rushes out to his neighbour to borrow some, but his neighbour is reluctant, saying that he too had been given the chance to plant trees in the EU/KAZP project but had refused saying there was no need for such things. Now he could see the consequences. The first man, contrite and desperate, agrees to return the following day to learn how to plant trees and how to look after them. He does, and, as an impromptu extension, brings his son with him so that he too can learn. After all, tree-planting is about the future as well as the present.

At one stage during rehearsals in the morning – which the young men had insisted take place in a series of locations – moving from one tree farm to the next, a thief had crept up to steal some plants and crops. He was caught by the actors and immediately tried, found guilty and given a warning. This incident was incorporated into the drama and, once in performance, the 'beating' they gave the 'thief' occasioned much laughter in the audience.

It is this kind of flexibility in Theatre-for-Development which confirms for people that the drama really is theirs to make as they wish.

This Workshop was held in an area where women could not perform in public without being perceived negatively, so although the Workshop was directed at the concerns of women and children, it had been necessary to find a way that young men could perform and thus bring the central issues to the attention of the men in power. However, a demonstration of how to build a particular kind of fuel-saving mud stove still needed to be given. Women extension workers were trained to demonstrate the technique, but a dilemma remained on how to enable the extension workers to carry out the task without their having to 'act' in the drama. A storyline was invented whereby a man comes home for his evening meal and it is not ready. He goes across to his neighbour's house and bemoans his wife's idleness. His neighbour points out that although the man's wife has been cooking for several hours, not only does the fire burn up a great deal of wood, but it does not even give off much heat, so food takes a long time to cook. He, on the other hand, has had one of the new stoves built for his wife, so his food is cooked much more quickly and economically. The first man is at first incredulous that this factor can make any significant difference, but eventually agrees to let some extension workers demonstrate the stove. At this point in the drama, the women extension workers who had been waiting quietly in the audience, get up and begin to prepare the clay (which they had earlier placed strategically on the stage area) to build the stove and demonstrate its cooking prowess. In this way, three significant moves were achieved: firstly, the stove was demonstrated 'officially' and therefore had the blessing of the elders of the community; secondly, the fact that women were seen publicly to have learnt new skills which they could then impart to others, was important; thirdly, the fact that women were demonstrating in public was also important. In this instance, in a very subtle way, local practice had been accommodated and the women, whilst not directly in the drama, had contributed to the performance.

It was significant that the women were enabled to be part of the drama as it moved into its 'real' not fictional, phase. Whilst the issues might be presented in a fictional form, the engagement of the women in the process could only take place at the point where fiction merged back into reality. This appears as the antithesis of much that is considered to be one of the strengths of Theatre-for- Development, i.e. the 'safety' offered by fictionalizing. However, when one realizes that in dramatizing, not only does the *character* assume the attributes of the fictional status, but these rub off on the performer. It is this power from 'real to non-real' and doubling back to 'real' that Boal identifies as 'rehearsing' (Boal (trans) 1979: 155).

The young men who had provided the personnel for a largely improvized drama – there had only been one or two run-throughs because of the constraints of time – unexpectedly also had to entertain the audience as the cooking demonstration was taking place. The young men sang quite a risqué song warning women to beware, that there was a 'bachelor on the loose'. Some of the spectators commented that this was very courageous of them to perform in front of their mothers and sisters. However, when the young men turned away from that part of the encircling audience where their mothers sat, they introduced other even more risqué elements into the song.

Theatre-for-Development relies at every stage of the process on the contribution of participant-spectators to *create* the drama. Their interactions and reactions are not optional extras without which the drama will go ahead anyway, but the *sine qua non*, the very basis of the drama, without which there will be no drama. In Theatre-for-Development, everyone who is present at rehearsal or performance is a participant-performer *and* a participant-spectator. The opportunity to shift more than once between the two positions is yet another of the mechanisms which gives Theatre-for-Development its power. Through transferring responsibility for the creation of a performance to non-specialists and by combining a continuing process of analysis and performing, Theatre-for-Development offers the opportunity to explore new relationships within the drama and a further possibility of re-enacting them outside the fictional world of the drama.

The Katsina Workshop was an altogether more relaxed affair for the participants than the earlier Benue Workshop. Away from the host locations, interactions within the group were largely discussion sessions, usually through reviewing the video filming of the day. Perhaps the most striking difference between the two workshops, however, lay in the use made of local performance genres. In Benue, these had been added on at the end of each performance in the form of a dance or song; in Katsina, they were central to the articulation of the issues raised by the pre-performance discussions. The discussion and analysis of current issues took place in familiar performance genres – surely an ideal achieved.

NOTE

1. Here I use 'Theatre-for-Development' to refer specifically to the technique of dramatising *from* material that has been generated *by* the community and in which members of the community share in or take over the enactment. This interactive and participatory approach and techniques at all stages from pre-performance discussion to post-performance action distinguishes it from the more general use of the term 'Theatre for Development' (or Theatre in Development) often used to refer to the entire corpus of drama work from the use of role-play to profes-sional/semi-professional presentational drama within a development context.

REFERENCES

Boal, Augusto, 1979, *Theatre of the Oppressed* (Toronto: Pluto).
Frank, Marion, 1995, *AIDS Education Through Theatre* (Bayreuth: Bayreuth African Studies Series).

Practice & Policy in Theatre & Development
London seminar, a personal response

JAN COHEN-CRUZ

The brochure for the Theatre and Development Workshop/Seminar immediately enticed me on three counts. The first was the 'and' instead of a 'for'. Clearly the reference was Theatre for Development (TfD). But the notion of Theatre AND development invited a reconsideration of the ways that the two fields might interact, and a concommitant opening vis-à-vis the range of theatre genres that might be utilized.

Secondly, the event was billed as a seminar/workshop. By including the working methods of both development specialists and theatre people, the format implied an interchange between the two. Theatre people would learn about trends in development funding, model projects, and translation of ideas into grant language. Development professionals could experience theatre, appreciate its value, and understand why it does not easily lend itself to quantitative assessment. And indeed, the intensive five-day schedule included daily theatre workshops, hands-on development seminars and presentations, performances and slide shows.

And thirdly, the brochure featured a photo of a big broad tree, evoking that traditional performance venue in African villages, and a centrality that we in the West most marvel at. This centrality underlines how much non-Africans stand to gain from African colleagues, their coming together an opportunity for both to develop.

The theatre approach of choice, as reflected by the number of sessions during the week (four), was Theatre of the Oppressed (TO).[1] Barbra Santos, one of the five '*coringas*'[2] or jokers from Augusto Boal's Centre for the Theatre of the Oppressed in Rio, led two of them. The first was an image theatre workshop on the theatre and development theme. The second was a fascinating presentation on legislative theatre, a technique initiated by Boal upon his election to the Rio de Janeiro City Council. Through legislative theatre, issues discovered by way of forum theatre are translated into proposals for new municipal laws. Cardboard Citizens, a theatre company of homeless people directed by Adrian Jackson, performed a work-in-progress using forum theatre intended for audiences in homeless shelters and schools. Ali Campbell and Liz Porter of Graeae Theatre led a forum workshop highlighting the adaptation of

TO techniques for disabled populations. This was followed up by an option for a fifth session on TO, also by Campbell and Porter, featuring discussion and more sharing of stories.

While I'm a great advocate of TO, I found the ratio vis-à-vis other techniques excessive. Only one session, up against Campbell and Porter, treated play devising (Gerri Moriarty's description of a project she facilitated in Northern Ireland). Using indigenous art forms was only mentioned in passing. Storytelling with Bantu Mwara and writing for non-actors with Noel Greig were each offered just once and at the same time. Only celebratory performance, as richly initiated by Welfare State International (WSI), was given an equivalent stretch of time, with groundwork laid the last evening and activities taking place all of the last day. Quibbling aside, this was still a stunning array of theatre techniques to taste in one short week. Moreover, the diversity signalled respect for having many approaches within one's grasp.

Central to the seminar/workshop was enhanced understanding between NGOs, funders, traditional development agencies (UN *et al.*), and TfDers. The operative strategy was familiarization with each other's vocabulary and *modus operandi*. A frequent refrain from theatre workers was that they can't know beforehand and hence write in a project proposal exactly what they are going to do in a given situation. Only after some exploratory contact with villagers can they identify all of the factors: what techniques they are going to utilize, on which segment of the population they are going to focus, how long the project will take, and on what problem they are going to zoom in. But this is too vague for most funders. In a market where funds are increasingly tight, where more and more decisions are made by multi-national organizations (i.e., UNESCO rather than a single country's agency), there is more pressure to fully articulate projects upfront. Funders demand value for money that they can comfortably anticipate from the proposal.

Over the course of the week, development specialists offered some helpful suggestions, such as using the term 'process-planned project', understood by funders as allowing limited but legitimate latitude to make decisions en route. Also helpful for theatre people were presentations on current issues in the development field. Clearly there needs to be an on-going dialogue between theatre people and development people.

James Thompson and Jane Plastow (the week's co-organizer with Paul Heritage) led a session entitled 'From Planning to Evaluation'. First they provided proposal guidelines. Then we formed two groups of twelve, each with a hypothetical project for which we had to develop a proposal, following those guidelines. At the end of 90 or so minutes, each group presented their proposal orally to the other group, Plastow, and Thompson, and answered questions. What made it work so nicely in our group was the mix of development and arts professionals. Christine Skinner and Gregory Nash from the British Council explained the difference between aims – big idealistic long-term goals – and objectives – the specific intentions and activities of a particular project – within this concrete context. They applied their criteria for assessing objectives, called SMART: specific, measurable, achievable, realistic, time bound. Frances Harding's years of experience in African settings made her practical contributions equally invaluable.

At a more informal group brainstorming session, Barbra Santos succinctly and eloquently summed up three relationships between theatre and development:

1. Theatre itself is development. Affirmation of the value that comes to people through a whole range of theatrical practices. Interestingly, several of the NGOs remarked that their theatre trustees were more suspicious of TfD than were their development trustees. Overall, the seminar had the healthy effect of relinking TfD to the whole field of theatre. At the same time, the week focused on theatre that functions as a form of research, discovering/rescuing problems, rendering them available for discussion, and initiating a dynamic search for solutions.

2. Theatre's role in personal development. People so engaged become producers; people affected one way or another can be transformed.

3. Theatre's role in social or community development. Through identification of problems, prioritization, mobilization and awareness, development in terms of solving collective problems can be enhanced by theatre.

Thinking of theatre and development so broadly evokes the various modes of 'applied theatre' that have circulated since the late 1960s. Applied theatre is the array of practices that essay to ameliorate situations through such means as building positive identity and community cohesion through the arts. Take, for example, community-based theatre, a popular mode allied with identity politics and targeting under-represented groups in quest of collective expression. While related to TfD, there are important differences. Community-based theatre is partisan, dealing with a particular group: TfD is bi-partisan, dealing with a particular population AND a 'civil society' institution. For example, co-organizer of the seminar/workshop Paul Heritage described working with Gay Sweatshop in the 1980s as partisan, community-based theatre, but bringing Gay Sweatshop into a partnership with a gay adoption agency in the 1990s as bi-partisan, theatre for development. One of the week's presenters, James Thompson, uses the phrase 'theatre in prisons' rather than 'theatre for prisoners' to include guards as well as inmates, cutting across levels of privilege. An ecology, a whole picture of the field, and who might contribute to change is thus arrived at, not content with the rhetoric that only those most obviously oppressed will be willing to change a system.

It's difficult to balance agendas in brief, intensive, workshop/seminars. While practitioners are needy themselves for a chance to sink into their own issues, leaders often try to demonstrate their techniques. For example, one of the stated issues of the week was adapting theatre for people with disabilities. The TO workshop on this theme advocated practices like stamping a foot as a signal when dealing with the deaf, and describing physical images when dealing with the blind. But the workshop leaders did not adjust to the limitations that actually existed in our group. One woman who walked with a cane sat the workshop out, while the sub-group preparing a scene with non-English speakers did not have time to finish and present it because they had to spend so long translating. The more workshops can adapt to the real group – such as how we might have incorporated the woman with the cane and the non-English speakers more successfully – and still point out significant variations (like the foot stamping for the deaf), the better. That's what Noel Greig did in the writing workshop. He put the actual participants quite specifically through his exercises, explaining how they could be adapted for children or the elderly. We got much needed nourishment and clear techniques that we can use in other circumstances.

Another suggestion is in response to the 20 of the 30 or so participants who had no formal, even brief platform to identify themselves and their work to the group. Hearing an outline of how choreographer Royston Muldoon, for example, does not deal with local music and dance but brings what he loves into a situation, would have expanded the models we encountered, identified him to interested parties, and acknowledged his presence and contribution to the field. We've all been so moved by Freire; we all want to be *subjects* of the work, not positioned solely as *receivers*. Some of the artists regretted that no time was set aside to brainstorm failures, something they were loathe to do in front of potential funders. Of course, there were terrific informal opportunities, such as during our collective meals.

Indeed, it was the many and various occasions for exchange between development and theatre professionals that made the week so worthwhile. A breakfast conversation between Helen Nordenson of the Swedish International Development Corporation Agency (SITA) and John Fox of WSI in which the former admonished the latter for how much they spend on fireworks was as educational as a formal presentation. One of the happiest refrains came from development people marvelling that this could be called 'work'. The clarifying of issues to explore more deeply at subsequent gatherings is also of value. At least two of the participants in positions to do so stated their desire to initiate similar seminar/workshops over the next few years. Using the SMART assessment approach, I'd say that's 't', a time bound objective. We learned to get more 's', specific, which in turn will render 'm', measurable outcomes: we also experienced the slipperiness of the measures we have. The 'co-education' that took place was definitely 'a', achievable and achieved, and hence 'r', realistic.

The Theatre and Development Seminar/ Workshop was also successful according to less tangible means of assessment – leaving me both satisfied and hungry for more.

NOTES

1. Theatre of the Oppressed is a body of techniques created by Augusto Boal that positions people as subjects, not objects, of their circumstances, and that are used to express and solve problems.
2. *Coringas*, or 'jokers', are the people who facilitate Theatre of the Oppressed techniques. The term 'facilitator' is inaccurate because the joker's role is not to make the situation easier but, if anything, help reveal its complexities.

Noticeboard

Compiled by JAMES GIBBS

PATTERNS OF THEATRE IN DEVELOPMENT

Nigeria i

A classic document in the area covered by this first volume of *African Theatre* is the *Training Manual in Community Theatre for Social Mobilization* issued by MAMSER Head Quarters, Abuja. The undated, 34-page booklet is a collector's item, a classic summary and statement. Although the authorship is not indicated on the cover or title page, there is, on page iv, the following acknowledgement: '*The Chairman and the Directorate for Social Mobilization is grateful to the following for writing of this manual.*' Then follows a roll-call of Nigerian theatre activists: Iyorwuese Harry Haghar, Yakubu Nasidi, Tunde Lakoju, Tar Shura, Bonat Tagwai, Oga S. Abah and Yusuf Abba.

A vast amount of experience is condensed under eight headings which draw attention to historical experience, processes, factors, models, skills, relation to 'Traditional Cultural Forms', and 'Evaluation and Follow-up'.

In addition to Nigerian examples – the Unife Guerrilla Theatre, A.B.U. Community Theatre Project, the Samaru, Maska, Tudun Sarki, Palladan, Gboko and Katsina-Ala Projects, the document refers to pioneering work carried out by Chikwakwa in Zambia, and Laedza

Batanani (Botswana). Mention is made of achievements in the Cameroon and Sierra Leone.

Nigeria ii

It would be an oversight not to draw readers' attention to Vol. 1, No. 1 of *Focus on Theatre: A Quarterly Journal of Theatre Discourse* edited by Chris Nwamuo and published in September 1994 by Median Communications, of 39 Hart Street, Calabar. In the present context, it is particularly worth noting for Hansel Eyoh's contribution entitled 'Community Theatre Revisited'.

In addition to providing a brief history of Community Theatre in West Africa between 1976 and 1989, Eyoh looks at the political disruption and civil war that has distracted attention and stifled development during the nineties. Significantly, the most recent title by Augusto Boal cited is *Theatre of the Oppressed*, and Eyoh concludes his essay: '*No rural development programme can succeed unless it is anchored in the actual producer and peasants, and unless the peasants are mobilised, educated and organised to handle the programme from inception to implementation, there cannot be rural development without people's power.*'

Nigeria iii

The variety of patterns of Theatre in

117

Development even within Nigeria is indicated by an article on the Okwangwo Experience written by Anthony Bassey and Kenneth Aklah, Education Specialists, Cross River National Park, Nigeria. Their concern is conservation and their audiences are made up of 'Support Zone inhabitants who are pre-dominantly farmers and who survive on hunting and gathering from the forest'. The Education Specialists use a drama unit that 'functions through an Environ-mental Theatre Club, made up of volunteers who are school-leavers trained 'in basic acting skills and … encouraged to write scripts that are then vetted by the Drama Officer and used in village performances.' In addition to conven-tional drama, several other types of drama are included … dance drama, and, recently, 'total theatre'. Puppets are also used and they attract large audiences 'because of their rarity in this part of the world. … Responses to performances have been positive, the turn-out high and the messages well received.'

The full account can be read in the February 1997 edition of *The Science Education Newsletter*, published by the British Council, Medlock Street, Manchester M15 4AA, UK, and spon-sored by Shell International Petroleum Company Limited!

Nigeria iv

The playwright should not be forgotten in all this. One of the most responsive Nigerian playwrights, a co-editor of this publication, Femi Osofisan, has given considerable thought to the issue. Speaking to 'Africa 95' at the School of Oriental and African Studies, University of London, in September 1995, Osofisan shared his 'Reflections on Theatre Practice in Contemporary Nigeria'. The text, published in *African Affairs* 97 (1998), opens with two quotations. The first is from Bertolt Brecht, whose writing must detain anyone concerned

about the political role of theatre in the twentieth century. Osofisan selected the following from 'Theatre in the GDR.':

'It is not enough to demand only cognition from the theatre, instructive images of reality. Our theatre must arouse pleasure in cognition and organise the joy of changing reality. Our audiences must not only hear of Prometheus freed from his bonds but must school them-selves in the enjoyment of freeing him. Our theatre must instil all the enjoyment and pleasure of the inventor and discoverer, the liberator's feeling of triumph.'

He followed this with a statement of his own position, an extract reproduced from Muyiwa Awodiya's *Excursions in Drama and Literature: Interviews with Femi Osofisan* (Ibadan: Kraft Books, 1993):

'Literature can entertain, in fact must entertain, but it is only the dim or brain-washed artist who is content merely to entertain, to play the clown. The primary value of literature seems to me to lie in its sub-versive potential, that explosive charge which lies hidden behind the facade of entertainment and which must be controlled and made to [explode] for the use of our people, of mankind… Literature must be used to play its role in the advancement of our society, in the urgent struggle against neo-colonialism and the insidious spread of fascism.' A little later, on the task he saw confronting the play-wright, he quoted an even more vivid statement of the committed writer's position from the same collection:

'… as to my aim in writing, and mainly for the stage, I want desperately to get close to the spectator, to each and everyone I have trapped in the darkness or half light, to penetrate very close and intimate, like a knife in the ribs. I want to make that spectator happy but uncom-fortable. I want to tear him open, guts and all, spice him, cook him in the filthy, stinking broil of our history. I want him washed inside out, in the naked truth, and then I sew him back again a different man. I believe that, if we wound ourselves often enough and painfully enough with reality, with the reality all around us, if we refuse to bandage our sensitive spots

away from the hurt, that we can attain a new and positive awareness.'
Osofisan is aware of the place his work occupies on the contemporary Nigerian stage, and lists plays, that, like his, confront terror and establish a 'space of surreptitious insurrection'. He includes titles by Ola Rotimi, Olu Obafemi, Wole Soyinka, Oladejo Okediji, and Bode Sowande. In his final paragraph he confronts the 'present crisis of the theatre, at least on the campus,' and concludes: *'What we may need to bring into consideration however, is the question of 'packaging', for in the new orientation towards a capitalist economy, what we may be ignoring (because it is painful for us to accept or assimilate), is that even a revolutionary theatre must sell itself nowadays as a commodity, and therefore learn to present itself like all products, if it must sell, as a necessary and glamorous item of consumption to its consumers.'*

Ghana
For the repercussions of ABU's Community Theatre along the West African coast, readers are recommended to read Sandy Arkhurst's contribution to the *Newsletter* published by Legon's School of Performing Arts. (See Sandy Arkhurst, 1994, 'The Community Theatre Project: A Rethink', *SPA Newsletter*, 2 (April–June): 4-6.) Under Arkhurst's supervision, students have worked with communities throughout the length and breadth of Ghana, encouraging the use of drama to raise awareness of issues concerned with health, education, family life and the environment. Partly through Arkhurst's influence on his erstwhile colleague, Yaw Asare, the National Theatre Company has come to see part of its role in terms of providing theatre for development.

Sudan and Kenya
Puppets were included in the work undertaken by Small World Theatre. Based in Wales and initially commis-

sioned by the Centre for Alternative Technology, Machynlleth, Small World has contributed to community theatre projects in many parts of the world – including the Sudan and Kenya. Largely through their work large-scale puppet plays, performed by a team of Sudanese men they had trained, became an integral part of a Village Extension Scheme in 48 villages in Northern Sudan. Apparently the plays 'proved an exciting stimulus to community participation which gained an unprecedented level of community involvement in the project.'
More recently Small World's directors, Ann Shrosbree and Bill Hamblett, have been involved with ventures involving 'Parking Boys' in Nakuru and the Nairobi Family Support Centre, Kibera, which works with children with disabilities. Their report observes: *'Despite political sensitivities in Kenya towards community theatre in shanty towns, this was a big success on a small scale and the Family Centre staff were delighted with the result.'* Those familiar with the experiences of Ngugi wa Thiong'o and Micere Githae Mugo will read a lot into the opening clause of that sentence! Small World Theatre can be contacted at Fern Villa, Llandygwydd, Cardigan, Dyfed, SA43 2QX, UK.

Tanzania (via Texas)
In 1994, *Theatre Insight*, which is published by the Department of Theatre and Dance, The University of Austin at Texas, devoted an exciting and imaginatively compiled issue to 'African Theatre and Performance'. Articles included Inih A. Ebong on Ibibio Theatre, Tracy Sutherland on the educational potential of Theatre for Development, and Rob K. Baum on 'The Geography of Containment in Sande Society'. In the illuminating coverage of performances and publications there were also interviews with Biyi Bandele(-Thomas) and Penina Muhando Mlama.

Dr Mlama was pressed about sensitive issues connected with development agencies. Laura Edmondson followed up an answer on these insistent questions on a key topic: '*So the donor agencies that you've solicited have not had their own agenda in mind? They realize that you let the people decide what issues to address, and you just act as facilitators?*'

Mlama replied: '*Yes, because that's what we tell them: if you want to work with an agenda, you're just using the people as a means. You can have an agenda that is also the people's agenda. For instance, if your agenda is clean water, I don't think the people are opposed to having clean water. However, most people say, 'What we want is clean water, not you going in and saying, what we want for you is clean water.' Many times the [agencies] have their own agenda, but we say, no, we are going to the village and [allow] the people's own issues [to] come out. In most cases, in the people's agenda, they will find their own interests. It is up to the organisation to be flexible, to look at the health issue from the people's point of view. What we are trying to do now is to educate and encourage the development agencies to get the ideas of the people before deciding on the projects.*'

The interviewer, Laura Edmondson, also contributed an account of The Lighters Theatre troupe's performance in Dar es Salaam, to the same publication. Once again the questions of authority and power came to the fore. It seems that in August 1993, sponsored by the Tanzania Media Women's Association, The Lighters worked on the problem of domestic violence, raising the issue of rape with a group of school children. Edmondson described the style of performance as 'participatory agitprop' as defined by Zakes Mda. She carefully noted the points at which the troupe's work followed, and diverted from, Boal's practice, specifically from his provocatively structured Forum Theatre, presentations in which the actors perform a drama based on the selected issue and incorporate within it deliberately disturbing 'errors'. Having completed the sketch, they then start again from the beginning encouraging members of the audience to participate, to offer suggestions about the way in which the problem should be approached, to become 'spect-actors,' that is to say to step into the drama, take over a role and divert the drama in a more productive direction.

Edmondson observed that: '*... the performers unintentionally communicated the sense that some of the students' suggestions were 'better' than others, which would have established a sense of competition that conflicts with Boal's goal of solidarity.*'

However, after a wide-ranging discussion, she concludes her fascinating account: '*Authoritarian or not, the performance was bound to create some level of empowerment, and I refuse to condemn the whole enterprise simply because it was not by the [Boal] book. Indeed I found it a privilege to watch.*' (p. 40)

These kinds of developments will be long and often discussed since they confront fundamental questions about how to adapt an imported form for local use.

South Africa i

With the work of Mbongeni Ngema we are far from that of Boal or Mda. Indeed, following recognition at the Edinburgh Festival and in Los Angeles, in the wake of an Obie Special Citation, Tony nominations and Hollywood contract, the performer-director who first came to fame through the acutely observed and deeply felt *Woza Albert!* has become more and more concerned with New York audiences of 'ladies with fur coats'. A few weeks after his *Township Fever!* opened in the US in 1990, he was quoted as saying: '*You see, when people pay $70 for a ticket, they do not want to hear about the sufferings of black people from a strange country in Africa. They want to be entertained .... They are not gonna be bored by you* *telling them about your struggle in South Africa. Those people want to go and see a good theatre piece. Finished. Whether it's a South African piece, a Jamaican piece, a British piece, they just want to see good theatre. In fact, they are a harder audience to entertain. Most of the time they do not see political theatre anyway; they refuse to go to fringe theatre in New York City. They do not go off-Broadway or off-off Broadway because they don't want to hear politics. Those are the ladies with fur coats.'*

During 1995 and 1996, the story of Mbongeni Ngema's sequel to *Serafina*, of his lavishly funded contribution to AIDS education, was told in the headlines. The background is provided by the award to Ngema by Health Minister Dr Nkosazana Zuma of a contract worth 14,247,600 Rands (about £2.5 million or $4 million then) taken from funds given by the European Union to combat the spread of AIDS in South Africa. What happened has been briskly and eloquently recorded by Bernth Lindfors, in his essay 'The Rise and Fall of Mbongeni Ngema' (see Lindfors, 1997, *African Textualities: Texts, Pre-Texts and Contexts of African Literature*, Trenton: Africa World Press). The story is told partly in the April 1990 interviews by Dolores Mendel and Sol Makgabutlane quoted from above, and partly from the following newspaper items arranged in chronological order. An eloquent bibliography:

January 1996
Khumalo, Reginald, 'Sloppy Show Disappoints', *Natal Witness* ,11 January: 7.
March 1966
Simon, Janine, 'Puppet Players Query Serafina Costs', *Star*, 1 March: 1–2.
Coan, Stephen, 'Serafina: There's Never Been a Theatrical Budget Like it', *Natal Witness*, 5 March: 9.
Anon., 'AIDS Message not effective', *Cape Times*, 11 March: 1.
Makoe, Abbey, 'Serafina Not a Total Sham, But waste of R 14-m', *Argus*, 11 March: 3.

Robbins, David, 'Experts Slam AIDS Play,' *Star*, 11 March: 1.
Cull, Patrick, 'Serafina 2 terminated by SA Government,' *Mail and Guardian*, 22–28 March: 14.
June 1966

South Africa ii
At the very time when the melodrama of *Serafina 2* was unfolding in the pages of the newspapers, drama was being used in a much less obtrusive way for conflict resolution. The objective of the Themba Project was to provide 'training for trainers' workshops to explore conflict using drama processes and thereby to help extend the skills of church and community leaders, people working in prisons, teachers, women and youth workers. During Themba sessions participants work 'experientially' and the outcomes include: greater awareness of non-verbal communication; sensitivity to tone of voice; greater confidence in handling conflict situations creatively; improved listening skills; knowledge of and experience in using drama-based processes for conflict resolution.

One of the participants commented '... it was acting *ubuntu* all the time instead of debating or pretending we can wish things away.' As preparations towards the major Ubuntu Festival (1999) gather pace, we can expect to hear the word *ubuntu*, glossed as Xhosa for 'togetherness', 'bonding', 'connectedness', with increasing frequency.

Anglophone–Francophone
There have been various attempts to bridge the gap between Anglophone and Francophone theatre in Africa. These date to the forties as is apparent from Gibbs's contribution to this volume. Eckhard Breitinger in Bayreuth has been at pains to work through bi-lingual publications on Theatre for Development – and to make available German research on the use of drama to spread knowledge

about AIDS in Uganda.

By the time this appears, the proceedings of a conference on the relationship between Anglophone and Francophone Theatre organized by Anne Fuchs will have been published in *Matatu*. [The subsequent issue of that journal will, incidentally, be entitled *Fontomfrom: The Performing Arts in Ghana*.]

The idea of a bi-lingual acting company has taken deep root in Accra. Surprisingly, in view of the situation in Ghana and the extensive work in English and Twi undertaken by Efua Sutherland and Abibigromma, the two languages the company has been using are English and French! Clearly, note has been taken of the position of Ghana as a country surrounded by states in which French is the major European language. (See Jean-Pierre Wurtz quoted below.)

PUBLICATIONS

Publications of particular interest include: Anne V. Adams and Janis A. Mayes (eds), 1997, *Mapping Intersections: African Literature and Africa's Development*, (Trenton and Asmara: Africa World Press) ISSN 1093–2976, p. 316.

The volume consists mainly of papers presented at the 12th Annual Meeting of the African Literature Association held at Cornell University in Ithaca, New York from 9–12 April 1987.

It has taken a decade to bring these papers together and publish them in a volume. However, there is much that remains fresh and, particularly in view of the topic of this issue of *African Theatre*, very pertinent. Contributors of papers and participants in the lively round tables include key figures in African drama: Femi Osofisan, Biodun Jeyifo, and Micere Githae Mugo. The last is represented in *Mapping Intersections* by a paper entitled 'Women and Books' that she delivered as the keynote address at the Women's

Writers' Workshop, Zimbabwe International Book Fair, 1985.

The creed expressed at the end of her paper will give pause for thought to many who consider drama, like literacy, a means of empowerment. She concludes '… *I believe that there are women writers, critics and publishers here today, who, in the struggle to break though into a male dominated world, will see it as logical to espouse the cause of the most oppressed in our societies. It is because all of us, men and women, need to address the problem of women and books within its context – the class struggle.*' (p. 59)

The 24th African Literature Association Conference was held in Austin, Texas, during March and April 1998. In addition to panels and papers on Hybridity in the South African Theatre, African Performing Arts, and Werewere Liking, there were theatrical performances of *Une Tempête* by Aimé Césaire and of Efua Sutherland's *Edufa*. The latter, acted by members of the African Students' Association, demonstrated the continuing links between Austin and Legon. It is to be hoped that there will not be a delay of ten years before the best of the conference papers appear!

The problems faced by playwrights wishing to see their work in print remain acute. Playwrights share with novelists the problem of interesting reliable publishers in what they have written. But it is good to note an encouraging development: Bode Sowande's *Ajantala-Pinocchio* was issued in an English–Italian edition by la Rosa (Via l. Ornato 8, 10131 Torino) during 1997.

In a prefatory interview to the text, Sowande speaks of the social problem which he addressed in his drama, making a point that links the play tenuously with drama that draws attention to social issues: '*We have in Nigeria today an acute problem, acute level of delinquency on the streets. And the juvenile delinquency that we have is as low as age seven or age six, and by the time the child is ten or eleven, the street wisdom is of an evil kind, or is of a malevolent kind, or is a street wisdom, a street genius that magnifies the totality of the kind of neglect and greed that the society has done. And I've seen Ajantala and Pinocchio combining their own personalities into this metaphor to shock the contemporary human society.' (xxx)*

Critical writing on playwrights remains in relatively short supply, but a particular welcome should be given to studies from Africa such as *Telling the Truth Laughingly: The Politics of Francis Imbuga's Drama* by John Ruganda (Nairobi: East African Publishing House, 1992). And Muyiwa P. Awodiya's *The Drama of Femi Osofisan: A Critical Perspective* (Ibadan: Kraft, 1995) – a companion volume to the collection of interviews mentioned above.

As will be obvious from the dates of many of the items mentioned so far, this issue of *African Theatre* has a lot of catching up to do – and passing on relevant information is the function of this discursive and eclectic round-up. It is not easy to get any idea what is happening in the theatrical life of the member states of the Organisation of African Unity. The least one can do is to draw attention to some of the publications and performances – hoping that the inadequacy of the list will provoke readers to become writers and send in news about the dramatic life around them for the next and subsequent issues. It is envisaged that *African Theatre* will carry an increasingly authoritative annual round-up of drama in the continent. You are invited to send in material.

PRODUCTIONS

Achebe & Bandele in the UK

Things Fall Apart has been through various transformations. One of the more recent – 1997 – was that prepared by Biyi Bandele and presented at the London International Theatre Festival by the West Yorkshire Playhouse in association with the Royal National Theatre Studio and Collective Artistes, Nigeria. Chuck Mike, inevitably represented in this issue of *African Theatre*, directed, Chukwuma Okoye did the choreography, and Yomi A Michaels and Janice Acquah were among a versatile and hard working cast. In the past those trying to keep abreast of theatre in Africa have been grateful to the now sadly folded *West Africa* for its occasional coverage of theatre on the continent, and for the glimpses it provided of African theatre elsewhere. In the case of *Things Fall Apart*, the gratitude was also due to Mercy Ette for her 'Memories of tales by moonlight' (*West Africa*, 23–29 June 1997: 1019). Her review included the assessment that the production was: '*essentially the original author's, but with a noticeable difference. Staged in a sand-filled courtyard, the performance evokes memories of tales by moonlight. With a sparsely designed stage set and functional costumes, the presentation concentrates highly on the imaginative.*'

She draws particular attention to the fact that the doubling and trebling sometimes involved cross-gender casting – '*an irony, considering that in Okonkwo's time, it would have been an insult to compare a man to a woman.*'

The production of *Things Fall Apart* is on a triumphant tour as we go to press. The production has focused considerable attention on the increasingly widely acclaimed adapter, Biyi Bandele. Bandele's youth in Northern Nigeria, his education, that included drama studies in the Theatre Arts Department at Obafemi Awolowo University, and the success of his one-act play, *Rain*, which won the 13th International Student Playscript Competition in 1988, caught the imagination of journalists. Winning the competition enabled the author, who gradually shrugged off a 'Thomas' from his surname, to spend time in England. His play *The Female God and Other Forbidden Fruits* was broadcast on the

Service in 1991. Two years later, the BBC screened *Not Even God is Wise Enough*, and *Marching for Fausa* was premiered at London's Royal Court Theatre. The following October, *Two Horsemen* opened in London. In January 1999 the BBC broadcast his adaptation of *Things Fall Apart* in its Classic Series on Radio 4.

Of *Resurrections* put on at the Cochrane Theatre, Jeremy Kingston wrote in *The Times*:

'*This play is not likely to be chosen by his country's present rulers for issue to schools. It declares that corruption is endemic at every level of society. Businessmen become millionaires by drug-dealing; a defence counsel bribes a judge. Money does not just talk, it drowns out all else. One young criminal envies the previous generation's luck: "All that oil money to steal."* ' (5 October 1994: 36)

Bandele's adaptation of *Oroonoko* from Aphra Behn's original playscript is at Stratford with the RSC during 1999. (To keep abreast of the prolific Bandele and his career, readers are indebted to another magazine, *New African*, and to the profile prepared for it by Ola Sheyin, December 1994. Incidentally, some of Bandele's stage plays have been published by Amber Lane Press of Oxford.)

Soyinka in Washington

The University of Washington DC presented Soyinka's early festive comedy *The Lion and the Jewel* at the beginning of April 1998. In a large theatre before a jungly set, with greenery that invaded the Bale's bedroom in the form of potted plants, an enthusiastic cast made heavy weather of a text that should be played with speed and confidence.

Inexperienced actors were clearly ill at ease for much of the time, desperately in need of props to hold, stools to sit on and things to do with their hands. An ominous note was sounded at the very beginning when Sidi entered with a pot – not a bucket – on her head, and wearing a printed cloth that was clearly not the product of the village loom. When the final dance sequence was performed by a company dressed in the height of Lagos fashion with women in towering headties, it was clear that the careful balance of cultural forces established by Soyinka's stage directions and by Lakunle's despairing questions, such as 'Who here can give a cocktail party?' was absent. On the evidence presented, there were probably regular cocktail parties in Ilujinle.

Soyinka in Jamaica

The progress of Jude Kelly's Anglo-Swiss-Nigerian production of *Beatification of Areaboy* around the world has not been easy to follow, but those with interest and access to the Internet have found material posted from various quarters. In due course, the production's peregrinations will no doubt be written up.

There are intriguing references to a performance in Jamaica, with Rex Nettleford listed as choreographer. It seems, however, that hopes of producing a video using a Caribbean context that could be widely distributed, not least in Nigeria, were thwarted by the mysterious disappearance of vital tapes.

The theatrical exchanges have continued in other directions and, as a footnote to this section, it is intriguing to read Samson Mujuda's review of *A Play of Giants* presented by a US University which 'went on stage at Ridgeway campus in Lusaka and Chongwe' in late April 1996. He described the production as offered 'to the people of Zambia towards the realisation of good governance.' (See 'Zambia's Leading Independent Newspaper', March 1996.)

WHO PAYS FOR WHAT?

Articles elsewhere in this issue raise the question of funding for theatre in Africa.

Who is paying African pipers and actors, and are they calling the tune? Inevitably the debate has roots in the past, many manifestations in the present and numerous implications for the future. In this context, it is useful to recall the opinion expressed by Kwesi Akpabala during 1964 in an article entitled 'The Theatre in Socialist Ghana' and published in *The Ghanaian* (April 1964: 14). Akpabala observed that: *'The imperialists, acting as impertinent cultural arbiters, have employed among other powerful means the theatre as a means for recolonizing Ghana.... The Theatre in Ghana ... must utilize the same means to combat neo-colonialist culture by resuscitating the rich cultural heritage of the African and crush it once and for all.'* Akpabala was writing at a time when there was money in the coffers of the Ghana government, and when other sources of funds were accessible. The Farfield, Ford and Rockefeller Foundations were supporting the work of Efua Sutherland and paying for part of the construction of the Drama Studio. Through the 'too good to be true' Congress for Cultural Freedom, the CIA was putting money into publications and organizations, including *Black Orpheus*, *Transition* and the Transcription Centre which, inter alia, produced *Cultural Events in Africa*.

In recent decades personal circumstances, economic conditions and World Bank policies have sent African activists and writers to seek funds from various sources. In her penetrating analysis of the 'Evolution of Theatre in Ethiopia, Tanzania and Zimbabwe', the Reviews Editor of this publication includes the following paragraph: *'The costs of underwriting the workshops and administration behind the massive growth of theatre in post-independence Zimbabwe have almost all been met by non-governmental sources. Moreover, most of the major funding agencies have come from outside Zimbabwe. The Ford Foundation paid for much of ZIMFEP's*

theatre work. The British Council and the Canadian agency, CUSO, have funded workshops and sent trainers to Zimbabwe. More recently, the Swedish aid giants, SIDA, have given approximately £35,000 for a three-year project on training and promotion with the NTO, while aid from HIVOS (The Humanistic Institute for Cooperation with Developing Countries) was secured in 1990 to run a two-year administration and training programme for ZACT. The greatest coup by a single company to date occurred in late 1993, when Amakhosi Theatre productions secured a grant of Zim $1.4 million from Scandinavia' (Jane Plastow, 1996, *African Theatre and Politics*, Amsterdam: Rodopi).

Plastow notes that Stephen Chifunyise and Robert Kavanagh have used the pages of *Zimbabwe Theatre Report* to raise questions about whether the acceptance of such aid maintains a neo-colonial dependency on the West, and this is a debate that David Kerr contributes to in his report between these covers.

It has been fascinating to watch Nigerian authors accepting commissions from non-African bodies, whether it be Soyinka scripting versions of *The Bacchae of Euripides* for the National Theatre in London, and of *The Blacks* for a Jean Genet season also in London, or Sowande marking the anniversary of a European revolution, and responding – in the play mentioned above – to Italian encouragement.

In Lagos, director Bayo Odeniyi has received support from banks, such as NBL. And, in the context of a crisis in campus theatre, the radical Osofisan has been quoted above using the language of capitalism – 'packaging' and 'commodity' – in his discussion about the direction the theatre will have to take.

In Ghana, director Sam Ansong Manu benefited from US backing for his production of James Baldwin's *Amen Corner*, and numerous Accra-based theatre groups have taken advantage of the performance areas made available by the British Council and the Goethe Institute.

It is clearly difficult to preserve unfettered theatre movements in nations that are deeply in debt. The absence of local sources of funding for the arts and for development projects makes collaboration with bodies that have very different cultural and other agendas inevitable. One has only to visit the Daniel Sorano Theatre in Dakar, or the national theatres in Accra and Lagos to feel that outside pressures, some of them intimately linked with financial conditions, have affected the way that bricks and mortar, concrete and steel have been deployed in African theatre buildings. Perhaps, the architecture is only part of it, only the outward and visible form of an increasing degree of inward and invisible dependency.

It is good to read in Jane Plastow's interview-article with Alemseged Tesfai that the Eritrean situation is being closely monitored.

Théâtre Utile

The Internet has been described as 'a great hunter-gatherer' and those interested in African theatre should take advantage of it. The Paris-based cultural organization Afrique en Créations has been particularly active in establishing relevant web-sites and in bringing together material on African theatre groups. The following account, under the sub-heading just cited, is an indication of one useful site to visit: '*Nous avons regroupé sous le terme générique de 'théâtre utile' les différentes pratiques théâtrales (théâtre d'intervention sociale, théâtre pour le développement, theatre-forum) qui se saisissent des problèmes de développement et de societé: problèmes de santé – notamment lutte contre le sida – condition féminine, protection de l'enfant, problème de l'eau, nouvelles méthodes d'agriculture, protection de l'environnement, sans*

oublier le thème, malheureusement récurrent, des droits de l'Homme. S'étendant progressivement, depuis une vingtaine d'années, à travers le continent africain, du Botswana (qui a connu la première experience, en 1974) au Nigeria, du Zimbabwe au Cameroun, de la Tanzanie au Mali et au Burkina Faso, les spectacles de 'théâtre utile', joués en règle générale dans les langues nationales, s'adressent en priorité aux communautés villageoises, fréquemment analphabètes, et aux populations défavorisées souvent des paysans déracinés – des périphéries urbaines. Ces initiatives bénéficient fréquemment de l'aide financière d'organismes internationaux, tels que l'Organisation mondiale de la santé, l'Unicef ou des organisations non gouvernementales, qui soutiennent ainsi des actions de sensibilisation, par le théâtre ou la danse, en faveur de leurs programmes sociaux ou de santé. Ce n'est pas la moindre contradiction, que de voir ainsi des équipes theatrales parmi les moins reconnues, constituer le support privilégié de la diffusion de programmes internationaux, vitaux pour la sociètè toute entière, de voir les équipes les moins 'médiatisées' jouer, en somme, le rôle de mass média en direction des populations les moins accessibles à la télévision. Le théâtre utile a son rendez-vous biennal à Ouagadougou (Burkina Faso), au Festival international de théâtre pour le développement, mis en oeuvre depuis 1988 par l'Atelier théâtre burkinabé, dirigé par Prosper Kompaoré.' Jean-Pierre Wurtz. *Envoyez nous vos commentaires sur le serveur:* <aec@pratique.fr> Copyright © 1996 *Afrique en Creations /INA.*

Writers will be interested in the material Afrique en Créations has been collecting on publishers. Those involved in studying African drama will be delighted by the lists of African drama groups and societies. As with all such electronic 'notice-boards', up-dating is a constant requirement.

Babalawo: Mystery-Master

AGBO SIKUADE

ORIGINAL CAST
As recorded by the BBC Africa Service, 1997, and directed by Penny Boreham

Umar (Police Superintendent)	*Jude Akuwudike*
Lape (woman in distress)	*Zenga Lonhmore*
Olisa (Police Sergeant)	*Tunde Babs*
Babalawo (medicine man)	*Peter Badejo*
Taju (Babalawo's assistant)	*Valentine Nonyela*
Mrs Babu (complainant)	*Jeillo Edwards*

SCENE ONE

(Forest noises, Babalawo's shrine)

Babalawo *(Muttering in a chanting voice)* Only briefly does the eye see the nose, few prisons can hold the snake: must the chameleon …

(Footsteps on twigs and grass)

Babalawo *(Gasps)* Who is there? Is that you, Taju? Why do you insist on practising your creepy, crawly … Step forward, from the bushes and quickly …

Taju I greet you master, great Babalawo, master of the mysteries, keeper of the secrets of deities, the …

Babalawo Taju, I know what or who I am, and right now I'm very busy.

Taju I must pay my respects to the …

Babalawo You should, first, pay for the last medicine I made for you …

Taju Most certainly, great master. I have the money now… I have brought it with me …

Babalawo Good. I see … well, put it down then and tell me why you have come to pester me again, so early in the day.

Taju Certainly, master … Here it is … I have … *(Taju approaches)*

Babalawo *(With distaste)* Wait, wait, wait!… You smell, Taju. Where in hell are you coming from? You smell, horribly!

Taju *(Sniffing)* Yes, you are right, master. I wondered what it was when …

Babalawo Spirit of my fathers!... Your feet ! Look at your feet! What is it?

Taju *(Crestfallen)* I believe it is some waste matter, Babalawo ... we took the path by the river ...

Babalawo Such respect for my shrine ... Genius, why can't you place your elephant feet? Careful! Don't spread it all over my floor!

Taju Sorry master. The villagers must not let their dogs and their children ... onto the ...

Babalawo I am holding my breath, Taju. What have you come for? Say it and be gone, please.

Taju The woman is here, master.

Babalawo Which woman, Taju? Who is she and what is her problem?

Taju Her children will not stay, master. I don't know who she is. Someone brought her to me in the town; she will not reveal her ...

Babalawo How much have you extorted from this woman's misery, Taju?

Taju *(Indignant)* Me? Master! How...

Babalawo You wish to lie to me? In my shrine? Shall we test the...?

Taju *(Very quickly)* She gave me five thousand naira.

Babalawo What! You took five thousand and ... Taju, are you a thief?

Taju A gift, master, she gave willingly... I ... she ...

Babalawo Please ... please just show her in.

Taju Master she brought you gifts ...

Babalawo *(Wearily)* Taju, show her in, please ... and go! ... And wash your feet before you return ... the woman as well.

Taju Yes master.

SCENE TWO

(General noise of police station, voices in background, etc....)

Mrs Babu Something must be done, it is very urgent, Sergeant.

Sergeant *(Exasperated)* Yes madam, I am trying to write down your statement. You are Mrs Babu and you want us to arrest a medicine man, because he put a curse on your husband.

Mrs Babu That's right. The father of my six children is lying there at the hospital, like a vegetable ... like a piece of wood ...

Sergeant That's all right, Mrs ... er ... Babu ... I'm trying to write all this down, so let's keep to the ...

Mrs Babu What are you writing down? What is the matter with you? I say go and arrest this husband-killer and you waste time practising your a.b.c. ...

Sergeant Madam, I understand your stress, but we have to follow certain procedures in these matters...

Mrs Babu Are you taking an exam this week, or do you just like scribbling grammar early in the morning?

Sergeant I hope you're not talking to me like that!

Mrs Babu Unless you have a twin brother standing here, then I am talking to you and now I want to talk to your superior officer. Where is he?

Umar *(Coming on)* Good morning, Sergeant.

Sergeant Ah, Superintendent, good morning sir.

Umar As soon as you can, get a few detectives to the royal palace. The Commissioner phoned me at home, very early this morning... The Aremo, prince and heir to the throne, says one of his wives left the palace this morning, carrying her only child ... Please, open a file ... missing persons ... What's the matter? Madam, you look as if ...

Mrs Babu Yes, I need someone to save me from this counterfeit policeman ... Please, are you an officer?

Sergeant Madam, you don't need an officer, you need a lawyer ... Hey! You two! Constable! And you, corporal, come. Take this woman away and lock her in the detention room.

Mrs Babu What? I am the complainant! *(Led off protesting)* Are you going stupid?... Look, you two robots, don't push me like that...

Umar *(Laughs)* Sergeant, what was that all about?

Sergeant That, sir, is Mrs Babu. The wretched woman was here first thing in the morning ... I had been stalling for time so that the policewomen could get here to detain her.

Umar Yes, but what did she do? I'm sure it's not just for being rude to you!

Sergeant *(Laughs)* Well, I might add that to the list of charges. No sir, she has more or less confessed to poisoning her own husband, but is trying to blame it on one medicine man!

Umar How is that so?

Sergeant She says she wanted to stop her husband 'fooling around', so she got this 'cure' from the medicine man, and it worked. Her husband lost all interest in the women outside, and stayed at home. The trouble is after a few weeks he not only stays at home, but stays on the bed! Just doesn't want to do anything at all; not even to get up and clean himself ... not even to eat!

Umar I see. She's collected and given the poor man some voodoo medicine for some purpose and it has probably backfired.

Sergeant That's what I say too, sir. But this ... er ... lady ... thinks the medicine man put a curse on her husband, as a sort of revenge.

Umar And why would he...

Sergeant She's a very rude woman, sir and, believe me, one could be tempted to teach her a lesson or two ...

Umar *(Short laugh)* It's really not so funny, you know. Poor man, I hope you've investigated the affair thoroughly

Sergeant We're working on it, sir. I've contacted the hospital; the man is there, but the doctors don't seem to know, yet, what's wrong with him ... only the symptoms ... he doesn't want to do anything ... absolutely nothing. I believe the voodoo was probably too effective.

Umar Have you talked to the medicine man?

Sergeant I was waiting for authorisation, sir.

Umar You can have that as soon as you open a file on the man. Don't forget the detectives ... for the Aremo's wife. We'll invite this Babalawo for a chat, 'to assist the police'. *(Going off)* Prepare the authorisation and bring it to me in my office. Does he have a name? I mean, does Mrs Babu know his name?

Sergeant She doesn't know his name, sir ... she says they just call him 'Babalawo'.

SCENE THREE

(*Forest noises. Babalawo's shrine*)

Babalawo Come in, woman, I am over here ... let your eyes get used to the darkness ... then you may.

Lape (*Emotional, urgent*) Babalawo, father of secrets, master of mysteries, save me ...

Babalawo Please ... be calm ... Nothing falls from the sky that the earth cannot receive. Now, tell me your troubles.

Lape Father of cults, I speak of something that is beyond trouble, beyond ... distress ... six times, in less than so many years, I have buried the rewards of my womb ... six children ... born to tease their mother with hopes and gentle caresses from loving little fingers ...

Babalawo The 'Abiku' children will not stay ... woman, what is your name?

Lape My name is 'Lape' ... but you may call me 'iku-run-mi'... Death has ruined-me' ... for Death has impoverished me, after six calls ... Death has clothed me in rags! I am torn ... broken ...

Babalawo Please, you distress yourself...

Lape Seven times I have knelt at the feet of Olodumare, and he has given me the reward of life ... (*Amongst the forest noises, a baby crying*) Babalawo, I thought I heard!

Babalawo Do not be afraid ... just tell me, tell me!

Lape After the first died, they consoled me. The water is spilt, but the calabash is unbroken' ... 'you will bring forth another' ... Then came the twins; two boys, in their beauty for all to behold the wonders of the heavens ... The demons took them from me and brought others. We named them in hope ... 'Banjoko' ... 'sit, stay with me', hold your mother's hand. Tiny fingers grew cold in the night. Then came 'Jekinniyi'. 'Let me have respect'. Respect, in this compound, respect, among the other wives, the other women. Furtive glances, hushed voices ... 'Jekinniyi' passed on heedless to my pleas ... Others followed. (*Breaks down*)

Babalawo Peace, woman, you must ...

Lape Six times, the demons of the iroko tree, cursed growth of evil gods ... six times, they have snatched my rewards.

Babalawo Six have left ... but you say seven; therefore, one child is still alive?

Lape Yes, she is alive. (*The sound of wind chimes*) We have named her 'Duro-ori-ike': 'Wait-and-see-how-we-will-pet-you' ... Wait, please ... see how your mother will braid your hair, see how I will bathe you in soft, warm scented waters; how your skin will glisten with oil from the richest perfumed seeds ... Wait, 'Duro-ori-ike', stay and be loved, there is love to spare ...

Ah, Babalawo … you should see her; you must see her … Beautiful beyond all my dreams. Olodumare himself had pity on this most pitiful of his daughters … and he gave me 'Duro-ori-ike' because Esu had eaten enough of his children, and Olodumare wished him to spare their mother …

Babalawo (*Sniffs emotionally*) Woman, I am moved by your joy … Olodumare is merciful …

Lape Babalawo, you should see 'Duro-ori-ike'! She is at the edge of the forest with her nursemaid … Your brother had said I must come alone, or else I would never have left her side … My life stands still, when her large, slow, gentle eyes quiver and close in sleep, and I breathe only when I can hear her breath, I live each …

Babalawo You have travelled a painful road, woman. What is it that I can do to …

Lapo (*Fervently*) Babalawo, you must stop the demons! I will give anything … This child must stay, for I have tied the stone onto my wrapper, and the waters of the great river will end this evil life, if the demons should call her to their homes …

Babalawo The spirits forbid … Please, let me examine the child. Where is she? If she is sick, then …

Lape (*Alarmed*) No! The gods forbid it…! She is not sick … The health of the gods themselves is on her … (*Calms*) Master, please, you mention sickness and my soul leaves this world in the agony of …

Babalawo I am sorry. I thought that was why you have come.

Lape The potion, great master of all cures … the potion to keep the evil demons from my child … Your brother said we …

Babalawo My brother? The man who brought you here … Taju. (*Mutters*) My 'brother' will suffer … (*Clears his throat*) Erm … Where is your daughter?

Lape At the entrance to the forest … Your brother gave me his young sister as a nursemaid for my child. She is with her … Your brother said you were …

Babalawo Taju … er … my 'brother', has been your 'doctor'?

Lape Yes, Babalawo … He has been helping me ever since the death of the sixth child … I owe him a lot.

Babalawo (*Mutters*) I am sure … Of course, he has sworn you to secrecy … about the … er … special … er … ceremony, or ritual you performed before this child was born?

Lape Oh yes … you have my oath, great one. I have not spoken of the er … ceremony to any living person.

Babalawo Not to your husband.

Lape Your brother said most especially not to my husband.

Babalawo Just as I thought. Well, that's very good to hear. Now, let me ask my 'brother' to bring his sister and the child to the shrine. (*Calling out, amused*) Taju! My brother! Where are you? We have some work to do …

SCENE FOUR

(*Noise of police station. Superintendent's office*)

Umar What did you say, Sergeant? You don't know his name?

Sergeant I'm sorry sir, but that's the truth ...

Umar Well, does anyone know where he lives?

Sergeant (*Laughs*) Somewhere in the middle of the forest.

Umar (*Laughs*) That's perfect. Well, I suggest you just open a file, conclude things with the hospital. I'm afraid you'll have to let the lady, Mrs Babu, go home to look after her family.

Sergeant They may not want her.

Umar (*Laughs*) Sergeant! Perhaps this Babalawo will do you a favour and cast a politeness spell on her!

Sergeant Perhaps. But how can we invite him over?

Umar You'll probably have to take the lady along with you as a guide.

Sergeant That was what I was afraid you might say. How I wish this Babalawo would just walk in and ...

(*Knock on the door*)

Umar (*Laughs*) You would be lucky.

(*Knock on the door, more urgent*)

Umar Yes. Come in.

(*Door bangs open. The Babalawo enters ... Wind chimes?*)

Babalawo (*Coming in panting, urgent*) Good morning, gentlemen, I have come to report a kidnapping, or an abduction ... a definite fraud and, if all goes well, an immediate and decidedly painful death! I shall despatch the criminal to...

Sergeant Calm down, please.

Babalawo Calm down?! You don't know what you are saying.

Umar Sir, please, who are you and wh ...

Babalawo What do I look like? Look at my outfit! I am a babalawo!

(*Pause*)

Sergeant Sir! My wish came true.

(*Pause*)

Babalawo Is this the police station or the asylum? Why are you two staring at me like that? I am a babalawo, not a TV set.

Umar How did you get past the constables at the desk?

Babalawo Oh, come on. Which true African dare stop a babalawo in full dress? Now, if you ask me one more (*Screams*) STUPID QUESTION!

Umar Take it easy, please.

Babalawo Don't tell me to take it easy!... (*Hushed*) I have a gentle, beautiful, innocent woman, under powerful sedation, at my shrine. She has had ...

Sergeant Why have you put her under sedation?

Babalawo I can read your mind ... and I forgive you, because in your other life you were a he-goat! (*Takes a deep breath*) Now, I shall say what I have come to say, and the two of you will please, just listen. The woman at my shrine has had seven children, six died, a few months after birth. Through my assistant, I treated her case and the seventh child has survived for three years. Now the child is quite healthy, but my assistant brought them both to my shrine this morning for what he called a talisman, to prevent evil spirits. Whilst the woman was in conference with me, my assistant, with the help of someone he called his sister, abducted, kidnapped the child. I have not told the woman of this tragedy, because of her unstable condition. She would kill herself, at my shrine. Now. Please, in the name of all that is sacred, help me bring in my assistant and this woman's child.

(*Pause*)

Sergeant Sir, shall I arrest this apparition?

Umar Sergeant! Please, fetch Mrs Babu and bring her here.

Sergeant Very good sir.

(*Footsteps. Door opens, closes*)

Babalawo Now, where have you sent that 'jackass' to?

Umar He's gone to fetch someone I want you to meet.

Babalawo Social introductions now? Are you two normal?

Umar You don't sound like a babalawo.

Babalawo What does one sound like?

Umar I really don't know, but definitely not like you. You sound like a university professor I once met, somewhere. We were quite close, in fact.

Babalawo I have never seen you in any of my several lives. However, I am one of the rarer variety of babalawo – the educated ones. In fact, I have doctorate degrees in several sciences. You're stalling for time until your jackass gets back. I'd better sit down and rest my weary legs.

(*Chairs drawn up*)

Babalawo By the way, did you know that 'babalawo' means – Master of the Mysteries? Mystery-Master, or something to that effect ... (*Breathes deeply*) What a day! Our wonderful police! Such prompt and urgent service! No wonder the country is full of criminals.

Umar I've known someone just like you. The same looks, the same manners. It's not possible, but you bear an incredible resemblance to a professor I knew, a long time ago, but he must be dead by now, or at least well over a hundred years old.

Babalawo That must be me. My real name is Methusela.

Umar He was a professor of science. He must have been ... I don't know, something like ninety-five when we met! He lived on our street when I was nine years old.

Babalawo How old are you now?

Umar Forty-two.

Babalawo No, I think you're still nine years old.

(*Pause*)

Umar How did you save her child?

Babalawo (*Short laughs*) Ha! Now we can start the probing.

Umar Well?

Babalawo It's none of your business! Trade secret!

Umar No, I'd really like to know. I'm quite a believer in traditional medicine.

Babalawo You are also a believer in delay tactics. You're setting up some form of arrest. All right, let's play the game. What's your name?

Umar My name is Umar. Police superintendent.

Babalawo I know all that. There's a nameplate on your desk and your name is also written on that wretched tag you are wearing on your left breast. If you haven't noticed, I have. And your rank is on your shoulder. I meant your nickname? The name the boys gave you at school. It tells a lot about a man his nickname. I can bet you didn't like yours. What did the professor call you? Did ...

Sergeant (*Offstage, struggling with Mrs Babu*) Get inside, you this woman, before I get...

(*Door opens suddenly and Sergeant and Mrs Babu enter*)

Mrs Babu Leave me alone! I want to see another police ... (*Cries out*) Hah! Who is this? You have brought a Shango priest to kill me!

Umar Madam, please control yourself! All right, Sergeant, let her go.

Mrs Babu (*Whimpers*) A Shango priest. In the name of all the spirits, why? I will repeat. Please, I confess. I collected the potion from the babalawo in the village, it was to stop my husband from going to see that useless woman every evening, leaving me and the children alone. I did not know it would do that to him.

Sergeant We had worked that out for ourselves. What we want to know is if this man here is the babalawo you...

Mrs Babu This man? No, no, no! This man is nothing like him. The babalawo wore fine clothes (*Hastily*) I mean no offence, master ... you know what I mean ... your clothes are wonderful! The babalawo's clothes were ordinary ones, not ... oh please, let me go back to the detention, or to prison ...

Umar Did the man have a name?

Mrs Babu Everyone in the village called him 'Babalawo' ... I think I have heard someone call him 'Taju'.

Sergeant Then why, in your statement, did you say you got it from a babalawo in the forest?

Mrs Babu That was where the Taju always took me, but I always waited at the edge of the forest, whilst he went into his shrine, to collect the medicine. Please, can I go? I can go back to the cell ... I ...

Sergeant Why are you looking at her, Mr Juju? Are you trying to intimidate the witness?

Babalawo Do you want to see the meaning of intimidate?

Mrs Babu (*Wails*) Let me out of here, in the name of God!

Babalawo Shut up!

Sergeant Now, you stop that ... you ... who do you think you are?

Umar Sergeant, that's all right ... Please take the lady away.

Sergeant Yes sir ... Come on Mrs Babu, let's go.

Mrs Babu Thank you.

(*They go*)

Babalawo Now, could you please go and arrest this man and rescue the child he has stolen?

Umar That terrible woman was so afraid of you … why?

Babalawo Was she afraid of me? I thought it was just a sort of healthy respect. She probably knows that our own form of 'God Punish You', is with immediate effect. Now, why don't you hurry up and let's go and arrest this man? I have a woman in the middle of the forest, who should very soon be brought out of sedation.

Umar I will ask the sergeant to send a team of experts to mount a search …

Babalawo I know where the wretched criminal has taken the child! I don't need any experts! I need several, hefty, brutal policemen, with little brains and plenty of muscle … surely you have a lot of those around and don't give me any tired-out, overweight, desk Sergeant!

Sergeant (*Coming in*) I heard that, mister Magic, and you had better behave.

Babalawo I know you heard me, prince pepper soup. I could hear your wheezing, as you were listening at the door.

Sergeant Wh …? I was not …!

Umar Sergeant, please arrange for six men … should they carry weapons?

Babalawo Guns? Certainly not! The usual police fist, boots and belts will be quite enough … thank you.

Sergeant Sir, you don't intend ...

Umar I do, Sergeant. We're going to catch this assistant, but first we'll solve our little puzzle about Mrs Babu's husband, won't we, Mr Babalawo?!

Babalawo It's so funny. No-one ever refers to the poor man as Mr Babu. It's always Mrs Babu's husband. As if his very existence depended on her.

Umar You may carry on Sergeant.

Sergeant Very good sir. (*Goes*)

Babalawo Your sergeant takes bribes. (*Chuckles*) Yes, 'he's on the take'.

Umar He's a very honest, hard-working and dedicated officer.

Babalawo I don't disagree. Honest. He doesn't steal, only takes bribes. Hardworking. He makes sure you see him early in the morning and after closing time, but all the little constables do the real work, or they don't get their benefits on time etcetera, and yes, what again? Oh yes, dedicated. Dedicated to his superintendent, by remembering Mrs Superintendent's wedding anniversary and forgetting that she was thirty more than ten years ago.

Umar All right, now, let's get to work. This 'Taju' was apparently your front in the village.

Babalawo You've lost me. My what? Front. I like that … 'front' as like a mask.

Umar He started to do a few half-baked babalawo tricks himself, but they seem to be going wrong. But you don't know, because he doesn't tell you.

Babalawo Spare me your practising investigation tactics and just ask me the questions. I don't have time. If you haven't realised it, I'm rather desperate. You should see the poor woman at my shrine.

Umar Okay. But how do you know where they have taken the child?

Babalawo Privileged information, that criminal clients reveal to their most trusted priest.

Umar I see. Who is Taju?

Babalawo (*With irony*) Taju is my 'front' in the village. (*As if reading a text*) It is important for the babalawo to maintain some mystery, if his work is to be effective. Just like the policeman. The criminal and the hero-worshipping public must not know that behind that uniform and that badge is just another frightened …

Umar That's how he used to talk in those days, too. You could never tell when he was just horsing around.

Babalawo What are you…? Oh my, we're back to your professor again! How do you remember all those things about him, anyway? You say you were only nine years old …

Umar I can remember. You couldn't forget someone like that.

Babalawo He's probably forgotten all about you

Umar Not 'probably'. He has to have been dead, at least thirty years ago or he'd be well over a hundred. By the way you're very well educated and quite up-to-date, for a forest babalawo.

Babalawo Yes. I was born an orphan, brought up by some European missionaries, who educated me and sent me to school for as long as it took me to get a doctorate in animal science and medicine. I chose the profession of the babalawo, because you can be as mercenary as the lawyer or the businessman, without being tied to some hypocritical oath. Yes, I also have a satellite dish. I traded in the old divination necklace of cowrie shells. The trouble is, I keep seeing … ghosts!

(*Wind chimes*)

Umar Just like the prof. You never knew if he was serious. Now. You say Taju was treating Mrs Babu's … er … treating Mr Babu.

Babalawo (*Laughs*) Let me help you. Taju must have been assisting Mrs Babu to keep Mr Babu at home, then something must have gone wrong.

Umar What went wrong, Babalawo, Mystery-Master?

Babalawo How would I know? You'll have to ask Taju.

Umar I will, but right now I'm asking you.

Babalawo Because you know Taju was getting all the medicine from me.

Umar Yes, that's right. So. What went wrong?

Babalawo Nothing went wrong.

Umar Mr Babu is lying critically ill in the hospital, because you and that … Taju … were playing with something serious and sacred – medicine! I have a good mind to throw you into the cell, just to let you…

Babalawo (*Bristling*) And who do you think you are speaking to? What do you know about medicine? What idea do you have about what is 'sacred'? (*Changes tone*) Take care, little boy, I quite like you, but you must not let me give you a spanking. I've got very rough hands …

Umar (*Hushed*) Professor, is it you? Have you found the secret of perpetual youth or something? Those are the very words you …

Babalawo I really believe you are a lunatic … No, no, I'm serious. You need help. Come to the shrine … I will cure you – for a fee.

Umar This is unreal. Who are you? What are you? You are not just another juju man.

Babalawo When will your fat cop get here? I'm stifling … and you're so … so … so …

Umar Go on. You were about to say my nickname, weren't you? Somehow you know it, don't you? Go on, say it.

Babalawo (*Laughs*) You are so … look, if you don't stop s..s..s..scaring me, I shall …

Sergeant (*Coming in*) The boys are ready sir.

Umar In a minute, sergeant … er … I'd like you to go along with them, if you think you can.

Sergeant (*Delighted*) Certainly sir … very good, sir!
(*Goes*)

Babalawo You're giving fat man the chance to be a real policeman for a change. Was that his carrot? Or is it just to annoy me?

Umar I want the two of you to get to know each other. You'll like him, I'm sure. He's just a …

Babalawo Yes, I know. Now. About Mr Babu … or Mrs Babu's husband. I suspect it was a case of an arrested disease. Taju must have given her a potion for him that would start a disease whose symptoms would be lethargy.

Umar Wait a minute! You mean that was the 'cure'? To inflict some disease …

Babalawo Sometimes, in medicine, we have to use what we have without much thought for 'niceties' … Oh, it would be quite safe … controlled. Taju should then have given her the drug or is it antidote, to arrest the disease.

Umar But why do you think your Taju didn't?

Babalawo Simple. Mrs Babu didn't come back for the antidote, because she probably wanted to cheat Taju of the balance of his fees, and if I know Taju, the fee was too high. I suspect his was the case Taju came to collect some medicine for a few months ago. If so, then I can give an antidote.

Umar You mean you know of Mr Babu's case?

Babalawo We never mention names …

Umar And you don't bother to examine the patient yourself?

Babalawo Taju has been with me for a long, long time. He is a babalawo in his own right. He knows the job.

Umar He seems to have gone bad.

Babalawo Just like anyone else, without the moral strength to handle power. It doesn't mean he can't do his job.

Umar Will the disease progress any further?

Babalawo I don't think so, but he should take the antidote, just in case.

Umar Now, just as a matter of interest …

Babalawo (*Chuckles*) I knew it! You want to know what the disease was?

Umar Yes.

Babalawo It was leprosy.

Umar What!?

Babalawo It must have been. Primary symptoms, capable of arrest at the stage of initial lethargy, without any real debilita …

Umar I think that is criminal! Dangerous!

Babalawo That's because you're a policeman and not a doctor.

Umar Neither is Taju ... and neither are you for that matter!

Babalawo I shall ignore that ... statement.

(*Pause*)

Umar What really went wrong ... in the case of this woman at the shrine?

Babalawo Money. Taju is a very good assistant ... but I knew he couldn't resist money.

Umar I don't believe it.

Babalawo You don't believe what?

Umar I saw the effect you had on Mrs Babu. Taju would never risk your anger ... unless there was a stronger attraction. It could never be money.

(*Pause*)

Babalawo Go on ...

Umar I don't know. What is it? Can you tell me?

Babalawo One day, maybe. Right now, we have to move quickly.

Umar Yes. (*Shouts out*) Sergeant!

Sergeant (*Enters*) We're ready sir.

Babalawo Good. Let's go.

Umar I'll wait here till you return, Sergeant. Be careful.

Sergeant You can count on me sir.

Babalawo Oh, come on, before I throw up! It's just a routine arrest!

(*They go*)

SCENE FIVE

(*Police station. Superintendent's office. Umar is breathing deeply. Snoring ... sleeping ... dreaming. Spooky voices taunting as in playground*)

Babalawo (*Offstage, in dream Babalawo is 'The Professor'*) Wake up, Spook, you lazy wretched little boy. Ah, but you're not so little now, are you? Well, anyway, wake up Spook, you lazy wretched grown-up boy! (*Laughs*)

Umar (*As boy*) Professor, why do you call me Spook, I don't like it. My name is Umar.

Babalawo Ah, Spooky, you look so serious! You're not meant to be sleeping are you, you're meant to be studying!

Umar (*Earnestly*) Yes, because I want to be a doctor. I want to save lives.

Babalawo Save lives maybe, (*hesitates*) but not as a doctor, I think. AND NOT AS ANYTHING ELSE, EITHER, IF YOU DON'T STOP SLEEPING!

(*Knock on door*)

Umar (*Waking, confused*) Yes, who is it?

Sergeant (*Enters*) It's me sir. You should have gone home sir. It's well after nine o'clock.

Umar Oh Sergeant, you caught the ... Taju?

Sergeant He wasn't doing much of hiding sir. It was very peculiar.

Umar (*Regaining composure*) ... Just as I thought. Please go on. What happened?

Sergeant Well, the Babalawo took us to this place ... some clearing in the outer parts of the forest. There we found Taju, his sister, an old woman who they said was their mother, and a little girl, probably three years old, who must have been the abducted child. The Babalawo pulled Taju aside, they spoke a few words and believe me sir, Taju just burst into tears! It was the most amazing thing I have …

Umar   What did the Babalawo do?

Sergeant   He just collected the child from the girl sir, got into the police car and said 'Let's go'. No arrest, no explanation … I totally ignored him and clamped Taju and the girl in handcuffs. They're in the cell right now. We'll charge them.

Umar   Where's the Babalawo?

Sergeant   We followed him to his shrine … spooky place … to give the child to its mother. She didn't even know the Babalawo had been away!

Umar   What has Taju got to say for himself?

Sergeant   He hasn't said a word, sir.

Umar   And he never will. Set him free … and the girl. No-one is going to press charges, so …

Sergeant   Sir?

Umar   That's right. What did the Babalawo say? Sometimes, in medicine, they use what they have … without too much thought for niceties.

Sergeant   I don't understand, sir.

Umar   The woman, the child's mother, is the missing person, wife of the Aremo, the crown prince, the …

Sergeant   Yes …

Umar   From records, we know she has the sickle cell disease … so does the Aremo. That was why their children were dying in their infancy. How do you think this little girl survived?

Sergeant   I don't quite get it, sir.

Umar   That's because they didn't teach you a little medicine at the police college, Sergeant. Two persons with the sickle cell will always have a child with the disease★ … but if they change partners … if one of the parents is not a sickler …

Sergeant   The child is … the child does not belong to the Aremo …

Umar   That is very good, Sergeant!

Sergeant   Then whose …

Umar   Taju wanted to show the child to his own mother, when he began to suspect what had …

Sergeant   You mean Taju is … Sir, you don't mean the wife of the Aremo was unfaithful?

Umar   No, she would be afraid of all the oaths they swear to at their marriage. But she wouldn't refuse some 'ceremony' at the hands of a babalawo she trusted. Some 'ceremony' that the master Babalawo might have taught and told Taju to perform.

Sergeant   Ceremony, sir?

Umar   Yes. That's what they would call it. The medical world would describe it as 'artificial insemination'.

★ Umar's medical knowledge is inaccurate at this point. His use of 'disease' shows his ignorance. Eds.

Sergeant Goodness me.

Umar Yes. Remarkable. Their little secret, eh? Only Taju had a little moment's emotion, poor man. His child belongs to the Aremo and he's probably sworn to some oath of silence. Let them go, Sergeant. There's no harm done and we'd only cause a lot of distress. It's going to be one of our little secrets.

Sergeant (*Big sigh*) Well, well ... Very good sir. I must say I'd have wanted that Babalawo here, just to let him know he isn't such a smart old jackass ...

Umar (*Chuckles*) Jackass. Yes, so would I. I had always wanted to ...

Sergeant Oh yes. There was something very odd ... the Babalawo said I should tell you ... your ... your nickname.

Umar (*Breathless*) ... Nickname ... Yes, what did he say my nickname was?

Sergeant SPOOKY. He said you never did like it, but he ... Sir? Is everything all right, sir? Superintendent, you look as if you've seen a ghost ...

THE END

Reviews

Every attempt has been made to provide full bibliographic details with the help of the Africa Book Centre, 38 King Street, Covent Garden, London WC2E 8JT. UK prices have been provided where available. All editions are paperback except where otherwise stated.

Jane Plastow, *African Theatre and Politics: The Evolution of Theatre in Ethiopia, Tanzania and Zimbabwe, A Comparative Study*
Amsterdam & Atlanta: Editions Rodopi B.V. 1996, 286 pp.
ISBN 90-420-0038-4 £24.95 ISBN 90-420-0042-2 £58.00 (cloth)

African Theatre and Politics belongs to a Dutch/United States series of book length publications with the self-explanatory, general title 'Cross Cultures: Readings in the Post Colonial Literatures in English'. The emphasis of this book is in comparing Ethiopian, Tanzanian and Zimbabwean performing arts, and much of its success depends upon the fact that little of its focus is on literature and few of the targeted performances are in English.

Plastow's book ranges from pre-colonial times to the present, but the emphasis is on post-colonial theatre. The three countries are chosen partly because of the author's familiarity with them, an important factor since she privileges field work rather than secondary sources for her evidence. Another reason for the choice is that the post-colonial governments of all three countries have professed allegiance to socialism at some stage. An additional similarity is that the theatrical dialogue in all three countries has been predominantly in the indigenous languages of Amharinya, kiSwahili, chiShona and siNdebele, rather than in the former colonial languages. Plastow is careful to explain, however, that in many ways Amharinya, the dominant language of Ethiopia, is a colonial language.

Despite the word 'evolution' in the subtitle, the structure of *African Theatre and Politics* follows a dialectical pattern, loosely modelled on Fanon's well-known periodization of cultural struggle. Thus, after a survey of pre-colonial theatre in the three countries, Plastow presents chapters on Colonial Theatre ('Conformity, Christianity and Suppression'), Theatre in Liberation Struggles, The Theatre of Independence ('A Time of Hope'), and Contemporary Theatres ('Disillusion and Debate'). Given the wild cards of Islam in Ethiopia and Tanzania, and the very short period of Italian colonialism in Ethiopia, this might seem a rather artificial grid. Plastow manages to make it seem plausible, however, by casting the Amhara empire as a form of colonialism, with the 1974 coup by the Provisional Military Administrative Council (PMAC) as the equivalent of a nationalist liberation victory. Questionable though this comparison may be (and Plastow makes a thorough interrogation of the concept herself), it has the merit of providing a clearly periodized framework for the comparative exercise.

Predictably, the chapter on pre-colonial theatre is the least exciting. To her credit, Plastow acknowledges the limitations of *any* analysis of pre-colonial theatre, relying as it must on very flawed secondary sources. Significantly, she scarcely attempts to make serious comparisons in this section, except to establish the importance of certain socio-economic structures for generating specific performance modes (such as the relationship between Feudalism and praise poetry).

The chapter on colonial theatre also relies heavily on secondary sources, but the comparative framework is more firmly in place. This chapter has some very valuable material on early literary drama in Ethiopia and Rhodesia, linking them to the psychosocial dynamics of imperial occupation. I had some doubts about the section in this chapter which dealt with indigenous theatre's reaction to colonialism, where I felt the explanations seemed to slot rather too neatly into the historical pigeon-holes. Although I agree that Tanzanian *Beni* and Zimbabwean *Mapira*, for example, can usefully be seen as manifestations of indigenous resistance to colonialism, I think the author might have done more to convey the contested nature of that resistance. Ranger's study of the struggle between ZANU Chimurenga cadres and Rhodesian government intelligence agents to access the symbolic power of pre-colonial *Mapira*, shows how willing some sections of colonial regimes were to appropriate the popularity of indigenous African performance.

It is in the last three chapters, dealing approximately with the post-1960 period, that Jane Plastow's research techniques pay most dividends. It is here that she is able to rely either on her own observation, on unpublished student dissertations, or on the information drawn from her extensive interviews with theatre practitioners, to make the description of theatre events and their political significance come alive. She is admirably prepared to risk arbitration where informants give contradictory opinions, or to suspend judgement when arbitration is in danger of descending into guesswork.

One of the great merits of *African Theatre and Politics* is Plastow's acute feel for the theatricality of performance styles. In a type of analysis all too rare in studies of African theatre, she frequently links a study of stagecraft, the class background of performers or the evolution of acting styles to the imperatives of political control and resistance. For example, the very stylized rhetoric and feudalistic working relations found in Ethiopian professional theatre under Haile Selassie are convincingly linked to the authoritarian and paternalistic nature of the Amhara empire.

By interviewing theatre activists from different sides of ideological or factional divides, Plastow is able to support her own observations to reproduce the smell of gunpowder in the acrimonious clashes of personality which mark all three countries' cultural wars. She is also acute at disentangling the ideological and personal interests which inform these debates.

One lacuna in this account of theatre personalities is Plastow's coyness about her own role in the theatrical history. It is quite clear from the book blurb and from one rather shy revelation in her account of Ethiopian theatre, that she had quite an active role in some of the theatre events. Although many critics feel scholars should, as far as possible, keep their own experiences and value judgements out of historical accounts, I, for one, would have appreciated more information about how Plastow herself fitted in with the debates and conflicts which were taking place while she taught, acted, and directed in the various countries.

One major pleasure for the reader, arising from the dialectical structure of *African Theatre and Politics*, is to trace through different chapters the careers of specific individuals at various stages of political development. Tsegaye Gebre-Medhin cuts a particularly fascinating swathe through Ethiopian theatre history, as we see him lionized but distrusted by the Haile Selassie regime, then become a fierce champion of the Dergue, followed by a growing period of disenchantment with the PMAC government, and finally, after the victory of the Ethiopian People's Revolutionary Front, attaining the status of eminent, but slightly marginalized and again rather distrusted, guru.

I have a few misgivings about *African Theatre and Politics*, though I'm not sure whether all of these are really about the book itself, or whether there is an element of vicarious auto-critique of my own book, *African Popular Theatre*, which came out at the same time as Plastow's, and which uses a rather similar dialectical structure.

Plastow takes a very hard line against intellectual radicals who assert their identity with the masses while neglecting the praxis of popular (especially commercial) theatre. Her scepticism is well founded in that intellectuals, with their easy access to publicity, donor funding and academic communication channels, can easily give the impression that they are not only the dominant, but also the most popular voices in national theatre. Although Plastow's willingness to champion the less articulate, non-elite forms of theatre is a welcome corrective, I think some of her judgements are excessively harsh.

It may well be true, for example, that the University of Dar es Salaam's *Paukwa* theatre, closely associated with Penina Muhando (née Mlama) as author, and Amandina Lihamba as director, rarely performed off 'the hill' (the University campus). I'm not sure, however, if it's fair to label *Paukwa* elitist on that account. In a 1992 on-campus performance which I saw of a Muhando play about toxic waste, there was a keenly participant audience of well over a thousand, who were clearly not all from the academic community, and who obviously enjoyed not only the message, but also, what Plastow feels is debilitatingly absent from Muhando's scripts, the humour of the play.

Similarly, the reduction which Plastow makes of Stephen Chifunyise's theatre work (partly aided by Preben Kaarsholm's analysis) to that of a monologically preachy 'theatre for development' is hardly fair. Some of Chifunyise's published polemics or play scripts may seem to have the exhortatory stiffness of a Marxist apparatchik, but, having worked closely with him on several projects, I feel confident in saying that Chifunyise's theatrical practice is very participatory, democratic and open.

Despite these basically minor and rather personal quibbles, I do value Plastow's interest in popular commercial theatre, and in some ways wish she could have pushed that analysis further. For example, I wonder why, other than for reasons of space, she has left out drama created for the mass media of cinema, radio and television. Some of the Zimbabwean authors she refers to, such as Chifunyise, T.K. Tsodzo, Aaron Moyo and Tsitsi Dangarembga have done some of their most fruitful work for the mass media, either directly or through adaptations of their stage plays. The polarities of elitist/popular become even more complex, contested (and therefore interesting) when they are combined with those of media imperialism/indigenization.

Another issue which arises from the question of commercial theatre is that of determining precisely what is 'political'. Plastow offers succinct and useful definitions of 'drama' and 'theatre' in her introduction, but avoids defining 'politics', settling instead for an assertion that culture and theatre provided a very important domain supporting the liberation struggles in all three countries.

In her analytical practice Plastow seems to view politics mainly as the factional conflicts relating to elites or parties in power and the forces opposed to them. There is very little probing, however, of the way apparently non-political, 'common-sense' beliefs (in the Gramscian sense) which permeate popular theatre, can have much wider ideological significance in the realm of class or gender relations. There is almost none of the analysis which, for example, Karen Barber has achieved in her teasing out of Yoruba Opera's hidden ideology, whereby Barber links the stereotypes and narrative silences of popular commercial theatre with the transformations taking place in post-Civil War, Nigerian, social and economic relations.

I realize, of course, that some of my apparent complaints about *African Theatre and Politics* could only have been addressed by making the book considerably, and perhaps unmarketably, longer. As it is, the reader should be very grateful that Plastow has managed to compress such complex, detailed and difficult-to-access information into a coherent comparative narrative of 286 pages, which achieves theoretical consistency, without ever losing sight of particular theatrical personalities and performance modes.

A final issue, which is more of a hopeless wish than a real criticism, refers to the dialectical structure of the book. I have already said that this framework bears its theoretical and factual weight surprisingly well. One qualm that I have, however, arises from the revolutionary, Fanonian origins of the structure. Plastow seems to dissociate herself from a Marxist (or at least a vulgar Marxist) perspective in the book, and thereby attempts to provide a more complex periodization than was available to Fanon. Without a revolutionary perspective, however, (where post-revolutionary socialism is the final term) it is somewhat difficult to see what is the destination of dialectically rendered, historical developments. In the case of *African Theatre and Politics* the last chapter is entitled 'Disillusion and Debate', and I feel the reader is entitled to wonder if disillusion is the final term of the dialectic, or a synthesis which will provide the thesis for yet another spiral of dialectical progress.

I am probably very sensitive to this issue because of lingering dissatisfaction with my own book, which also used a kind of unconsummated dialectic as its structural framework. In the long run the question is probably unanswerable. A book must have an ending, however artificial; history, ineluctably, does not.

David Kerr

Christopher Balme, *Theater im postkolonialen Zeitalter, Studien zum Theatersynkretismus im Englischprachigen Raum*
Tübingen: Niemeyer Verlag, 1995, 260 pp.

David Kerr, *African Popular Theatre from pre-colonial times to the present day*
Oxford: James Currey, 1996, 278 pp.
ISBN 0-85255-533-4 £12.95

Christopher Balme and David Kerr cover – at least in part – the same terrain of dramatic texts, and they both focus on the key issue of syncretic theatre, but their approaches are totally different. David Kerr, himself an old hand in practical theatre in Africa with more than 20 years' experience as director, scriptwriter, facilitator etc., concentrates on theatre and performance as a social phenomenon and a medium for political expression. His descriptions of popular theatre as 'providing a theatre form which could mediate conflicts arising from rapid urbanisation and embourgeoisement' (76), or 'popular theatre could mediate the experience of modernisation and class formation' (59) testifies to his dialectical view of historical development. Christopher Balme's interest focuses on theatre as a cultural and an aesthetic phenomenon that can be best approached through cultural semiotics – a concept that represents a cumulative and integrated view of the various facets of the theatrical semiosis (visual, aural, kinetic, spacial etc.).

One of the prime achievements of Balme's work is the precision with which he defines those terms that have already been introduced into the critical debate, but have been used with broad, vague and sometimes contradictory meanings by previous critics. Balme is equally concise and precise in the description of critical criteria which he newly introduces into the debate and by means of which he broadens the critical terminology (e.g. the term *semiosphere* for the variety of cultural implications of a performance space, or *cultural text* as ideologically neutral compared to *performance text*). The point of departure for Balme's critical analysis is the complexity of his material, which according to Balme can only be adequately approached through a complex system of various methodologies, derived from different disciplines. It is no surprise that Turnerian terms of theatre anthropology are re-written. For a graded system to categorise syncretization, Balme borrows from the systematizations which have been already achieved in religious studies for the classification of categories of syncretic religions. The most influential source for critical concepts is of course semiotics in general, theatre semiotics in particular. But with the introduction of the concept of cultural semiotics, he introduces historical and geographical criteria: he re-introduces temporal/diachronic and spacial/synchronic concepts into a semiotic framework, i.e. relativistic concepts which semiotics have previously eliminated from their theoretical structure.

Balme first gives a survey of the history of indigenous performance theories, beginning with Dholomo's essays from the thirties and his proto-negritudinist view of African performance as dominated by rhythm and patterns. Theory formation in the fifties and sixties is dominated by the Nigerians Adedeji, Clark and Rotimi who argue in favour of the secularization of ritual in theatrical performance, and Soyinka's mythopoesis. From the Caribbean, Walcott and Erroll Hill contributed the view of carnival as the foundation of the theatrical.

The main body of Balme's book consists of a systematic synchronic analysis of the principles of theatricality: the voice, the body, the stage. Talking about the delicate relation between ritual and theatrical performances, Balme emphasizes the change of paradigm from communal participators in a religious ceremony to a contrapuntal actors/spectators relation in theatre. A similar change of paradigm is seen with masquerades when they are moved from the sacred space to the performance stage. Here, spirit possession acquires comparable importance: just like the relation between the mask and the masquerader, the relation between the spirit and his medium/actor occupies a liminal space that blurs clear definitorial ascriptions. Particularly chapter 6 on 'the body as text' with its own semiotic structure, both as static appearance (make-up, mask, costume) and as kinetic expression (dance, mime) provide new insights that one missed with other works on post-colonial theatre. There are a few details, where I would disagree, e.g. that the Market Theatre in Johannesburg caters for a predominately white audience, or that Walcott's *Ti Jean* is based on Anansi lore: folklore yes, but Caribbean Anansi-lore is restricted to Jamaica and follows a different pattern from the *Ti Jean* trickster story.

David Kerr organizes his material differently. He begins with a historical survey that describes various forms of precolonial and colonial performance practices, both ritual (e.g. Egungun) or secular (Alarinjo, Apidan Theatre). When he is dealing with colonial theatre, Kerr distinguishes three forms of syncretic theatre: the militaristic mime in Eastern Africa, the Yoruba opera cum travelling theatres in Nigeria, and the concert party of Ghana and Togo. To each form, he ascribes different social functions and different political intentionalities. Kerr rejects earlier criticism (including Martin Banham's) that interpreted the development of African theatre and performance as a teleological process which leads from pre-colonial ritual performance to post-colonial art theatre with defunctionalized ritualistic elements (e.g. Soyinka's *Death and the King's Horseman*). On a different plane, Kerr reinstates teleological concepts: popular performance proceeds from pure entertainment through class awareness to the formation of an instrument in the liberation struggle.

The early chapters on Yoruba opera, concert party and the travelling theatre movement summarize what has been delineated in specialized studies. Chapter 7, 'Literary Drama and Popular Theatre', offers fresh views, since it compares East and West African theatres (e.g. Byron Kawadwa's operas and Ogunde's). He looks at practitioners of art theatre who lift material from popular performance traditions into works that cater for an elite audience. Kerr also touches on the dilemma of the radical Ibadan dramatists Osofisan, Sowande, Omotoso 'discussing peasant issues through the filter of radical intelligentsia' (124). Kerr is at his best when dealing with those theatre and media forms where he was himself directly involved: 'Popular Theatre and Macro Media' (chapter 9) describes the endeavours of people like Duro Lapido, Soyinka and Saro-Wiwa to develop a distinctly African idiom in TV films, warning at the same time that 'popular dramatists [who want] to avoid media imperialism have to accept the ideological confines imposed by national governments ... or finding alternative media structures ... at the risk of censorship or artistic persecution' (194). The chapters on protest drama in South Africa and Ngugi's Kamirithu project illustrate Kerr's concept of a truly popular art form that grows from grass-roots participation as opposed to the government promoted National Dance Groups, National Theatres with their vulgarized neo-negritudinist concept of culture, that 'makes it a populist rather than popular folk theatre' (208).

David Kerr focuses his attention on organizational structures and their political implications, government policies, class or sponsor's interests. He looks at liberating, emancipative aspects of popular art forms in the process of creating theatre, of bringing it to an audience with a political message, but, more important, as a show that is in itself a political statement. Christopher Balme, on the other hand, focuses on performative aesthetics, on techniques and mechanisms of syncretic theatre 'as creative re-interpretation of heterogenous cultural materials in order to produce new semantic and cultural configurations' (35). Both books – each in its own and very different approach – offer new perspectives on post-colonial theatre – as an art form or as a social institution.

Eckhard Breitinger

Olu Obafemi, *Contemporary Nigerian Theatre: Cultural Heritage and Social Vision*
Bayreuth: Bayreuth African Studies and Ilorin: Joe-Noye Press, 1996, 289 pp.
ISBN 3-927510-32-7 £19.90 ISBN 3-927510-49-1 £25.95 (cloth)

In this book, Olu Obafemi has written the first comprehensive study of contemporary Nigerian theatre. He achieves a historical account of its emergence and development, as well as tracing its different ideological and aesthetic strands. Other studies such as Chris Dunton's *Make Man Talk True* (1992) and Yemi Ogunbiyi's *Drama and Theatre in Nigeria* (1981), while covering similar material, do not apply the classification which Obafemi has employed to make *Contemporary Nigerian Theatre* comprehensive and yet easy to read. There are three chapters which, though individually broad, are united by the headings under which the author has argued his subject.

Chapter One is in three parts, with each looking at the major practitioners of Yoruba Opera, a theatre which the author remarks:

> ranges widely between the serious historical-mythological dramas of the late Duro Ladipo, through Hubert Ogunde's political satires and morality plays, the late Kola Ogunmola's comic fantasies, and the comedy theatre of Moses Olaiya (alias Baba Sala) and his Alawada Group. (13)

Obafemi observes that despite the difference in training, approach to theatrical art and subject matter between the operatic and literary traditions, the two share a practice of integrating 'themes, materials and the form of traditional drama with additional elements adopted from western dramatic experience'(13). It is this deployment of the traditional performance elements, which roots their plays firmly within the cultural soil of Nigeria. For the operatic artists, this artistic sensibility is variously employed to create a theatre concerned with the quest for 'socio-cosmic harmony' in a world constantly on the brink of disaster.

Part One uses Ladipo's handling of his material in *Oba Ko So* to suggest a correlation between form and meaning in his theatre. Whereas critics such as Ogunba, Adedeji and Armstrong find Ladipo's theatre lacking in depth of characterization, Obafemi argues that 'a reliable critical mode needs to be employed in the appreciation of the "religio-historical dramas", such as Ladipo's, which abound in Nigerian folk operatic tradition' (19). Structurally, Obafemi finds the play neither weak nor episodic as claimed by critics because Ladipo achieves organic unity by employing 'recurrent repetition of episodes, music realised in drumming, songs and dance as well as language' (21). There is, argues Obafemi, a 'closeness between the statement and the aesthetics in Ladipo's plays' evidenced by 'his success in using myth, ritual and history through theatre to appeal to the sensibility and perception of his audience' (35). Thus in Ladipo there is a marriage of form and content which makes his drama appealing.

Part Two looks at Ogunde's *Strike and Hunger* (1946). Its topicality and dramatic technique, Obafemi argues, is very much inspired by the Yoruba travelling theatre. The play reveals the syncretism of Ogunde's theatrical enterprise, as well as his 'role as a guardian of society's conscience, a role which he inherits from the traditional artist, especially the Alarinjo Masque-dramaturge' (37). Obafemi finds that the play observes the travelling theatre structure of opening glee, the play and the closing glee – something which Ladipo's plays shun. Obafemi praises Ogunde's courage in dedicating himself to the search for and exposition of the truth and to satirical comment on social ills. Ogunde, it must be remembered, had brushes with different Nigerian governments.

The section on Olaiya is stimulating, especially locating the source of his theatre in the *Efe* or *Yeye* tradition of Yoruba popular culture. Obafemi writes,

> Olaiya lacks the profundity of the late Ladipo and the latter's deft handling of mytho-historical material. He equally lacks the political commitment of Ogunde. Yet his ability to treat the excruciatingly funny, the farcical, is unparalleled on the Nigerian stage. His most valuable assets are his ability to provide laughter and popular entertainment. (55)

It is highly debatable whether any work of theatre can be totally apolitical as Obafemi seems to suggest Olaiya's is. That he ostensibly goes for slapstick comedy does not mean that a unique ideology underpins his creative process, and neither does it mean that his plays lack a distinct moral universe. That he succeeds in making people laugh is reason enough why he, as the book agrees, is indisputably the most popular, the most commercially viable theatre practitioner in Nigeria of his time. Still, the author disapproves of Olaiya, the popular artist who attracts large audiences, but 'aborts' the traditional role of the artist as instrument of communal will in pursuit of commercial success. Obafemi feels that Olaiya's 'lack of seriousness' poses a danger to the 'supposed' useful employment of the theatre for serious concerns. One feels that he is, in fact, in danger of becoming like the elitist critics he cited earlier who dismiss Olaiya because of an essentially monochromatic conception of theatre.

Chapter Two looks at Soyinka, Clark, Rotimi and Sofola – the first generation of university trained dramatists. The book asserts that the literary theatre of the 'animist metaphysical' dramatists and the popular tradition are not mutually divergent as a superficial glance might suggest, for both are products of artistic sensibilities inspired by the oral tradition and cultures of Nigeria. However, Obafemi sees the movement from the popular as: 'a move from a celebratory communally-orientated, robust theatre to self-conscious, individualist and metaphysical dramatic theatre creations' (67). He finds the main difference between these two theatre traditions to be that while both 'draw from the common back-cloth of traditional theatrical performances, the literary dramas are quite different in their dramatic vision' which often tend towards 'metaphysical and tragic interpretations of the social and mythic materials' (67). He attributes this to the playwrights' Western education which has exposed them to Western theatre aesthetics and a Western tragic vision. They developed their dramatic and aesthetic visions by fusing their traditional African performance heritage with Western dramatic models. The result is that while 'the works of Ogunde, Ladipo and Olaiya are popular, vital and celebratory, the dramatic creations of these later playwrights are exotic, profound and esoteric' (68).

Part One of this chapter focuses on Clark's use of folklore to articulate an essentially tragic vision. Obafemi identifies two major strands of Clark criticism – the neo-classical and the neo-African. He completely rejects the neo-classical critics who seem not to be 'totally mindful of the extent of the influence of the Ijo metaphysical concepts on Clark's tragic vision, as well as the imprint of the indigenous theatrical forms on his drama' (70). They are, he argues, 'limited in their perception and lose sight of the hybrid nature of Clark's artistic … fusion of Western form with an indigenous theatrical style and themes' (70). The neo-African critics, on the other hand, contend that although Clark's plays are informed by Ijo cultural material, his tragedies have a lot in common with both classical and Elizabethan tragedies. Using *Ozidi*, Obafemi moves away from these earlier critiques to analyse the play's ritual/folklorist structure derived from Clark's Ijo cultural background. This is fruitful since it leaves aside any comparative ideological baggage to concentrate on the play's structure and its effectiveness in expressing Clark's tragic vision.

The book acknowledges Rotimi's attempts to draw tragedy out of the facts of history in *Kurunmi* and *Ovonramwen Nogbaisi*. In the former, Rotimi explores the Ijaye war from the perspective of Kurunmi's role in it. And in the latter, he recreates Benin history and the encounter with the colonizing British forces from the perspective of Ovonramwen Nogbaisi. In both, Obafemi suggests, Rotimi is able to make what were essentially social and communal events into episodes in the personal tragedies of the two protagonists.

But, as Obafemi says of Rotimi's drama, while the general critical response has been mostly favourable, reviewers find his language pedestrian and unsophisticated. This view I agree with, even though Rotimi has on numerous occasions tried to explain his use of language as an attempt to evolve a new English whose phraseology has been tempered with nuances and colouring of Yoruba. But where writers like Chinua Achebe succeed in achieving this domestication of English through a sophisticated colouring, Rotimi is 'over the top', and occasionally borders on the banal.

Obafemi feels that while all the playwrights – both popular and literary – have emphasized the quest for harmony between man and his cosmic environment, only Soyinka has succeeded in evolving a revolutionary vision for society based on traditional African mythology. There are also three strands of Soyinka criticism. The conventional critics concern themselves with the profundity and universalism of Soyinka's drama.

The second group, which he calls the materialists, are consciously ideological and dialectical in their approach and they 'reject as conservative and unprogressive, Soyinka's vision based on animist metaphysics' (119). The materialist critics though, have, in the past few years, produced the most exciting criticism of Soyinka. Jeyifo's analysis of the unspoken class tensions in *The Road* is the most stimulating interpretation of the play that I have read. The third group of critics, represented by the famous troika of Chinweizu, Onwuchekwa and Madubuike, the book calls 'legislators' because, 'their criticism is both prescriptive and declarative'. They accuse Soyinka of not developing a uniquely African aesthetic derived purely from his Yoruba cultural inheritance.

Obafemi identifies a new form of criticism which fully takes 'into consideration both Soyinka's metaphysical and materialist perspectives in evolving a dramatic aesthetic' (122). Taking all these on board, the author sets out to highlight Soyinka's persistent exploration of the potential inherent in myth and ritual to facilitate an understanding of contemporary human behaviour and society. His quest for breaking what he sees as a cycle of human stupidity, errors and tragic history is at the centre of his drama and is why he repeatedly creates heroes who alone are destined and equipped to intervene to stop that cycle on behalf of society.

Obafemi's treatment of individual plays is incisive; especially good is his view of ritual as a technique in Soyinka's plays. He argues that at a deeper level ritual in Soyinka serves as a vehicle of theatrical expression – that it functions as a language, episode arrangement, music and also as a means of emotional and moral interaction between performer and spectator (147). The book extols Soyinka's sophistication as a dramatist, especially his mastery of language and use of other art mediums in the realization of his dramatic structure. Music and dance form the pivot, in conjunction with flashbacks, for character development and story intensification. It is a technique,

> which allows him to move back and forth in time and space to achieve this 'animist interfusion'. The result is the achievement of a dense structure: a complex atmos-phere which invites the audience to build their responses to whatever their minds can grasp. (154)

The final part of this chapter examines Zulu Sofola, Nigeria's first female dramatist whose plays appropriately provide us with the first crop of female protagonists fully developed in their own right and not as foils to their male counterparts, as was hitherto the case. Sofola has been heavily criticised as being conservative and by feminists for her anti-feminism. According to Obafemi, hers is a

> vision grounded more on her abiding conviction of the inviolability of cultural and traditional paradigms, myths, rituals and mores. She expounds the resultant tragic consequences that await defiers and rebels of traditional systems, codes and ethics … (159)

This is evident in the tragic fate of her protagonists in *Wedlock of the Gods*, *King Emene* and *Old Wines are Tasty*. But, whatever is said of her works ideologically, all agree on the theatrical effectiveness of her plays. Adelugba praises her mastery of theatrical language, and others 'her dramaturgic competence and the accessibility of her linguistic mechanics' (160). What I find admirable in Sofola is the structuring of her plays, partic-ularly *The Sweet Trap* in which her skill in dramatic ordering of character and event is most evident. Content and form merge in a delightful theatricality. However, she remains an apostle of old values which individuals defy at their peril and it is in this respect that she is, as Obafemi concludes, a traditionalist steeped in the animist meta-physics of the first generation of Nigerian dramatists.

Chapter Three looks at the 'political' theatre in Nigeria, represented by Osofisan, Sowande, Omotoso and Onwueme. Obafemi argues that the conscious ideological commitment of these dramatists forms the 'significant point of departure' between them and the old breed. Their work urgently addresses contemporary social problems in Nigeria in a manner designed to achieve a mass awareness of the possibility of alterna-tives to decadent contemporary social structures. These writers, the book states, having all been influenced by Soyinka, transcend this influence to fashion a revolutionary aesthetic based on their perception of art as an instrument for social change. However, the danger, as the book rightly cautions, with such socially relevant theatre is that it tends to creak and limp in places (many of the plays, including Obafemi's, are guilty of this). Moreover, this kind of theatre often lacks the philosophical depth which charac-terizes most of the work of the first generation. In comparison to Soyinka's or Clark's depth and mastery of language, Osofisan or Sowande appear shallow and pedestrian. However, their plays are theatrically effective because their simple language and their employment of traditional theatre forms and styles make them easily understandable and emotionally accessible to the average Nigerian audience. Another reason why their theatre is successful is that in 'their effort to achieve a degree of reality of the Nigerian situation on stage', they opt to produce a performance orientated theatre instead of the literary dramas of their predecessors. They also seek to involve their audiences in the action – sometimes the direction of action is dependent on a decision elicited from the audience as in Omotoso's *The Curse* and Osofisan's *Once Upon Four Robbers*. Obafemi sees this as a combination of influences from Soyinka, Brecht and the *avant garde* movement.

Of this generation, Osofisan is the most prolific – certainly the 'most articulate and ambitious in using the subversive potential of the theatre to shape audiences' percep-tions' and consciousness of society. His radicalism lies in the fact that he aims to develop in the spectator a critical consciousness, a questioning attitude and the ability to challenge history, myths and rituals, and not to be dazed by them. He thus employs history or myth or ritual only to subvert them so that the whole superstructure upon which they are built can be exposed.

All the new generation dramatists, according to Obafemi, are committed to a socialist ideology and use theatre to articulate this ideology. Omotoso in *The Curse* and *Shadows in the Horizon* aims to 'open up the society's awareness to a socialist alternative'. His use of 'characterisation, stage objects, mimes and gestures' and, especially, his absurdist caricatures to actualize his social vision is very effective. Sowande, using his philosophy of 'spiritual nationalism', occupies the middle ground between the animist metaphysics of the first generation and the radical iconoclasm of the 'new'. One, however, detects in Obafemi's comments a certain disapproval of Sowande's treatment of myth and his use of ritual symbols and language in *A Sanctus for Women*. Obafemi feels that this persists in later plays thus making him as obscure as Soyinka and Clark. To some extent, Obafemi is right because one finds that some of the weaknesses in Sowande's plays arise because of an untidy marriage between the mytho-poetic and socio-realistic elements of his dramatic aesthetics. This is especially the case in *A Farewell to Babylon* – a play high on conceptualization, but limping in its performative trajectory.

The book sees Onwueme as a latter-day playwright, and one whose topicality, relevance and experimental attitude places her comfortably in the same ideologically committed bracket as Osofisan, Sowande and Omotoso. Three of her plays, *A Hen Too Soon*, *The Broken Calabash*, and the award-winning *Desert Encroaches*, are discussed. She has since written *The Reign of Wazobia, Ban Empty Barn* and *Mirror for Campus*. Obafemi finds the first of the two plays structurally and thematically weak with poorly developed characterization, coupled with an over-zealous enforcement of theme. But he considers *Desert* more accomplished with a mature 'theatrical inventiveness' evidenced in success-ful allegorical symbolism and anti–illusionism while dealing with a difficult and abstract theme.

The book ends with a postscript in which the author re-assesses his earlier views – given that the main bulk of this research was done prior to 1980 – in the light of developments in Nigerian theatre from 1980 onwards. The categorization of 'political', Obafemi acknowledges, has since expanded to include the later Soyinka, Clark and Rotimi, and the generation of playwrights that emerged after Osofisan and his group. The popular travelling theatre tradition has taken on board recent developments in technology; as Obafemi says 'it has retreated from the roads and the stage to appear instead on television and cinema screens' (265). And that is not quite all, for even the earlier themes and concerns with 'socio-cosmic harmony' have made way for a 'certain animist and mytho-magical escapism' in the video and film dramas of the eighties and nineties. I must note that at no point in the discussion does the book show any concern for the danger to live theatre which this surrender to technology entails.

For the first generation of dramatists, the reality of neo-colonialism and post-colonialism has compelled them to re-evaluate their earlier concerns and commitment to 'issues of cultural nationalism, race-retrieval and the general ideology of liberal humanism to engage in topical, politically committed dramas' (269). The result is a narrowing of the difference between them and the second generation. The latter have, in conjunction with the newer breed, gone on to perfect their dramatic skills and idioms. Writers like Osofisan now reveal 'a sobering, reflective and somewhat compromised approach to dialectical materialism as an alternative vision to both the metaphysical mythopoesis and bourgeois reformist standpoints' (273).

But for certain mistakes – such as very loose sentence structure, spelling errors and choice of words which at best were mild irritants to flow and at worst obfuscants to overall coherence and meaning – this a very timely book, the first comprehensive gaze at contemporary Nigerian theatre. Its strength is its identification of the trends and aesthetic strands of Nigerian theatre. In doing this, Obafemi is able to provide a very valuable guide to Nigerian theatrical culture. Analyses of playwrights and plays is both fresh and competent. The book shows a writer who knows his subject very well and whose passion for theatre is in no doubt at all.

Osita Okagbue

Karin Barber (ed.), *Readings in African Popular Culture*
Oxford: James Currey and Bloomington & Indianapolis: Indiana University Press, 1997, 192 pp.
ISBN 0-85255-236-X £12.95

Karin Barber, John Collins & Alain Ricard, *West African Popular Theatre*
Bloomington & Indianapolis: Indiana University Press and Oxford: James Currey, 1997, 310 pp.
ISBN 0-85255-244-0 £14.95 ISBN 0-85255-245-9 £40.00 (cloth)

'It would be … unfortunate', Michael Etherton said in 1975, 'if the literary theatre became the main criterion within Africa, particularly in the minds of those dispensing patronage' (1975: 5). He was pointing to one of the major deficiencies which Africanist intellectuals displayed towards performing arts during the 'pioneer' period of African criticism in the 1960s and '70s – an obsession with eurocentric, literary theatre forms, and an almost total disregard of the performing arts which were actually popular with 'the people'.

In recent years a considerable body of academic work has been produced which has attempted to redress the problem Etherton observed. Ground-breaking books on regional forms of popular African theatre by Ebun Clarke, K.N. Bame, Biodun Jeyifo, David Coplan and Zakes Mda, have been supplemented by several comparative surveys such as those by Jane Plastow, Penina Mlama, Christopher Kamlongera and myself.

In addition, however, there has been a considerable body of localized and often specialized primary research into a wide variety of African creative arts. Africanist scholar, Karin Barber, particularly in her seminal, frequently cited 1987 article, 'African Popular Arts', has played a key role in advancing a theoretical framework on which much of this empirical research could be built. Barber is also central to the two books under review, as a co-author of *West African Popular Theatre* (WAPT) and editor of (as well as contributor to) *Readings in African Popular Culture* (RAPC).

The two books, though sharing many aspects of the 'Barber approach' to African performing arts, have quite different purposes. RAPC is a collection of articles on a wide variety of oral, musical, graphic or performing arts from different parts of sub-Saharan Africa. In addition to its interest to the general reader, the book is presumably intended as a collection of sources for students of African performing arts. A few of the articles in RAPC have been specially commissioned, but most are reprints of previously published work. WAPT, on the other hand, consists of much more extensive, specially commissioned analyses of specific West African forms of popular theatre, linked to translations of three play texts, which are reproduced in full.

One of the major attractions of RAPC is its extraordinary eclecticism, both in its subject matter and in its style of presentation (including some useful photographs). The book is structured around six broad general topics, though the categories are highly permeable; it is easy to imagine the articles being re-arranged according to totally different principles.

The first section, 'Views of the Field', with an Introduction by Barber herself and articles by Ulf Hannerz and Johannes Fabian, focuses on theoretical issues interrogating terms such as 'popular', 'mass', 'tradition', 'indigenous' and 'authentic'. The boundaries separating African from non-African and the nature of hybridity/syncretism in Africa are put under scrutiny. There is also a wide-ranging discussion of the way popular arts relate to more formal instruments for examining African reality, such as economics, kinship, religion and politics.

Section 2, with its fairly self-explanatory title, 'Oral Tradition Revisited' provides innovative anthropological or ideological analyses of music and song, or in the case of Mamadou Diawara's article on Mande griots, examines the impact of electronic media on oral traditions.

Section 3, 'Social History, Social Criticism and Interpretation' is a very broad category which looks at music, literature, theatre and painting, with several articles, such as Pongweni on Zimbabwean Chimurenga music and Vail and White's history of a Mozambican plantation song, illustrating the important role art played in the struggle against colonialism. Others discuss art's role in popular negotiations of class, ethnicity or gender in post-colonial Africa.

Section 4, 'Women in Popular Culture', contains articles which address the depiction of women by both male and female artists, linking gender stereotypes to wider processes of modernization, class-formation and the anti-colonial struggle.

The fifth section, 'Little Genres of Everyday Life' seems to have been designed as a catch-all category for articles which could not conveniently fit into the other sections. It contains two papers on popular urban folklore in Nigeria, and a brilliant dissection by Achille Mbembe of Cameroonian post-colonial politics, as seen through the lens of newspaper cartoons.

The last section, 'The Local and the Global' contains two articles about South African performance, one by Ulf Hannerz on Sophiatown, and one by Veit Erlmann about South African music's impact on and reception by 'Northern' consumers. Despite their apparently parochial point-of-entry, these two articles provide an appropriate conclusion, in that they refer back to some of the key theoretical issues raised by Barber's Introduction, in particular, the complex cultural articulations linking centre and periphery which mark the development of modern, popular, artistic forms in Africa.

Despite the appearance of almost frenzied eclecticism displayed by RAPC, there are some common preoccupations. An attitude which almost all the articles project, either explicitly or implicitly, is a distrust of elitist (especially academic elitist) conceptualization. A typical example is provided by Werner Graebner's article on the artistry of popular Tanzanian musician, Remmy Ongala. Defending Ongala from attack by Tanzanian intellectuals that his songs 'supposedly strengthen a passive outlook on life', Graebner suggests that: '[The] critics are ... too ... concerned with transparency and linearity of discourse, overlooking the possibility of ruptures, multiple meanings and interpretations, the juxtaposition of different topics in a song' (Barber 1997: 114–15).

Similarly, Jane Bryce defends, against accusations of 'escapism', romantic fiction written by African women (and some men): 'In spite of prevalent critical attitudes of disapprobation, many of the texts categorised as popular/trivial do, in fact, subvert their own genre, against all expectations and the requirements of the formula' (Barber 1997: 122).

Such distrust of preconceived academic categories is similar to that which emerged in British Cultural Studies during the 1960s, in reaction to a Leavisite emphasis on 'discrimination'. Barber refers to British Cultural Studies in her Introduction and it is perhaps more than a coincidence that its main academic focus was the University of Birmingham, which also hosts Karen Barber's current academic home, the Centre for West African Studies.

The recent academic approach to Cultural Studies in Africa is, however, far from being a mere transplant. The main difference between Western approaches and the emergent Africanist cultural studies is that the latter is able to base itself on an anthropologically derived revalorization of the 'oral' as a vigorous source for African popular culture. Several articles in RAPC suggest that literary or graphic cultural forms based on Western elite models have failed to extend strong roots in African soil. Instead, complex popular forms have emerged based on indigenous, oral models, but synthesized with a variety of occidental influences. For this syncretic popular art, the critical tools and criteria which Africanist academics inherited from Euro-American sources are largely inadequate. As Barber eloquently explains:

> When the distinction between 'folk', 'traditional' 'popular' and 'mass' or that between 'high' and 'low' culture is transplanted to Africa, then, the already porous and ambiguous classifications seem to turn around on their axes and reconfigure themselves into an unstable, almost unusable paradigm. (Barber 1997: 4)

The articles in RAPC provide important examples of the reorientation both in subject matter and methodologies required to build on indigenous foundations a new paradigm capable of supporting academic approaches to syncretic African popular culture.

Another common theme running through many articles in RAPC is a resistance to simplistic ideological interpretation of 'texts'. The two examples above (Graebner and Bryce) illustrate not only a distrust of academic criticism, but also of the demands by political or academic apparatchiks for African popular artists to provide instrumental weapons in an anti-imperialist struggle.

In article after article the researchers comment on the way subaltern African artists construct critiques of dominant culture, not by direct polemic or open appeals to mass solidarity, but through what Barber, in her article on Yoruba Opera, calls 'chinks of dissent' (99). Such slivers of resistance are to be decoded in metaphors, allusions or a mode of character patterning whereby moral condemnation of oppression is expressed through displaced or vicarious stereotyping.

Vail and White, for example, in their analysis of 'Paiva', a woman's work song from the Portuguese sugar estates in Sena, Mozambique, emphasize that the song never 'emerged into a strike or open rebellion', but allowed the 'apparently docile' workers to preserve 'in an image or slogan or even a curse one small region of the mind which refuses to capitulate completely' (Barber 1997: 62). More pessimistically, Achille Mbembe describes the way newspaper cartoons provide an artistic correlative for the 'mutual brutalisation' which constitutes recent Cameroonian politics, with oppressor and oppressed locked in a circular dependency: 'The hallucinated subject only sees, hears and believes power at the price of an original arbitrariness that those dominating and those dominated must constantly reiterate' (Barber 1997: 161). Mbembe notes that the cartoons are both commentaries on and an expression of neo-colonial hegemony, but do not provide any clues about how to 'break the demon'.

Even in a context where cultural forms are linked to active resistance, as in the Zimbabwean Chimurenga songs, Alex Pongweni is at pains to refer to a Shona artistic 'predilection for innuendo' rather than 'direct statement' (Barber 1997: 66), a subtle approach which song-creators continue to find useful for critiquing the post-independence ZANU PF Government.

The only article which provides a blatantly militant exception to this emphasis on African popular culture's ambiguity and its oblique approach to protest, is Ngugi wa Thiongo's piece on 'Women in Cultural Work'. This not only describes the role women played in the Kamiriithu theatre process, but also ends with a clarion call for cultural struggle against the undemocratic culture of the Moi regime in Kenya.

The sore thumb exceptional tone of Ngugi's article points to a significant lacuna in RAPC. There is a large body of recent cultural theory which has strategized about ways African popular art can be modified and/or mobilized for purposes of political or socio-economic struggle. Barber does refer to this tradition in her Introduction, but there are no articles by authors like Stephen Chifunyise, Ndumbe Eyoh, Ross Kidd, Robert McClaren or Zakes Mda to support the Ngugi article as examples of popular culture mobilized against state hegemony. Given that RAPC is likely to become the main source book for African cultural studies during the next decade, I am a little concerned that its relative neglect of what Barber calls 'the intervention of committed activism' (Barber 1997: 2) might lead the new discipline into a purely reflective, theoretical and analytical approach. There is a danger that it might retrace the direction of British Cultural Studies, which, as Tomaselli *et al.* point out, has moved from the combative role it assumed in the 1960s under the leadership of Stuart Hall, to a more quietist stance where it 'has divorced itself from the actual politics of culture' (Tomaselli *et al.* 1996: xiv).

A far less serious problem that I encountered with the book derives from the mixture of previously published articles and those specially commissioned for RAPC. Some of the papers, such as Ngugi's on Kamiriithu, and Horn's closely researched 1986 survey of South African theatre, are clearly dated, whereas others, such as Diawara's account of Mande orality transposed for the radio, or Mbembe on Cameroonian cartoons, are much more recent. In some cases, research dating from an earlier period has been modified for present circumstances. For example, Pongweni's analysis of the Chimurenga songs, derived from his 1982 monograph, *Songs that Won the Liberation War*, has been updated in the last paragraphs, to show the post-independence transformations of Chimurenga songs.

I have no problem with RAPC's use of articles from an earlier period as a kind of frozen illustration of a particular era's ideology, analytic preferences or strategic methodology. I feel it might have been useful, however, if Barber could have provided a brief guide, which set the articles in their historical context, for the benefit of cursory browsers too lazy to closely read the acknowledgements.

These criticisms can, in no way, however, diminish the enormous value of *Readings in African Popular Culture* in bringing together such a heterogeneous selection of nuanced, well-researched, thought-provoking articles from the emerging field of African Cultural Studies.

West African Popular Theatre is a book which focuses much more closely than RAPC on a specific genre (theatre) and region (West Africa). Since there are only three authors, Karin Barber on Yoruba Opera, and John Collins and Alain Ricard on Concert Party from Ghana and Togo respectively, the book is able to have a more homogenized style and format.

The book is structured around three translations (by WAPT's three authors) of play texts: *Orphan Do Not Glance* (Awisia Yi Wo Ani) by the Ghanaian group, the Jaguar Jokers, *The African Girl from Paris* (L'africaine de Paris) by Happy Star of Lomé, and *The Secret is Out* (Gbangba dEkun) by Lere Paimo's Eda Theatre Company. Each text is preceded by an extended introduction which provides invaluable descriptions of the plays' creators, modes of theatre organization, performance conditions, and aesthetic analysis of the specific oral performances from which the written texts derive. In addition, there is an extensive jointly authored Introduction, which traces the theatre forms' histories and their broad socio-economic contexts.

Despite this homogeneous approach there are considerable differences between the three sections, most obviously in the play texts themselves, but also, to some extent, in the analytic approaches of the three researchers. The most noticeable difference in the play texts is between the two Concert Party plays. *Orphan Do Not Glance* is an episodic, rambling play, built on melodramatic, stereotyped characterization, and frequently punctuated by songs, dances, Highlife music and comic or sentimental stage business. By contrast, *The African Girl from Paris* is a much more smoothly constructed linear play, relying heavily on quick-fire dialogue and fairly subtle, psychologically rounded characterization.

The contrast is no doubt partly attributable to the tastes of the two researchers. *Orphan Do Not Glance* provides a perfect illustration of Collins' empirical preoccupation with theatrical synaesthesia, the integration of dialogue, costumes, make-up, music, song, dance and audience participation. Ricard, while not neglecting such aspects, seems much more interested in placing *The African Girl from Paris* within a theoretical (even philosophical) paradigm which helps unlock the problematic of First World/ Third World psycho-social dependency.

The translators struggle bravely with the linguistic complexity characteristic of West African popular theatre. For example, *The African Girl from Paris* retains French as the dialogue for Monique, the Afro-French title character who speaks no Ewe, while using English as a correlative for the original Ewe.

The translation problems in *The Secret is Out* are perhaps even more daunting, since English has to be employed not only as an equivalent of Yoruba, but also for very different Yoruba registers/dialects associated with the life-style of, among others, sophisticated nouveaux riches, urban thieves and the practitioners of traditional Yoruba religion. For a non-Yoruba reader it is difficult to decide whether the juxtaposition of American colloquialisms like 'good on you, baby' and the archaic, 'ye gods!' represents a contradiction in dialogue style, or is simply an accurate manifestation of a relentlessly shifting set of Yoruba argots.

For all three plays it is necessary for the translators to provide extensive notes, not only for linguistic terms (such as loan words from other languages), but also to explain potentially mystifying details of the socio-economic and cultural context. The extensive notes are an indication of the wide distance separating the local culture within which the plays were created and the assumed 'international' culture of the average, anglophone reader. If for no other reason this book is indispensable for its provision of playtexts from genres which, despite their apparently peripheral nature in global terms, have been extensively discussed, yet where almost none of the texts themselves have been previously published.

There are many other reasons, however, for recommending WAPT. Although previous books like Bame's *Come to Laugh. African Traditional Theatre in Ghana* and Jeyifo's *The Yoruba Popular Travelling Theatre* of Nigeria, provide excellent surveys of Ghanaian Concert Party and Yoruba Opera respectively, nowhere else is it possible to obtain such detailed in-depth information about specific conditions of play-creation, administration, rehearsal and performance, linked to psycho-social, ideological and aesthetic analyses.

In the process, the authors are able to dispel several existing preconceptions and oversimplifications. I find the book particularly useful, for example, in its critique of the stereotype promulgated by several theatre critics (including myself) that West African popular theatre is predominantly oral, in contrast to the literary nature of 'art theatre'. The authors (particularly Barber) are able to show that the relationships between oral and literary creativity in West African popular theatre are ambiguous.

Many popular theatre 'dramatists' are quite well-educated and see no major gulf between oral and literary methods of creating a text. Thus, even when a play is created entirely through discussion and improvisation, the actors perform to a clearly understood scenario, which Barber calls a 'virtual text' (Barber *et al.* 1997: xiii). Barber sees Lere Paimo, even when he encourages a collective, improvisatory mode of play-creation, as fully imbricated in 'the mystique of literacy ... part of a larger image of the theatre as a modern, progressive, educational force' (Barber *et al.* 1997: 195). Similarly, Ricard envisages Concert Party as belonging to a 'mixed orality which coexists with written sources and notes' (Barber *et al.* 1997: 144).

Parallel to the ambiguity the theatre practitioners display towards literacy and education, is the self-questioning role the researchers assume themselves. A refreshing feature of WAPT is that the authors do not attempt to hide their status as white outsiders behind an Olympian position of scopic omniscience. In a very helpful introduction Barber focuses on the combined difficulties and privileges of the authors' 'outsider' status as an entry point into their conceptualization of West African popular theatre. Each author has a specific entry point: Barber as researcher and actor in *The Secret is Out*, Collins as musician in *Orphan Do Not Glance*, and Ricard as an ethnographic film-maker of *The African Girl from Paris*.

Barber suggests that the urban, syncretic nature of West African popular theatre, mediating both indigenous and imported traditions, makes it easily accessible to foreigners. This permeable neotradition has 'produced an innovative hybrid opportunistic mode of expression in which the incorporation and containment of novelty is a constitutive feature' (Barber *et al.* 1997: ii). Provided they respect the form's features and procedures, Western participant researchers are welcome, because their association with modernity is easily incorporated into the aesthetics of performance in ways which are attractive to audiences.

The authors' awareness of potential 'outsider/insider' contradictions opens the book up to issues of 'World Theatre', which make it of interest to a wider public than the parochial-sounding book title might attract. In the last 20 years there has been increasing fascination in the way 'First' and 'Third' World theatre modes can interact and cross-fertilize, especially in the work of such theatre practitioners as Jerzy Grotowski, Peter Brook and Eugenio Barba. A major criticism which 'Third' world critics such as Wole Soyinka (1988), Homi Babha and Rustom Bharucha make of such hybrid theatre is that it is based on the power wielded by well known occidental practitioners who have little knowledge of the target 'Third' world theatre forms, but who appropriate superficial forms and devices to vivify the jaded conventions of Western theatre. (See also Williams [1991] for a useful collection of essays on this debate.)

The work of Barber, Collins and Ricard cannot be easily accused of such exploitative tactics. They are acutely aware of the benefits they derive from their interaction with Yoruba Opera and Concert Party, but it is clear that the theatre groups with which they engage also derive some benefit from the cultural exchange, while retaining the vigour and identity of the original theatrical conventions. The authors of WAPT offer an alternative model of cultural interaction, which is far less opportunistic than much of that displayed in current Western academic and media practice.

The self-reflexive interest in cultural boundaries shown by the authors of WAPT overlaps with many of the preoccupations displayed by authors in RAPC. In both books participant research proves a particularly useful tool for crossing the boundaries between popular art and academia, and, even more importantly, for mapping the ever-shifting, sometimes virtually meaningless boundaries between such categories as indigenous/imported, rural/urban, oral/literary and popular/elitist.

I believe it is possible to see RAPC and WAPT as symptomatic of a new paradigm, in which academics accept popular cultural forms on their own terms, rather than clinging either to imposed and largely irrelevant Western criteria, or to an equally artificial, exotic and reified alterity. The two books provide essential source material to help understand this paradigm and to use it as a basis not only for the analysis of popular African culture but possibly also as an inspiration for its practice.

David Kerr

REFERENCES

Barber, Karin, 1987, 'Popular arts in Africa', *African Studies Review*, 30, 3: 1–78. Etherton, Michael (ed.), 1975, *African Plays for Playing* (London: Heinemann African Writers Series). Soyinka, Wole, 1988, *Art, Dialogue and Outrage* (Ibadan, New Horn). Tomaselli, K., Muller, J. and Shepperson, A. 1996, 'Negotiations, transitions and uncertainty principles: *Critical Arts* in the worlds of the post', *Critical Arts*, 10, 2: 1–xxii. Williams, David (ed.), 1991, *Peter Brook and the Mahabarata: Critical Perspectives* (London: Routledge).

Mary Karooro Okurut, *The Curse of the Sacred Cow*
Kampala: Fountain Publishers, 1994, 65 pp. ISBN 997-002-034X, £4.95
(Fountain Publishers are distributed in the UK and US by African Books Collective, 27 Park End St, Oxford, OX1 1HU)

Steve Chimombo, *Sister! Sister!*
Zomba: WASI Publications, 1995

Kriben Pillay, *Looking for Muruga*
Durban: Asoka Theatre Publications, 1995 ISBN 1-874994-02-1

Two men in tight embrace drown themselves. The ultimate testimony of their friendship, so they say – and the ending of Okurut's play – because one of them, Mutumo, has
lost wives, cattle and homestead. What used to be prosperous fields are now covered by
a shimmering lake, due to the disobedience of Mutumo's spouses. Instead of giving the
sacred cow Kajeru a proper burial on her demise, the homestead followed the youngest
wife, Nyabwangu, and feasted on Kajeru's meat in the owner's absence. Mutumo
returns to find himself bereaved of everything but his life. In desperation he turns to his
friend Mwamba, first in disguise but is soon discovered, and together they revisit the
fateful site. For Mwamba, the lake is a burial place which symbolizes the loss of
Mutumo's manhood:

> My brother,
> What manhood
> Do you now speak of?
> What manner of man
> Are you ? [...]
> Let us not deceive ourselves,
> We are men no longer [...]
> When all our pride
> All that we were
> Lies at the bottom
> Of this water. (59)

   Ayeeeh, let us wail, for the loss of lives and the link between Mutuma's property and
his manhood. What kind of men are you indeed, Mutumo and Mwamba, if, in the face
of such calamity, suicide is your only option; an escape from reflection, imputation and
possible shame? And what kind of friend is this who urges his comrade to drown
himself, who is prepared to leave his own responsibilities behind, to have his 'clay
dissolved' 'Together with yours [Mutumo] / At the bottom of the lake '(64) so that 'we
find great happiness together / In the next world' (65)? Is that friendship?
   On the one hand, Mary Karooro Okurut's *The Curse of the Sacred Cow* is a simple
morality play, based on a legend from Western Uganda. The rules of the head of the
family are disobeyed, hence the family must drown in torrential rain, including those
who tried to observe the rules. It is, so the blurb instructs us, one of the ways to keep
order in society. The Law of the Father has to be followed or disaster ensues. No doubts
are left about the roles in this drama: Man embodies reason and command. Wife
number one knows her place and carries herself with the dignity of a 'woman proper'
and the mother-of-the-homestead. (Yet, she is not spared in the final disaster.) Wife
number three is the exact opposite – impetuous, nonsensical and unwilling to fit into
the place assigned to her. Instead of being the dutiful youngest wife, she tries to occupy

the place of man, signified by Mutumo's stool, from where she eagerly commands in his absence. This impudence cannot but end in tragedy. Wife number two shuttles between these two poles of womanhood, an insecure and cantankerous character who eventually succumbs to Nyabwangu's meaty temptations. What remains is the blood friendship of the two men, situated above all petty women's quarrels, dignified and committed until its very end – at least one could think so.

On second reading, however, the text perpetually deconstructs itself and the purported moral values begin to crumble. There is, for example, a homoerotic connotation towards the drawn out ending of the play – 'My brother, / I can only live / When my bones / Are lying next to yours / In close embrace [...] / Then I will know / Great happiness' (62) – and the outcome suggests that this form of male bonding, like the insubordination of Nyabwangu, also goes against the Law of Father. Hence it has to end in the lake. It also transpires that Mutumo is utterly unequipped to cope with the chores necessary for survival. When, in disguise, he seeks work with his friend Mwamba, he cannot fulfil a single task except one commonly performed by children. Perhaps his ineptitude is not only a sign of his noble status, it also makes him unfit for a life on his own, a life without the attention of wives, dancers and servants?

The above reading is, I admit, somewhat sardonic, but the text does indeed undermine its own moral intentions. Narratives of lakes and disaster are quite common in Eastern Africa and have also been utilized as material for drama in the English language. *Simbi Nyaima* (1982) by the Kenyan Asenath Bole Odaga is one such example. However, the difference between these two works is that Okurut neither offers theatrical challenge – the play is a linear adaptation of a folktale for a proscenium stage and loses the interactive vigour one might attribute to the 'original' story – nor does it transcend encrusted roles. Here, women are 'the source of all evil' and men occupy positions of unchallenged authority. There is also no reward, or at least mercy, for the obedient family members in the play and not once are the master's own actions questioned. The play thus cements a 'traditional' *status quo* which does not take into account possible gender and power dynamics, let alone dare to envision some form of transformation in (Ugandan) society.

Oral materials and their performance modes are not static. They can adapt older 'texts' to contemporary issues, as documented in the neighbourhood theatre of Kampala's suburbs, for example, and are thus capable of continuously remaking themselves. *The Curse of the Sacred Cow* is, however, a fossilization of stereotypes, where obedience to traditional authority is supreme and any attempted challenge is pilloried. Considering that the country has a long history of drama and performance in schools and educational institutions and that, in all probability, these will constitute the prime audiences of scripted English language plays (most plays are performed in Luganda), *The Curse* is moralistic in a conservative, even reactionary manner, without being genuinely thought-provoking for its audience. It also lacks the humour or innovative spirit found in other plays written by the small number of female dramatists in Uganda.

In contrast, *Sister! Sister!* by the Malawian Steve Chimombo is a play of a different sort. This short play, which was first inspired by the 'National Day of the Girl' and grew out of an epic poem, *Breaking the Beadstrings*, is an earnest attempt at tackling the tribulations of a young teenager, Mwali (meaning: uninitiated girl), on her way to womanhood. Infused with the spirit of the women's liberation movement, especially by her sister Chiphetsa who is an academic in town, Mwali attempts to rebel against reactionary customs and male domination. Above all, she is opposed to the impending initiation ceremony, *dzoma*, and the alleged misconduct of her boy-friend Mchanda. Breaking the traditional beadstrings collected and worn by women throughout their life seems the appropriate means to set herself on the road of freedom. Between Mwali and her oldest sister, Namagetsi, a heated argument evolves which is a fairly even-handed exchange of progressive and customary opinions. Mwali attacks with an antagonistic mixture of feminist and Christian tenets; she is against the determination of her life by restricting 'traditional' patriarchal patterns but fervently sticks to rigid puritanical maxims. Namagetsi, unlike her sister, is a woman firmly grounded in the customs of her people. This rootedness is literally inscribed onto her body in the form of beautifying tattoos. To Mwali, however, they are just another form of 'encasement' (12). The young girl is critical of certain practices supposed to help her turn into a fully-fledged woman, and at times quite rightly so. For example, she points out potential hazards when the *fisi* (literally: hyena, here: a ritual male figure) deflowers all girls on their initiation. Yet, she does so mainly for ethical reasons, not on medical grounds, and thus weakens her case quite considerably.

Throughout the dialogue of the two sisters Chimombo cleverly plays with the concepts of old-fashioned attitudes and presumed progressiveness. In Mwali's eyes, for example, Namagetsi is the oppressed and antiquated woman, bound by 'A lifetime of pots and plates by the fireplace, mortar and pestle under a tree' (11). Namagetsi, on the other hand, sees her work as necessary for the survival of the community and mocks the rigid, 'old fashioned' (3) sexual morals of her younger sister. She also knows how to manipulate custom for her own benefit and does not feel at all 'threatened by man' (8).

The audience or reader soon realizes that the emerging tensions cannot be neatly solved, that both arguments have their points, but that they are also limited in their vision. Namagetsi cannot look beyond her familiar life, yet there is equally no doubt about Mwali's vision of liberation being thwarted. For she merely parrots the mottos of her other sister, using words too big for her little mouth: 'The women are as good as dead, if they don't realise that the men are killing them mentally, crippling them psychologically and deforming them physically, as Chiphetsa says' (8). 'And she says women should smash, sweep and smother anyone who is going to block our progress to self-love, self-respect and self-determination' (11–12). It is sad that, again, feminist thoughts are reduced to such hackneyed, stereotyped slogans – 'Chiphetsa said we can do without man' (25) – whereas Namagetsi's 'traditional' ideas are rendered with much more grace and subtlety. It is, after all, an unbalanced verbal battle that is fought here, for the original representative of 'feminism' is conspicuously absent throughout the play and moreover abandons Mwali when she needs her support. 'Self-love' and 'self-determination' are thus unfavourably juxtaposed with the communal values and genuine concern of Namagetsi.

Deserted by her intellectual sister Chiphetsa, who, because of an international women's conference, fails to take her to town before the start of the *dzoma*, Mwali turns to her oldest sister for guidance. Then the surprising happens. Although Namagetsi encourages Mwali to undergo initiation, equivalent to the acceptance of the 'traditional' way of life, she too seems suddenly to have a need for liberation. In contrast to Chiphetsa, she decides on another approach, tackling the matter from within the system she was born into: 'You have another lesson, little sister. We can only liberate ourselves by accepting the beads and tattooes [sic] as part of our womanhood. We can only liberate ourselves by using the same beads and tattooes as weapons to fight our slavery' (27).

Elsewhere, Chimombo described his play as making 'suggestions on how women could liberate themselves from male bondage' (Chimbombo and Chimbombo 1996: 189). The sudden twist to Namagetsi's stance is somewhat amazing and her final vision – stringing human (woman) beads so that the whole world is 'joined by beads in a universal bond of womanhood' (28) – abstract and unconvincing. So is her final song, similar to the one with which she opened the play, yet this time not inviting but refusing man. Whether Namagetsi too has subscribed to the fallacious notion which equals women's liberation with the absence of men (she is not married and prevents herself getting pregnant) or whether it is meant to express a deeper understanding of her situation remains nebulous and unclear.

In the given context, however, the play has been timely and relevant. *Sister! Sister!* was produced at a time when protests against molestation, rape and violence against women swept over Malawian campuses, while proponents of feminism were subjected to student attacks. The play thus hit and still hits the raw nerve of gender issues, a hot topic not only in Malawian society, but important to other African countries as well, regardless of the play's cultural specificities. It also seems to signify the emergence of a new generation of plays which, after decades of socially passive works due to the stifling activities of the Malawi Censorship Board, addresses a topic of immediate concern to the community. Moreover it marks Chimombo's return to play-writing in the English language after some 20 years, though one might wonder whether an adaptation in Chichewa might not be more appropriate to reach a wider Malawian public, especially outside the urban areas.

Despite its ambiguities, *Sister! Sister!* will provide the audience with both entertainment and food for thought, without being in danger of becoming over-didactic or boring. The small cast invites touring the play, as does the fact that it will work equally well in intimate or larger spaces. Useful for a non-Chichewa-speaking company are the translation of songs at the end, though the glossary is somewhat incomplete and should be redone for a reprint.

The most complex play under review is Kriben Pillay's *Looking for Muruga*. An idiosyncratic pastiche of stand-up comedy, Indian dance drama and Beckett's Theatre of the Absurd, it is a piece which contrasts with the linearity of the other plays, exploring the situation of South African Indians, and especially of Hindu communities, in their multifarious, changing manifestations. The intricate quilt of personal stories and South African history – above all the Indian-African intercultural experience – combined with a plethora of conjuring tricks, dance rehearsals and crude jokes is sewn together by the story of Sherwin, a teacher and aspiring writer, who, after some ten years' absence, returns to the bar-cum-brothel he used to frequent as a theatre student. Now he is looking for the then waiter of the place, Muruga, in order to turn his life into a play. From there on we are taken on a journey through the lives of the protagonists by means of play-acting, variety show and flashback techniques. We experience the flow of time, its change and stability – or the illusion of both – in the perpetual pursuit of (self-) recognition:

[after a comic routine by Muruga]
Sherwin You were just like Muruga, I can't believe it!
Muruga I am Muruga.
Sherwin I mean the other Muruga.
Muruga Maybe all waiters are Murugas. [...]
Sherwin But he wasn't just an ordinary waiter. He did what you just did. He was an entertainer. He gave us something special on those Saturday nights. He made us laugh. (6-7)

Muruga has the role of the jester in the play, the Komali (or clown) of the Therokoothu, the Six-Foot Dance, a long, dramatic recital from Tamil scriptures which Pillay draws on recurrently. Muruga is the implicit Master of Ceremonies who guides the direction of the action, who teaches Indian dance to the African student Dante and his personal philosophy – a capricious mix of the religious and the profane – to Sherwin. He is rude, risible, serious and provocative, an 'extra-'ordinary being, yet Everyman at the same time, slipping into any role with admirable ease, behind whose masks he will always be Muruga – a person never to be fathomed in his entirety.

> **Muruga** Even when we are grown up, there's still many of us. My right name is Subramaniam, but my calling name is Muruga. And in the Cape they know me as China.
>
> **Sherwin** But no matter what's your name, you are still the same person.
>
> **Muruga** I also thought that. But when I was with my mother I was always Subramaniam. I was different. I felt different. Then the old Muruga was different. He was the joller, the fella you used to know. And China, he was for the Cape. Even spoke differently. [...]
>
> **Sherwin** And this Muruga?
>
> **Muruga** I can't tell you.
>
> **Sherwin** Why not?
>
> **Muruga** Because it's easier to see yourself when you look back. (22, 27)

Looking for Muruga, then, is about the never-ending quest for identity, an exploration of the human condition in one particular context. It is about personal identity, but also about the (collective) identity of South Africans of Indian descent. (Muruga, after all, is the boy-god of Hindu mythology who travelled around the world and can hence be read as a signifier for the Indian diaspora.) Not only do we meet the educated Sherwins and the menial Murugas, there are also the Indian upper-class ladies – the 'kuggles' – the beautiful, yet blemished Ranis, and the Africans who are part of their world. Pillay tackles Indian and Indian-African relations with a liberal portion of self-critique. Whereas Sherwin blames race riots or differences in social and economic levels on the now officially abolished apartheid system, trying to bring salvation with another – Marxist – ideology, Muruga believes in the responsibility of the individual and is prepared to address the community's share of the blame: class, caste, and inter-ethnic racism. The tragic story of Charlie, an African who worked for Muruga's family and 'could sing the Tamil numbers like a born Tamil' (37), then links the retrospection back to the frame, to Danté, 'Another Muruga' (42) and, as he himself proclaims, the 'token Black' (48) of the play. Nonetheless, he is the bridge along which an intercultural communication, perhaps even cross-fertilization, could be envisioned.

Looking for Muruga is a play without a closure. It's numerous layers unfold only bit by bit, and many will reveal themselves fully only to an insider audience because of their explicitly cultural or religious references. It is also a play which probes the state of what has come to be known as 'Indic' theatre in South Africa (a term strongly evocative of post-apartheid 'P.C.' but, I was informed, coined and preferred by the artists under discussion). It is a work which focuses on the attempt to write a play about a theatrically under-represented community. As such it raises many questions without offering an immediate answer, but it is certainly a well-crafted experiment in the theatre history of the 'new' South Africa.

Christine Matzke

REFERENCE

Chimombo, Steve and Moira Chimombo, 1996, *The Culture of Democracy: Language, Literature, the Arts & Politics in Malawi, 1992–1994* (Zomba: WASI Publications).

Don Rubin (ed.), *The World Encyclopedia of Contemporary Theatre. Volume 3. Africa*
London and New York: Routledge, 1997, 426 pp. (illus.) ISBN 0-415-05931-3 £95.00 (cloth)

The African volume of *The World Encyclopedia of Contemporary Theatre* (WECT) covers
very much the same ground already covered by Martin Banham's *The Cambridge Guide
to World Theatre* (1988), and specifically Banham *et al*'s *The Cambridge Guide to African
and Caribbean Theatre* (1994). But it differs from the two by not giving special treatment
to individual dramatists. It rather concentrates on providing a detailed political as well as
theatrical history of individual countries. Unlike the guides, *The World Encyclopedia* does
not concentrate on literary or scripted theatre, but rather attempts to provide information on diverse theatre forms and styles including traditional forms such as storytelling,
dance theatre, rituals, festivals, masks and puppets, theatre for young audiences, theatre
design, theatre companies, directors and general theatre/performance scholarship and
publishing. As the general editor, Don Rubin, points out, what the volume attempts to
do is conduct 'a broad-based comparative cross-cultural study' of a 'wide range of
national theatrical activity on a country by country basis and from a specifically national
stand point'.

What is interesting about the volume is the format used to present its material. The
volume opens with a series of introductory essays by different scholars on specific aspects
of African theatrical performances. The first of these is a general introduction by Rubin
in which he explains the genesis and scope of the WECT and provides a guide on how
to use them by explaining the thirteen section headings under which each national entry
is made . The really reassuring aspect of the project is the fact that the national entries are
provided in the main by scholars who are nationals of these countries, thus providing in
the volume 'a national view point' on theatre in each country and thus answering
questions such as :

> What ... does Romanian theatre look like to a Romanian in this post-modern
> world? Canadian theatre to a Canadian? What is of import to an Australian about his
> or her own theatre? To a Senegalese? A Brazilian? A Vietnamese? An Egyptian? ...
> What is the self-perception of theatre professionals in the new Germany where two
> totally different systems were uncomfortably reunited as the 1990s began?(4)

However, the project's 'international, intercultural working definition' of theatre as
a 'created event, usually based on text, executed by live performers and taking place
before an audience in a specially defined setting'(8) is problematic since it reinforces the
common confusion in much theatre scholarship between text and script. Rubin seems
to suggest that the text is a basis for theatrical performance when in actual fact a text only
comes into being in the act of performance. On the other hand, a script can provide a
basis for theatre becoming transformed into a performance text in the process. This distinction is particularly relevant in any discussion of African theatre since so much of it is
non-script based and oral in nature.

In a foreword, Wole Soyinka, Africa's first Nobel Laureate for literature, argues that
'theatre, despite its many masks, is the unending rendition of the human experience, in
totality, and its excitement lies indeed in its very unpredictability . . . [and] as a rehearsal
for real life'(13). Rubin's 'African Theatre in a Global Context' sets African theatre
within a global context in which its diverse nature is examined; first is the contempo-
raneity of traditional forms with the hybrid concert/popular and literary theatre forms,
the latter being direct products of the colonial encounter between Africa and her
European colonizers. The essay argues that: 'Purely spoken drama in Africa ... is still

very much a minority form, a late development that emerged as part of colonial impositions and missionary training within indigenous communities'(14). Moreover, the entertainment and learning dichotomy which took place in western art, did not happen in African traditional art and so art, particularly theatre, in African societies is not 'perceived as *either* educational or escapist but rather both simultaneously'(15). What the book does not however add is the fact that this perception of art in general and theatre in particular as being both entertainment and instructional simultaneously in traditional Africa filters through into modern theatre practice with the result that forms such as Theatre for Development are quite popular and present in most African countries and also that even the individualistic literary theatre is constantly striving for a function and relevance for its society, from Soyinka in Nigeria to Ngugi wa Thiong'o in Kenya and from the late Dele Charley in Sierra Leone to Dickson Mwansa in Zambia. The book finds the exciting experiments being carried out by contemporary African dramatists who are beginning to 'reintroduce indigenous traditions into their work' and the new theatre forms and styles emerging from these experiments, to be at the root of much intercultural and 'interdisciplinary science of theatre anthropology' which has preoccupied western theorists and practitioners such as Victor Turner, Richard Schechner, Eugenio Barba, Jerzy Grotowski, Augusto Boal and Peter Brook (15).

'Of Inner Roots and External Adjuncts' by Oumane Diakhate and Hansel Ndumbe Eyoh traces Africa's theatre history before and after contact with European colonialism and argues that 'early Africans never invented a generic term to designate' their theatrical activities. For them theatre was a lived experience which did not need naming for it existed at every moment or point of living such as rituals of birth, naming, initiations, harvest, marriage, status elevation and death, all being capable of giving rise to theatrical events where 'music, dance and verbal parody figure in equal parts'. Diakhate outlines the development of Francophone African theatre which he sees as a recent phenomenon created between the two world wars, and which followed, as it were, the French colonial policy of assimilation – 'making Africans into proper French citizens, reshaping the culture of the African world along French lines'.(21) To this effect, the theatre that was encouraged was a reproduction of French (European) theatre models and styles, and the central focus and origin of Francophone African theatre Diakhate traces to the Ecole William Ponty in Gorée, Senegal, where African students began to perform French-style drama and later were encouraged to write plays about their own countries. Many of the early, well-known Francophone African playwrights were products of Ponty and they were instrumental in the development of theatre in their respective countries through the cultural centres and circles.

Anglophone African theatre also began by copying western forms and later progressed to a period of 'experimentation and radicalization during which it assumed the language of Caliban'. It has now settled into a period of 'total theatre which in essence is a mixture of traditional African and western forms'. Equally, argues Eyoh, the theme of this theatre has 'gone from traditional celebration to colonial vilification and back to root sources and cultural affirmation, and settling, at the end of the twentieth century, into socio–political and economic appraisal' (25-6). The central thrust of this section thus is that African theatrical art before outside contact, and particularly before the encounter with European colonization, was rich and complex. But that both the Arab conquest and the later colonial encounter did interrupt the evolution of contemporary African theatre in many ways, as well as leave imprints on it. Contemporary African theatre, both Francophone and Anglophone, however, are once more returning to their roots, and it is this blend of African traditional sources with western imprints that give African literary theatre its vitality as well as its relevance. But, points out Eyoh, one needs to be aware that contemporary African theatre did not evolve 'smoothly from the past, but rather from a fragmented history of both traditional African and western influences' (29).

Atta Mensah's 'The Great Ode of History', although overdone and a mite romantic in places, in the end is quite a good introductory essay on the structure and function of African music and dance. His analysis of the 'time count for a *kadodi* initiation dance for Masabi youths' captures on one level the intricate beat/rhythmic patterns played out by the master drummer which the young initiates are expected to interpret and dance to. And, at another level, the essay captures the essence of the interrelationship between music and dance in African performance – the dancer and the musician hold a dialogue with one another. That is why music and dance are both seen as languages of communication with the audience. This is one of the best essays on African music and dance that I have come across, not only does it provide an analysis of music and dance patterns, it also provides a classification of the musical instruments into four broad categories: ideophones, membranophones, chordophones and aerophones. The essay also points out that as other aspects of African life and activities, including theatre, have taken on board elements of the foreign, to create hybrid forms, so have music and dance to give rise to forms such as the West African highlife, African pop, *beni* in Tanzania and *mbeni* in Zambia.

Henryk Jurkowski's essay is the only one written by a non-African (apart from Rubin's) and his claim that puppetry in Africa owed its existence to foreign influence is strongly contradicted by the case of the legendary Akpan Etuk from Uyo who went to the land of the dead and brought back knowledge of puppets, and by the Tiv *Kwag-hir* puppets which definitely did not result from foreign influences. His generalization is therefore rather unfortunate. But he is right to observe that puppetry is not a widespread form of theatre in Africa. Ato Quayson's reading of African theatre as a form of 'intermedium' provides a very useful term for negotiating the complex participatory relationship between audience and performer in African theatre performances. As he argues, African theatre 'creates an intermediary space by which audiences are drawn into an active process of meaning and making' and is a 'conduit for meditations on historical processes' (43). The last essay in this section is Sony Labou Tansi's 'Theatre in Africa' in which he challenges Eurocentric notions and definitions of theatre which allowed for the wholesale denial of the existence of theatrical art in Africa on the pages of colonial artistic discourse. For him theatre is 'a coming together of human beings who have agreed on a place, a time, a story and who take roles and wear costumes in order to act out for one another tales from and of existence' (46).

The remaining parts of the book are dedicated to closer scrutiny of the theatre of individual nations. As I have said earlier, the structure of the book and the headings under which theatre is analysed in the countries is interesting in itself. Each country is examined in terms of: a general history, structure of the national theatre community, artistic profile (companies, dramaturgy, directing and acting), theatre for young audiences (puppet and mask theatre), design (theatre space and architecture), training, criticism, scholarship and publishing. Some countries which probably do not have a very well developed theatre are treated under a broad heading of overview – countries such as Angola, Chad, Congo, Guinea-Bissau, Kenya, Rwanda and Togo. Of these, Kenya is the most surprising considering the level and amount of theatrical activity that has gone on in that country. I presume that is the fault of the national scholar who made the entry and the way he perceives theatre in his country. However, two things need to be said about these headings. The first, which is positive, is that the headings are broad enough to allow a detailed look at theatre in each country. However, some of the headings overlap and in the end become repetitive. For instance, some of the material under history is reproduced under artistic profile and then under criticism, scholarship and publishing. Perhaps a merging of some of the headings would have led to a more integrated discussion of each country. Having said that, the merits of the headings by far outweigh the flaws and the volume therefore has to be commended for its detailed look at theatrical activities in these countries.

On the whole, this is another useful contribution to the ever growing literature on African theatre. There are some shortcomings though, such as some errors in dates (a 1966 date instead of 1996 is given in connection with the Kendil Theatre Company, and the death of the South African director and playwright, Barney Simon, is given as 1985 when it should be 1995). There are also some spelling errors such as Enuga for Enugu (221), inconsistency in the spelling of Antananarivo on pages 177 and 179, Samora Machel is spelt as Samoira (200). One other thing is that some countries were left out altogether such as the Gambia, Lesotho, Mauritania, Malawi, Botswana, Gabon, Central African Republic and Equatorial Guinea. No reason is given for their omission.

Osita Okagbue

Eckhard Breitinger (ed.) *Theatre and Performance in Africa*
Bayreuth: Bayreuth African Studies, 1994, 216 pp.
ISBN 3-927510-31-9 £14.95 ISBN 3-927510-23-8 £25.00 (cloth) ISSN 0178-0034 (BASS)

This eclectic collection of conference papers brought together under the title 'Theatre and Performance in Africa', opens with an introduction by Breitinger which includes some words with which I must take issue. He picks up on 'mongrelization' as used by Rushdie who aligns it with 'newness in cultural expression, in social awareness, in aesthetic expression' then juxtaposes it with 'ethno-centrism and natio-centrism' which Breitenger says 'must stand for "oldness", for traditionalization and even fossilization' suggesting that these 'look into themselves and back onto themselves' (6). He explicitly contrasts this with 'Hybridity' celebrating, he says, 'selfhood and otherness at the same time.' It is these two, 'mongrelization' and 'hybridity', which he says demand a response from 'cultural workers and creators'. Before I comment further I have to say that there is another phrase which is pervasive and which I find offensive: it is the 'common man' and I don't know which I like less 'common' or 'man'. There may be an excuse for 'common' but none for 'man'. 'Common people' is available if indeed people need to be referred to as 'common', but of course it brings an entirely different meaning to the phrase, which is exactly why I dislike it in the first place. After all one is referring to the majority of people. Breitinger is explicit in his use of the category: 'Elites and commoners and their respective forms remained largely segregated, pointing into [sic] different directions in their intentionality' (8).

Happily, he goes on to describe Okot p'Bitek's philosophy which is a pleasure to read again in this volume. That it should be relevant a quarter of a century after it was written, is a testimony to p'Bitek's perception and a sad commentary on the pace of social change. But I like Breitinger's acclamation of the task of Theatre-for-Development: 'Breaking the silence of the rural masses, raising their voices beyond the village boundaries, reclaiming articulation and thereby participation in the control of their own destinies, has become the sociopolitical message of Theatre for Development' (9), though I would have preferred it if he had referred to people in rural areas as 'people' and not the dehumanising 'masses' so beloved in Marxist discourse.

The aim of the collection is clearly set out: the first group of essays aim to 'treat the question of intercultural theatrical practice in the context of the metropolitan North to the transformation of a dramatic text from the South...into a performance that communicates across cultural boundaries when performed in the north'. This essay is followed by one on masquerades and one on 'cultural mongrelization within the context of one nation-state [Uganda]'(10). His second group of papers explores issues of who is the most appropriate and able to 'effect liberation in the present political scenario', and asking, is this to be a self-generated process or does it require interventionist tactics? His third category is concerned with the wider political discourse and addresses issues of subtle dissent in live theatre and in the media.

The first section begins with an account by Alby James of his relationship with Temba Theatre company and the arts in Britain. He asserts his 'Englishness' and his right to whatever aspects of the culture he selects, and not just those to which society directs him because they see not an Englishman, but a black person. He concludes by observing that culture can be 'oppressive and exclusive', that governments can be 'too precious' about cultures, and that nations are made up of peoples from different cultures.

Breitinger's own paper on the production, *Mother Uganda and her Children*, is interesting. There are one or two verbal infelicities arising partly from his writing in a foreign language and partly from typos. For example he consistently adds 'ies' (in his introduction) and 'es' (in this paper) to his decades, so we get 60ies and 70es. Surely someone could have noticed before publication? He goes on to describe in detail the collection of dances and songs brought together for the production and how these formed part of a 'folklore' based presentation. The play is a tale of strife in spite of the efforts of 'Mother Uganda' to instill harmony into her 'children'. Breitinger says that the 'Mother Uganda' figure is 'shaped according to the traditional concept of the African Earth goddess, a universal mother figure who nourishes all her children' (24). This paragon of moderation is never tired of 'admonishing' her wayward children and finally succeeds in persuading them that hard work is the path to harmony. Even Breitinger has to call this final tableau a 'utopian vision'. He sees the value of this moralistic fable as being 'a play of conscientisation'. Rose Mbowa used mime and dance as the primary vehicles for the performance so as to build on 'non-verbal communication'. The visual message conveyed through costume and movement is reinforced by the dialogue rather than the other way round. The choice of English as the main language of the play is contrasted with the Swahili name of the central troublesome character, a language associated in Uganda with the military and the police. By choosing to give a Swahili name to her main protagonist, Mbowa enabled people to understand 'where the real source of discord and ethnic hatred in Uganda is located' (29).

There are three more essays in this section dealing with such diverse issues as black identity and a range of stage productions using African elements.

The second part of the book begins with Oga S. Abah's excellent article on Theatre for Development. This article is surely set to become a classic account of a synergy of established performance genres and contemporary issues in the best tradition of Theatre for Development. He surveys the genre historically and gives examples from several different countries before focusing on the dramatic contribution of a local singer from his own village in central Nigeria to the issues raised in the drama during a workshop in 1989. He then addresses the issues raised by published plays, whether those of Ngugi and Ngugi or of Femi Osofisan, and goes on to critique the paradox of the 'animateurs' and the playwrights who 'trigger the process' of Theatre for Development whilst the people 'create the total theatre in the village arena'.

Other articles address theatre in South Africa, in Zimbabwe, children's theatre in Cameroon and language in TV plays in Nigeria. Taken together the collection provides a useful source of material on performance in and about Africa. Its eclecticism is one of its strengths, as most people will find something of interest in the book whatever their particular specialism. This book forms an important part of the available literature on African theatre.

Frances Harding

Helen Gilbert and Joanne Tompkins, *Post-Colonial Drama – Theory, Practice, Politics*
London/New York: Routledge, 1996, 346 pp.
ISBN 0-415-09024-5 £16.99 ISBN 0-415-09023-7 £55.00 (cloth)

Brian Crow and Chris Banfield, *An Introduction to Post-Colonial Theatre*
Cambridge: Cambridge University Press, 1996, 186 pp.
ISBN 0-521-567-22X £12.95 ISBN 0-521-495-296 £35.00 (cloth)

Stimulated by the wide recognition of the post-colonial theorists (Said, Baba *et al.*), critics have now discovered theatre as one of the most thrilling art forms for post-colonial syncretisms. The two books under review here are part of a broad debate on post-colonial theatre forms from the South Pacific around the world to the Canadian Pacific coast (see Christopher Balme, 1995, *Theater im postkolonialen Zeitalter*), as well as regionally or nationally focused theatre histories (David Kerr, *African Popular Theatre*, Errol Hill, *The Jamaican Stage*, Chris Dunton, *Make Man Talk True*, Olu Obafemi, *Contemporary Nigerian Theatre* and many others).

Gilbert and Tompkins claim:

This book focuses on the methods by which post-colonial drama resists imperialism and its effects. We isolate possible ways to read and view theatre texts from around the post-colonial world as well as ways to interpret the strategies by which play-wrights, actors, directors, musicians, and designers rework a historical moment or a character or an imperial text or even a theatre building. (1)

And this is exactly where my problems with this book begin:

1. In the title, the authors use the term *drama*, here they talk about theatre, even per-formance. The plays are nearly always scripted and published drama texts, and dealt with in terms of drama rather than theatre. Talking about traditional or ritual components, the authors refer to the original performance style of rituals, rather than their representa-tional versions on the stage. Drama, theatre, performance are not perceived as clearly defined and distinct concepts with separate types of critical discourse.

2. The book 'focuses' on and 'isolates' practically every aspect of post-colonial drama, i.e., it rather sprawls than focuses. But while the claim to the broadest possible range of issues is maintained, an unclaimed reduction to the issues of the centre/margin controversy is practised. In line with the approved rhetoric of post-colonial criticism, the old binaries North and South, modern and traditional are refuted, only to be replaced by another set of undeclared binaries. Binary or antagonistic argumentation is a crucial issue in critical theory, including the basic question whether one can reason at all

without constructing oppositional concepts. My objection is not against dualistic reasoning *per se*, but against unacknowledged dualism.

Binary **no. 1**: the canonized written metropolitan text of the Great Tradition with its oppressive imperialist effects and the liberative, self-assertive informal text of the colonized.

No 2: the suppressive and marginalizing effect of colonialist historiography versus the reappropriating rewritings of the colonial encounter from the perspective of the colonised.

No 3: the oppressive, silencing, and alienating effect of the norm language vis-à-vis the self-assertive, voice-seeking endeavours of the colonials in their urge to express themselves in their mother-tongues or their appropriated forms and varieties of the master-tongue.

The list is not complete, but polemically simplified. The key example for the culturally dominating canonical texts is, of course, Shakespeare, in particular *The Tempest*. The Prospero-Caliban issue has been thrashed out extensively (including by myself, first in 1979), the consensus among critics is unanimous, which leaves hardly any space for new insights. I disagree with the presentation of Shakespeare as a unidirectional, petrified, inflexible text that stifles the colonial. This is a very simplistic argumentation: The 'metropolitan Shakespeare tradition' from Dryden to recent revalorizations of Shakespeare as a 'popular theatre practitioner', show that Shakespeare has always been handled with utmost flexibility. What Gilbert/Tompkins present here is the caricature of the Shakespeare tradition as it was practised and (mal)treated at parents' days concerts in the colonial school system. Tompkins/Gilbert's Shakespeare polemic is strategically supported by revealing omissions: translations of Shakespeare into Pidgin or Krio (the Creole of Sierra Leone) or into Swahili (by Julius Nyerere, then President of Tanzania), which testify to the flexibility of the 'Shakespeare tradition' are obviously unknown to the authors. Even more crucial in my view is the total absence of the Roman plays and the *Weak King Histories*: *Julius Caesar* with the topic of regicide, *Richard II* with the issue of good governance, civil disobedience and the right to 'destool' the governing prince, are issues of immediate political concern in many countries, and dramatists have used the canonized texts to camouflage their criticism of the political system or the head of state. Secondly, dramatists like Soyinka, Walcott, Fugard and many others, have worked at the Royal Court and the Royal Shakespeare Company; they have been exposed to a much more subtle style of staging Shakespeare and they are, both in their dramatic and their theatrical work, way beyond these simplistic forms of the Shakespeare school play.

Colonial and post-colonial history is presented in a similar antagonistic form. Gilbert/Tompkins refer to Hayden White and his concept of narrativity in historiography, and although historians throughout the world have theorized about the peripheral/metropolitan perspectives in the historiography of empires (and ensuing re-writes of history), they still write as if the mission school version of historical instruction had never ended or even been questioned.

With language, the same: apart from some erroneous explanations on the function of Creoles, Pidgins, Patois and varieties of English, the discussion concentrates exclusively on the debilitating effects of enforcing the metropolitan language on colonials. That polyglossic language usage or code-switching are functionalized in theatre, not only as a political statement but also as a representation of the linguistic realities in many societies, seems to be overlooked. Deviations from a metropolitan language as a means to represent marginalization (and rejections of marginalization) is no prerogative of post-colonial theatre, on the contrary, it is one of the few, really universalist strategies of theatre everywhere and anytime (viz. *Pygmalion, Look Back in Anger, et al.*).

The scope of Gilbert/Tompkins's book is ambitiously wide; it spans the whole

(English-speaking) world from the South Pacific through Asia, Africa, the Caribbean to the Canadian Pacific coast. To do so effectively, the authors have to strain the 'unanimism' (Appiah, *In My Father's House*: 24–6) of the post-colonial situation, rather than engage in the wide diversity of different post-colonial realities. The wide range also blurs the contours of a new and alternative canon of post-colonial plays, which is part of the agenda of the book. Some of the texts included here, do not convince as being representative: Under the heading 'Re-writing history in the Caribbean', the authors exclude Walcott's *Henri Christophe*, a widely performed seminal text in post-colonial theatre. Instead, they include C.L.R. James's *Black Jacobins*. As an academic book of historical criticism, *The Black Jacobins* (1938) was one of the most influential texts in the pan-Africanism debate throughout the 1950s and '60s. The drama version (1967) has remained largely unseen. Gilbert/Tompkins summarize the play as: 'giving theatrical life to the principal players in the slave rebellion' (112). This is a misrepresentation of James's intention. He wrote about the heroes of the first black revolution and the formation of the first black republic. James's *Black Jacobins* are seen to be of equal historical importance as their French counterparts, Robespierre, Danton, Marat. 'Principle players in a slave rebellion' is historically wrong. But what is worse: this is the lingo of the colonialist historiographer, against whom Gilbert/Tompkins antagonize so violently.

To this book applies what Appiah described as the failure of 'ideological post-colonial discourse': it antagonizes coloniality without stepping outside the systemic structures of originally colonial academia. It results in 'reverse discourse' (Appiah, I*n My Father's House*: 59), but it also reduces the theatre practitioners to simple 'reactionaries', whose creations arise only from opposition to what they feel as oppressive. There is nothing of the spirit of Salman Rushdie or Derek Walcott's enterprise of 'bringing newness to the world' through 'bastardized' cultural projects.

Brian Crow/Chris Banfield take a personalized approach, presenting portraits of seven dramatists – in this limitation apparently a much more manageable project. But I did not find the result entirely convincing. Brian Crow, who wrote the portraits of Walcott, Soyinka, August Wilson, Jack Davis, Athol Fugard, follows a fixed pattern: first a broad framework of political, historical, literary background of the 'national culture', followed by a close reading of drama as text, with hardly any references to theatrical aspects and practically no contextualization of the individual plays. The exceptions are the essay on Athol Fugard, whose workshopping technique of creating plays is looked at in its theatrical and political context, and described as a model with far-reaching consequences in the history of South African theatre. The other two exceptions are the essays by Chris Banfield on the Bengali dramatist Badal Sircar and his Delhi counterpart Girish Karnad. Banfield looks very closely at the interfaces with traditional Indian theatre on the one hand, and Indian film on the other, telling us much more about the theatre concepts of the two authors than about the plots of their plays.

Discussing Soyinka, both books focus on *Death and the King's Horseman*, and both ignore Soyinka's warning not to reduce this play to a simple presentation of the cultural clash. Brian Crow's image of Soyinka is limited and one-sided, referring exclusively to the mythio-poesis in Soyinka's work. The early political plays, *Kongi's Harvest, A Play of Giants, Opera Wonyosi* are dealt with in one single paragraph; the political implications of *A Dance in the Forests*, both in content and as a rejection of the Nigerian Independence celebrations are overlooked; Soyinka as founder/leader of different theatre companies, in particular the Guerilla theatre with its 'hit and run' dramaturgy of street theatre is not even mentioned. A look at Soyinka's autobiographical piece *Ibadan*, at the plays of the nineties up to *Area Boy*, the essays *The Open Sore of a Continent*, show us a completely different, highly politicized Soyinka. If bibliographies are an indicator of scholarly erudition, the articles are under-researched. Brian Crow lists Eldred Jones's *Wole Soyinka* (1981), but none of the numerous post-Nobel award scholarly books (including Derek Wright's *Soyinka Revisited*). The same is true for the Walcott article, where one misses the most important critical works such as Robert Hamner's *Derek Walcott* (1981) and Stewart Brown *The Art of Derek Walcott* (1992). What is listed for further reading is hopelessly outdated.

What both books present as debilitating effects of colonialism and neo-colonial cultural imperialism is in many ways true, but in no way new. After reading carefully argued, sophisticated and knowledgeable general criticism like Appiah's *In My Father's House* or specific theatre criticism like Balme's *Theater im postkolonialen Zeitalter* (1995) or David Kerr's *Popular Theatre in Africa* (1996), the two titles under review here are flat and disappointing.

Eckhard Breitinger

Marion Frank, *AIDS-Education through Theatre*
Bayreuth: Bayreuth African Studies 35, 1995, 183 pp.
ISBN 3-927510-37-8 £14.99 ISSN 0178-0034

This volume is a study of the use of Theatre for Development in Uganda, particularly in relation to its use in various AIDS campaigns. Frank selects Uganda because it is a country which opted to tackle the AIDS epidemic head-on without official coyness or evasiveness. She begins with a comprehensive overview of the form of theatre which has come to be best known as Theatre for Development, distinguishing it from other forms by its avowed intent to communicate, educate and to 'raise issues, find solutions and spark off collective action.'(13). Within Theatre for Development, she distinguishes a 'sub-genre' which she calls 'Campaign Theatre' which is a form of theatre 'concerned with raising consciousness in people on such topics as environmental issues, health care...' (13) and it is on Campaign Theatre that the book focuses. I personally like this term 'Campaign Theatre' but friends in Nigeria told me it would be taken there to mean a political campaign and so would not be useful to them. This is regrettable as good, distinctive, descriptive names are badly needed in this field of theatre.

Chapter 2 begins with a synopsis of the history of Theatre for Development as related through the various publications in this field and then goes on to give a history of selected performers in Uganda. This immediately begins to reveal new information. She describes the work of Jonathan Muganga with Vincencia Sserwadda in initiating a series of locally produced entertainments and dramas which addressed relevant health issues. Whilst she gives the history of the movement, she glosses over exactly how they 'composed plays with simple stories, poems and songs'. This is a pity because it is this crucial link between the message and the creative processes of utilising familiar forms of performance to address new and contemporary issues which constitutes x, the unknown factor between existing and new forms in African performance. The alternatives appear to lie between a mechanistic application of new words to well-known songs and dances and thus to embellish a new theme or the introduction of a dialogue drama which then carries the weight of the new information and is inserted between an array of familiar forms. If Frank has a description of *how* familiar forms accommodated new information, then this is what we want to know in detail. What we are given is a statement: 'At the end of the play, the women sang a song, "Endiisa" (Feeding) to emphasise their message.'

The accommodation of new themes in old forms remains unproblematized. It is assumed, taken for granted. At the end of the section on this particular project, she quotes from Muganga how the people were able to use 'community channels of communication and respected folk artists and communication in their own community.'(62) We still do not really know *how*.

Frank continues in this vein filling in substantial background to another of the many interesting social projects in and around Makerere and Kampala often resulting in specific, concrete projects such as the building of a clinic. Geoffrey Wadulo has operated on similar lines to Muganga with an easily recognized play formula: scene one – the wrong kind of behaviour; scene two: the results of such behaviour; scene three; the solution (64). This kind of drama aims to inform and to enable people to put their newly acquired knowledge to immediate use. Frank again distinguishes this kind of 'process-to-product' theatre from the 'consciousness-raising' genre which 'does not have any immediate impact' (65). It is rewarding, even at this early stage of her book, to see this distinction forcefully and repeatedly made. Her next focus is on a rural group called 'Crude Theatre' whose work went through various stages of popularity – almost fading as they became too heavily political and lost the 'entertainment' factor as their primary means of communication. A timely warning.

The following section addresses issues of theory. She surveys early linguistic models of communication and goes on to 'mass communication' and then finds her way back to theatre via some dubious phrases like 'Theatre as we know it'. Oh dear, oh dear, who are 'we'? Section 3 continues with information about Bagandan society and approaches to morality, polygamy, virginity, sexuality and intergenerational relationships. Something of an ideal society from a man's point of view is described as the 'precolonial state'. Frank refers to important issues when she introduces the idea of plays, usually developed by Ugandan artists who create a 'situation where TfD plays … are endogenous' (107), but notes the influence of 'exogenous' factors such as funding by outside agencies so that the problem being addressed within the play is not, in this form, entirely defined by the target group itself. This friction between funding bodies and the preferences of the activating group remains a problem.

From theorizing, she moves on to discuss case studies in Section 4. She offers a very useful distinction between Campaign Theatre and the 'project-oriented' plays with which she began. Whereas Campaign Theatre needs to be performed as often as possible in order to get a message across to as many people as possible, the locally specific plays need to be performed only as often as necessary, or even just 'once in order to solve a certain problem' (117). She further contrasts this specificity with the plethora of cassettes, films, radio broadcasts which are spawned from Campaign Theatre so as to 'reach large numbers of the population' (117).

It is only now that Frank addresses issues within the playform itself. She notes that the 'didactic plays – both project-oriented and C T – do not develop their characters.' Types of characters represent different sectors of society via age, gender, occupation. The dialogue is that of ordinary speech accessible to all Ugandans and the information is given in 'languages, images and metaphors which are relevant to a Ugandan audience' (118). These are important aspects to raise. For the rest of the book, she gives accounts of specific instances of localized performances in schools, on television and in the commercial urban public space before turning to her conclusion where she makes a final distinction between the 'two ways of dealing with the topic AIDS through theatre' and names the commercial theatre groups and those plays 'produced in cooperation with international organisations and NGOs' (164).

This is an extremely useful book for those who want to have an overview of theatre in the service of social communication or alternatively those who want to explore issues contained in the practice of Theatre for Development. There is much to enrich the reader's knowledge in many fields in this book and it forms an essential aspect of the literature on Theatre for Development.

Frances Harding

Kamal Salhi (ed.), *African Theatre for Development: Art for Self-Determination*
Exeter: Intellect Books, 1998, 188 pp. ISBN 1-871516-77-3 £14.95

Abah, Oga Steve, *Performing Life: Case Studies in the Practice of Theatre for Development*
Nigeria: Shekut Books, 1997, 115 pp. ISBN 978-125-106-9

These two recent additions to the literature addressed to the theory and practice of Theatre for Development are to be welcomed for quite opposite reasons; Kamal Salhi's collection particularly because of its abundant new material on North Africa and the contribution of women, and Oga Abah's because this leading and innovative practitioner has at last responded to pleas to record and analyse his work.

While one might challenge Salhi's suggestion that there is a 'general ignorance about African Theatre for Development, in university circles and even among theatre scholars' (on the contrary, the real ignorance is in government and NGOs, I suspect) his eclectic selection of essays certainly significantly extends our understanding. Salhi's own essay on Kateb Yacine's early work, while perhaps raising the question of whether it is what we think of as TfD, is nevertheless an excellent and informative record of this brave and radical playwright's work. That it ends on a relatively optimistic note ('Yacine's theatre provides the means for people to work out the complexities of social and cultural differences within their homeland') may look somewhat ironic in terms of present events in Algeria, but Salhi is right to bring Yacine into the broad focus of theatre and development. Laura Box contributes an essay on women playwrights and performers that again concentrates on francophone North Africa. She rightly says that 'virtually all of them are unfamiliar to speakers of English'. A great virtue of this essay, in addition to its shrewd analysis, is the listing and contextualizing of plays, playwrights and performers, with Box commenting that 'using a panoply of strategies both contemporary and traditional, women are writing plays which speak to the very issues which North Africa must face if it is to survive its present circumstances'. More relatively unfamiliar ground is covered by Valerie Orlando in her essay, 'Werewere Liking and the Development of Ritual Theatre in Cameroon: towards a new feminine theatre for Africa'. Orlando describes Liking as emerging from a 'wasteland of feminine artistic deprivation' in West Africa. The Ki-Yi M'bock theatre group created by Liking and the playwright's syncretic creativity are clearly and enthusiastically chronicled by Orlando. Two other essays in the collection point to specific activities: Jane Plastow's description of the extraordinary presence and status of theatre in the Ethiopia-Eritrea war (aptly titled 'Uses and Abuses of Theatre for Development …') and Juma Adamu Bakari's examples of 'Satires in Theatre for Development Practice in Tanzania'. The remaining four essays have a stronger historical, analytical focus, though in the case of Frances Harding's 'Neither "Fixed Masterpiece": nor "Popular Distraction": voice, transformation and encounter in Theatre for Development' and Osita Okagbue's 'Product or Process: Theatre for Development in Africa', the sense of the work of experienced and authoritative practitioners is very evident. Page Law contributes a detailed and comprehensive survey of TfD in contemporary South Africa, valuably updating (and illustrating) the situation in an area of the continent where the theatrical scene is evolving and responding to events in a manner that is often difficult to keep track of. Bala A. Musa's 'Popular Theatre and Development communication in West Africa: paradigms, processes a prospects' by contrast seems to stand a little aloof from practice and to be more at home with theoretical discussion. The assertion that 'popular theatre for conscientization is still a novelty in West Africa' would, I fear, not please Osofisan, Fatunde, Obafemi, Sowande, Rotimi *et al.*

This helpful and often important set of essays would have been improved by the inclusion of a 'who's who and who's where' of contributors, and by better proofreading – the worst example of which is the misspelling of Osita Okagbue's name in every place apart from the footnotes.

Oga Steve Abah, from his base at Ahmadu Bello University in Nigeria, and through the Nigerian Popular Theatre Alliance (NPTA), has been labouring at the practice of TfD for almost 20 years, and is acknowledged internationally as a leading authority. The slim volume *Performing Life* shows the thinking and the practice behind Abah's work, and his exhaustive concern that both should be rigorously pursued. Abah is a delightful mix of scholar and practitioner; his scholarship leads him into a desire to identify and label the ingredients of TfD. From this arises his coinage of the word 'perforaltics' – the oral and gestural amalgamation of a community's cultural systems into a dramatic representation of their own reality, as he describes it. It is, he again explains, 'writing the community's story through action'. Abah is stimulating in the way he wrestles to articulate the complexities of creating a TfD programme, but even more impressive when he describes his own experiences and actions. This, it seems to me, is always done with generosity (to other practitioners, to community participants, even to government agencies) and utter honesty. A substantial part of the book is devoted to a description and discussion of TfD workshops held under the auspices of NPTA in northern Nigeria in the late 1980s and early '90s. These produce the usual gamut of possibilities and problems, opportunities and frustrations, none more graphically so than those encountered in the village of Otobi. This is a long story, patiently and clearly told by Abah, culminating in the placing in the village of a grinding machine. This seemingly positive step of development, stemming from TfD workshop activity, turned into a nightmare. 'By 1995', Abah tells us 'the multi-purpose grinding machine had torn Otobi into splinters and it had become a community against itself'. Here is the nightmare scenario, where the intervention of a TfD team had apparently caused massive and dangerous communal tension. What to do in these circumstances ? Dear reader, as they say, read on! Abah shows, impressively, the self-examination of the TfD group and the ultimate resolution of the problem. This is a fascinating description of the best kind of practice at at work – full of dedication, full of constructive self-criticism, determinedly honest. Frances Harding's careful introduction and short contributions from Jenkeri Zakari Okwori and Egwugwu Illah enhance the value of the book. There is also a useful bibliography. *Performing Life* should become an essential handbook for TfD practitioners (*and* theorists). The problem, of course, is that it is published by an obscure Nigerian press and may be difficult to obtain. We shall attempt to persuade ABC in Oxford and others to stock this title; otherwise write to Dr Abah at the Department of Drama, Ahmadu Bello University, Zaria, Nigeria.

Martin Banham

Robert Mshengu Kavanagh, *Making People's Theatre*
Johannesburg: Witwatersrand University Press, 1997, 234 pp. ISBN 1-868142868 £12.95

In *Making People's Theatre*, R. M. Kavanagh is, as he says in his prefatory note, 'offering twenty-six years' of experiential work in people's theatre'. He goes further to caution that the ideas and methods therein are not '*the* right ones', they may be 'useful' but not '*definitive*'. The text reads as an attempt at providing a manual for novices interested in engaging in theatre activities, what Kavanagh has termed 'people's theatre' – a theatre that is practised by the broad majority in society, from institutions to organizations to the populace in the rural areas. His definition of 'people's theatre' is a theatre that is dissimilar from the conventional European theatre, which he has called 'dead theatre'.

Stating that Africa has had a long tradition of theatre which has been 'historically obscured', he laments the exportation to Africa of a tradition of this 'dead theatre' that was presented to schools as 'drama'. Though he does not take time to elucidate what he classifies as 'dead' and/or 'live' theatre, he laments the unimaginative and slavish recitations of Shakespeare's plays in African schools. At the same time he rightly states that the colonial forces consciously avoided any mention (in schools or elsewhere) of 'non-European Theatre' – like the Japanese Kabuki, Chinese, Indian or even African performing arts.

In making people's theatre, Kavanagh contends that one has from the very beginning to be motive-driven, and in listing the various motives that may inspire one, two identifiable categories emerge: (a) an individualistic approach to theatre with the explicit aim of personal gain; (b) a more pedagogic and community oriented approach. He then goes on to suggest a practical guide to the essentials of forming and/or running a theatre group. But the guide would only be relevant to amateur groups and in situations where theatre has not developed well enough to provide a wage big enough to live on. Issues of commitment, discipline, respect and group dynamics become tricky for the simple reason that theatre at this level is amateur and not professional in the sense that it does not provide a paid job. It becomes an activity that one engages in for sheer love of it or for lack of anything better paying to do.

Seen in this light and as much as one may agree with Kavanagh that any theatre activity will require a high sense of commitment, it would be difficult to demand this from members of a group if and when any other better paying activity arises, or even when they are prevailed upon by their benefactors. Kavanagh himself gives a good example when he says, '… if an actor has an important rehearsal or even a performance but is required somewhere on family business or to attend a family ceremony, like a funeral or a wedding, it is hard for the other family members to accept his or her absence'. The situation does not mean that the actor is less committed but rather points at the missing links. Kavanagh does not address the important question of how theatre can survive as a self-sustaining industry in this kind of situation.

In 'people's theatre' the ensemble arrives at decisions democratically, and in choosing the play to be performed or made it is suggested that prior decision be arrived at on what the intention is, who is the audience, and what are the available resources. Kavanagh uses examples of his own experience in South Africa, Zimbabwe and Ethiopia to suggest ways of play-making from the very beginning of script writing, to improvisation, to the choice of an already written play for performance.

In chapter four, titled 'Bringing it to life', the author deals with the elementary aspects of staging a play and even uses diagrams to elaborate stage positioning and movement. Staging is further discussed in chapter six, and it is here that one notices nothing exceptional in the manner in which the author has addressed theatre in Africa. Giving examples of forms of staging he very elaborately handles the issue when discussing European forms of staging. He uses diagrams to illustrate staging as understood in Western scholarship giving examples of classical Greek, Elizabethan, and the different types of stages, e.g. end stage, traverse, proscenium, etc. He even illustrates how particular Western practioners have designed their own types of staging such as Artaud and Growtosky.

His treatment of the African forms of staging is the least clearly researched. As much as it would be absurd to cluster the different forms of staging in Europe as 'traditional European', and thence the necessity to give examples of, say, 'Classical Greek' or 'Elizabethan', it is equally absurd to cluster African forms of staging as simply 'traditional African'. In illustrating the 'traditional African' stage, his diagram indicates where the King, his wives and elders would be positioned, where the cattle enclosure would be, where the ordinary people would be, and at the centre of all these, the performing area. As though all performances were designed with the King's presence.

The African continent is colossal, the African communities as varied as they are numerous, and the performance forms as variant as the communities are multifarious. The staging, if we may use Kavanagh's word, would of necessity differ from performance to performance. Consider rituals in performance and performance in ritual and the space dynamics involved. Our opinion is that the term 'staging' would not apply where such is the situation, and that 'performance space' would be a better substitute. This heuristic definition of the forms and practice of 'African theatre' is a typical cliché of the colonial legacy, the very question Kavanagh portends in his introduction. The book does not succeed in addressing the question beyond the introductory mention.

Chapter seven deals with lessons in stage lighting, sounds and set. Again making general statements about this aspect of the African performance, Kavanagh says, 'in the narrative or story telling theatre of Africa, performances were given at night by the light of the fire'. He then goes ahead to give elementary lessons in lighting, sound and setting as may be practised in housed theatres, complete with computerized mechanics. When he refers to 'functional' set and costume it is in reference to what he says is called in English theatre 'black boxes and leotards' still within the context of plays performed on set stages.

People's theatre in Africa would necessarily include forms of community theatre, Theatre for Development and related fields. As you read through Kavanagh's book, one keeps on waiting to come across a discussion of the issues presented (e.g. the chapter on lighting, sound and set or the one on staging) and their application in the various forms of Theatre for Development, forms that have gained a lot of popularity in the developmental and democratization processes. One dare say that the participatory nature of the Theatre for Development forms that are now widely practised relate closely with the forms that were practised in pre-colonial Africa, particularly in the sense that they endeavour to be entirely participatory.

The last chapter of Kavanagh's book is a useful step-by-step record of the process that was used in devising, rehearsing and staging of the play *Mavambo* by the Faculty of the Arts, Drama, of the University of Zimbabwe.

There is no doubt that anybody interested in making theatre in the manner Kavanagh has suggested will find the book invaluable. As said earlier, it is a manual that is elaborate with step-by-step methods of making theatre, from the point of devising to script writing to the staging of the made play.

By the end of the book though, one is left wondering whether the book addresses the agenda that the author introduces at the beginning. His suggestion that the African theatre is 'live theatre' as opposed to the colonial 'dead theatre' receives no further examination apart from the mere mention. The aim of the book he says in the introduction is '... to re-examine such [in reference to "dead theatre"] "rules". To the extent that they are valid let us use them. To the extent that they are not, let us discard them'. It is not clear which of the 'rules' of the 'dead theatre' we should discard and which we should use. One hopes that this is not a suggestion that the various forms of theatre found in Africa were or are without 'rules'. A thorough research into indigenous African forms of performance is left wanting.

Bantu Mwaura

Index